Residential Sales Comparison & Income Approaches

concepts and techniques

3rd edition, 2nd printing

Timothy Detty
Certified General Appraiser
AQB-Certified USPAP Instructor

HONDROS LEARNING™
4140 Executive Parkway
Westerville, Ohio 43081
www.hondroslearning.com

Published 2018. Printed in the United States of America

20 19 18 2 3 4
978-1-59844-255-7

For more information on, or to purchase, our products, please visit
www.hondroslearning.com

Table of Contents

Suggested Syllabus

RESIDENTIAL SALES COMPARISON & INCOME APPROACHES: CONCEPTS AND TECHNIQUES

COURSE DESCRIPTION: This course is designed to provide the student with a comprehensive knowledge of the development and application of the sales comparison approach and the income approach in residential appraisal assignments. The course begins with how the fundamental principles of valuation and appraisal standards apply to an assignment in which the sales comparison and/or income approach is relevant in the scope of work, and details the development steps in the appraisal process through reconciliation. As part of the progression, the student will become acquainted with accepted methodology and techniques that can be applied in the assignment using the sales comparison and/or income approaches. Included and emphasized, through numerous illustrations and application case studies, are choosing comparable data, derivation and application of adjustments for various elements, derivation and application of rates of capitalization, and the logic and rationale applied during reconciliation. Also included is an introduction to the HP 12c financial calculator as well as a discussion about using the sales comparison and income approaches in special situations.

COURSE OBJECTIVES:

- Recognize how the fundamental valuation principles interact with the sales comparison and income approaches.
- Relate how the performance obligations of USPAP apply.
- Identify the type and source of data required for the analysis and how the data is classified and chosen.
- Illustrate accepted valuation sales comparison and income approach methods and techniques, distinguish their common applications, and properly apply them for problem solving.
- Reconcile indications produced by the sales comparison and income approaches.
- Discover special situations in which the sales comparison and income approaches are applied.
- Demonstrate the functions of a financial calculator and how they are used for appraisal calculations.

COURSE TEXTBOOK: *Residential Sales Comparison and Income Approaches: concepts and techniques*, Hondros Learning™, Copyright © 2018

COURSE CREDIT HOURS: Qualifying education: 30 credit hours. Attendance is mandatory to receive course credit.

INSTRUCTION METHOD: Lecture, illustration, case examples, and workgroup case studies

COURSE OUTLINE with Suggested Time Increments:

DAY 1 (total classroom hours 7.5)

2 hours	Introduction and Overview
	Chapter 1 Introduction to Sales Comparison and Income Methodologies
1.5 hours	Chapter 2 Sales Comparison Analysis—Data Identification and Analysis
1 hour	Lunch
.5 hours	Chapter 2 Sales Comparison Analysis—Data Identification and Analysis (continued)
3.5 hours	Chapter 3 Sales Comparison Analysis—Adjustments and Reconciliation

DAY 2 (total classroom hours 7.5)

3.5 hours	Chapter 3 Sales Comparison Analysis—Adjustments and Reconciliation (continued)
1 hour	Lunch
4 hours	Chapter 4 Introduction to Financial Calculators

DAY 3 (total classroom hours 7.5)

.5 hours	Chapter 4 Introduction to Financial Calculators (continued)
3 hours	Chapter 5 Introduction to Income Fundamentals
1 hour	Lunch
4 hours	Chapter 6 Income Analysis

DAY 4 (total classroom hours 7.5)

2 hours	Chapter 6 Income Analysis (continued)
1.5 hours	Chapter 7 Using the Sales Comparison and Income Approaches in Special Situations
1 hour	Lunch
2 hours	Chapter 7 Using the Sales Comparison and Income Approaches in Special Situations (continued)
2 hours	Final Examination and Student Surveys

Preface

Hondros Learning[a] is proud to present *Residential Sales Comparison and Income Approaches: concepts and techniques,* part of the market-leading textbook series for appraisal qualifying education. Written specifically to correspond to the 2015 Real Property Appraiser Qualification Criteria promulgated by the Appraisal Qualifications Board (AQB), *Sales Comparison and Income Approaches: concepts and techniques* features **clear writing**, **real-world examples** and **case studies**, useful **illustrations**, numerous **practice questions**, and a **glossary of key terminology**, making this text the most up-to-date tool available for achieving mastery of the sales comparison and income approaches in residential appraisal assignments.

In addition to following the *AQB content guideline* for qualifying education, all texts in our appraisal series are *affordably priced* and feature a *clear writing* style and *numerous study aids* to assist students with comprehension and application of the material. Concepts range from simple to slightly complex, illustrating the application of the material in various appraisal scenarios. **Key terms** are highlighted and defined throughout, and compiled in a self-contained *glossary* to assist in learning definitions and concepts required for the AQB National Uniform Examination. **Important points** are highlighted throughout the chapters—a proven method to facilitate retention of key material. **Real-world examples** and **case studies** assist with understanding how appraisers use the sales comparison and income approaches in residential appraisal assignments. Selected USPAP Illustrations and Guidance references are included with most chapters to illustrate USPAP applicability and obligations in specific appraisal circumstances. The Appendix includes the most common forms used by residential appraisers for the sales comparison and income approaches, as well as handy flashcards for critical income approach formulas.

Instructor materials are available separately to make using this text in your classroom a seamless experience.

Text Outline

Chapter 1 amplifies how valuation fundamentals and principles interact with the development of the sales comparison and income approaches. The discussion includes an overview of the appraisal process and the performance standards of USPAP related to development of a real property appraisal.

Chapter 2 focuses on data identification and analysis in the sales comparison approach. Illustrated are common elements examined by the appraiser during the property inspection or as part of the research performed by the appraiser during the course of appraisal development. Comparable and competitive properties are defined, with the discussion leading to illustrated examples of the process and rationale used by the appraiser in choosing comparable and competitive properties for analysis.

Chapter 3 provides an in-depth look at how data is analyzed and processed in development of the sales comparison approach. This chapter illustrates how the elements of comparison are analyzed, the use and application of quantitative and qualitative techniques for deriving and applying adjustments for numerous conditions and characteristics, as well as various techniques for reconciliation of the sales comparison approach.

Chapter 4 offers an introduction to the use of a financial calculator in the appraisal profession. Specifically illustrating the HP12c financial calculator, this chapter provides detailed instruction of how the calculator operates along with step-by-step keystroke applications for the most common mathematical calculations used by residential appraisers.

Chapter 5 introduces fundamental principles of the income approach. This chapter explores and illustrates terms, concepts, and components analyzed and/or developed by the appraiser when the income approach is applicable in an assignment.

Chapter 6 examines and demonstrates the analysis performed by the appraiser for developing an opinion of value by the income approach. This chapter illustrates the development of a value opinion using multipliers and the direct capitalization method, using an overall capitalization rate. A detailed presentation of determining market rents as well as the techniques for deriving multipliers and rates of capitalization is also provided.

Chapter 7 discusses the appraisal of partial interests and special ownership situations. Also covered is the use of combined approaches and special requirements for appraisals for use in residential lending transactions. Fannie Mae guidelines and requirements that the appraiser agrees to observe in developing the sales comparison and income approaches in residential assignments are emphasized.

USPAP References Within the Text

USPAP references are based on the 2018-2019 version of USPAP ©The Appraisal Foundation.

Exam Prep

Additional appraisal products available from Hondros Learning to help students prepare for the licensing exam include the *Appraisal Review Crammer*™—a valuable self-study or classroom exam preparation guide and *Appraisal CompuCram*™ an online exam-prep program.

About the Author

Timothy Detty has taught thousands of real estate and appraisal students over the course of his teaching career at Hondros College. A practicing Certified General Appraiser, he has also written numerous real estate and appraisal courses and served as both author and expert reviewer for several real estate and appraisal textbooks. He has been awarded the designation of Certified Distance Education Instructor (CDEI) from the International Distance Education Certification Center (IDECC) and is a member of the National Association of Appraisers. In addition to being an AQB Certified USPAP Instructor, Tim has served as an at-large representative to the Education Council of Appraisal Foundation Sponsors (ECAFS), was formerly a member of the Education and Research Advisory Committee of the Ohio Real Estate Commission, and is a frequent guest lecturer and contributor to various real estate and appraisal publications.

Introduction to *Sales Comparison and Income Methodologies*

Valuation methods for real property can be thought of as avenues of analysis by which the need, desire, and expectation for a particular property is measured in numbers based on how well the need, desire, and benefit is satisfied by the property being analyzed.

Real property appraisers have three valuation methods (known as the approaches to value)—the sales comparison approach, the income approach, and the cost approach. In this text, we will focus on the sales and income approaches. Several accepted techniques for developing value opinions are available to the appraiser in each approach, which will be explored as we progress through this course. Focusing on residential applications of the sales comparison and income approaches, we will discuss in this chapter what prompts the appraiser to employ a certain methodology and technique.

Relevant Valuation Fundamentals

Fundamental principles and theories of value must always be included in the appraiser's thought process when developing value opinions. Let's begin by reviewing these cornerstones in the context of how they apply specifically to the sales comparison and income approaches.

Substitution

Probably first and foremost in the appraiser's mind when developing an opinion of value is the principle of **substitution**. In the sales comparison approach, **substitution** is rooted in *the premise that an informed buyer will not pay more for a property than they would be required to pay for a comparable substitute.* The principle of substitution can also be applied to features of a property. A comparable substitute is one of equal utility.

For Example: If an appraiser is determining the value of a property feature, the appraiser must be conscious that a knowledgeable buyer is not usually willing to pay more for the existing feature than the cost of adding the feature to a house that does not have it.

» *A knowledgeable buyer typically will not pay more for a feature than what it would cost to add that feature to a house that does not have that feature...or that an informed renter will not pay more in rent than he would in rent for a comparable dwelling.* «

One of the applications of substitution in the income approach would be applied in the determination of market rent—the informed market participant will not pay more for rent on one property than he will pay for a comparable rental. Or on the other side of the equation, an investor will pay no more for a property than what he can acquire another property for that has a similar return.

For Example: If a 1,000 sq. ft. property can generate the same return as a 1,100 sq. ft. property, the small property would be a better investment (substitution).

KEY TERMS

Anticipation An economic theory that says value is created by the expectation of future benefits, such as profit, pleasure, tax shelter, production, income, etc. Anticipation is the foundation for the income approach.

Appraiser's Peers Other appraisers who have expertise and competency in a similar type of assignment. *

Assumptions That which is taken to be true.*

Balance A condition that exists in the real estate market when there are slightly more homes available than buyers.

Buyer's Market A situation in the real estate market in which buyers have a large selection of properties from which to choose.

Change A principle affecting value in real estate that says all factors that influence real estate—physical, economic, governmental, and social—are constantly changing, and, thus, property value itself is subject to constant change.

Characteristics of Value Also known as D-U-S-T. The characteristics of value are Demand, Utility, Scarcity, and Transferability.

Client The party (or parties) who engage an appraiser (by employment or contract) in a specific assignment.*

Competition Two or more parties, properties, etc., trying to obtain the same thing.

Conformity The theory that says a particular property achieves its maximum value when it is surrounded by properties that are similar in style, function, and utility. Also called **Homogeneity**.

Contributory Value The theory that a particular item or feature of a property is worth only what it actually contributes in value to that parcel of real estate.

Credible Worthy of belief.*

Date of Report An indication of the perspective from which the appraiser is examining the market.

Effective Date Establishes the context for the value opinion.

Extraordinary Assumption An assignment-specific assumption as of the effective date regarding uncertain information used in an analysis which, if found to be false, could alter the appraiser's opinions or conclusions.*

General Data Information that covers the forces that affect property values, but are not directly related to a particular piece of property. General data covers **p**hysical, **e**conomic, **g**overnmental, and **s**ocial factors (**P E G S**) and can be local or national.

Anticipation

The principle of **anticipation** implies that *value is created by the expectation of future benefits*. It is easy to mistakenly associate anticipation as being related only to the income approach. While it is true that the actions of typical investors are most clearly based on the expectation of future benefits, such as an anticipated income stream (quite possibly the most obvious example), the principle of anticipation is embedded in other valuation methods, such as the sales comparison approach, as well. Individuals purchase their primary residence anticipating its benefit to satisfy their housing requirements. Vacation homes are purchased with the expectation of enjoyment. And of course, most all property is acquired with an expectation that equity will grow and the property will appreciate in value.

Change

Change is a principle that affects value; it suggests *all factors influencing real estate and property values are constantly changing*. In both the sales comparison approach and the income approach, change is a key consideration that is applied based on the determinations made by the appraiser during market analysis. Due to change, the necessity for adjustments in the sales comparison approach must be considered. Change will be reflected in the income approach through the determination of potential market rent and/or the net income projection for a property, as well as rates of capitalization that are applied. In either approach to value, the principle of change influences the relativity of comparable data for use in the appraiser's analysis of the subject.

» Change is an important consideration that appraisers determine and apply during a market analysis. This is true for both the sales comparison approach and the income approach «

Many of the analyses involved with the sales comparison and income approaches reflect the principle of change. We will explore these as we look more closely at the components of the individual valuation methods, but change is most

KEY TERMS

Highest and Best Use The most profitable, legally permitted, economically feasible, and physically possible use of a piece of property.

Hypothetical Condition A condition, related to a specific assignment, which is contrary to what is known by the appraiser to exist on the effective date of the assignment results, but is used for the purpose of analysis.*

Intended Use The use(s) of an appraiser's reported appraisal or appraisal review assignment results, as identified by the appraiser based on communication with the client at the time of the assignment.*

Intended User The client and any other party as identified, by name or type, as users of the appraisal or appraisal review report by the appraiser based on communication with the client at the time of the assignment. *

Jurisdictional Exception An assignment condition established by applicable law or regulation, which precludes an appraiser from complying with a part of USPAP.*

Limiting Conditions Statement by the appraiser explaining the framework used to reach the appraisal value.

Primary Data Data that is obtained directly by the appraiser.

Principle of Consistent Use Holds that land cannot be valued for one use, while the improvements are valued at another use.

Progression A principle that says the value of a home is positively affected by the other homes in an area. Usually said about the "worst" home in the "best" area.

Regression A principle that says the value of a home is negatively affected by the other homes in an area. Usually said about the "best" home in the "worst" area.

Scope of Work The type and extent of research and analyses in an appraisal or appraisal review assignment. *

Secondary Data Data that is compiled by other parties and used by the appraiser.

Seller's Market A situation in the real estate market where sellers can choose from a large number of buyers looking for property in an area.

Specific Data Information that is relevant to the subject property. There are two types of specific data.

Substitution Theory that an informed buyer will not pay more for a home than a comparable substitute.

**Definitions from most recent edition of USPAP*

commonly related to one or more of the broad forces of value known as **P-E-G-S**: physical, economic, governmental, and social forces, which are identified as part of the appraiser's market analysis.

Physical (Environmental) Forces

Physical forces are referred to by some sources as **environmental forces** because they refer to the environment in and around a property or area. Physical forces *apply to the land and any natural or man-made features or characteristics,* such as:

- Climate
- Condition and other physical characteristics of surrounding properties
- Topography
- Nuisances and hazards present in an area
- Change in use taking place in an area
- Street patterns and characteristics
- Aesthetic appeal or overall impressions of an area
- Maintenance levels of the area in general
- Linkages or convenience to employment, transportation, services, and other amenities
- Environmental hazards or potential environmental conditions
- Availability and adequacy of utilities
- Services available to the area
- Acceptability and quality of schools
- Typical building size, quality, and maintenance
- Uses of surrounding properties

In the sales comparison approach, physical forces are most often considered for possible adjustments for location, view, topography, site, quality, condition, appeal, or other physical characteristics. Potential market rent or net income is the most common area in the income approach to reflect on physical forces.

» *An appraiser's choice of comparable properties (and necessary adjustments) and potential market rent and rates of capitalization for the subject are all strongly influenced by physical forces* «

Economic Forces

Economic forces *reflect the health of a market area's economy and the economic state overall, including national and regional factors.* Like other things, economic forces can change quickly or gradually but of all of the broad forces, an economic force may be most likely to cause sporadic volatility in property values. Economic forces most commonly seen to affect property values include:

- Change in an economic base
- Income levels
- Interest rates
- Inflation
- Employment levels
- Trends of owner-occupied vs. tenant-occupied properties

- Development and construction activities
- Foreclosure rates and number of foreclosed properties
- Availability of financing

As a regular part of every appraiser's routine, they should have, at their disposal, numerous sources for gauging the economic climate and constantly monitoring the market for change that is either taking place or potentially on the horizon. The appraiser's conclusions resulting from the analysis of economic factors are the core of the appraiser's decision for market condition adjustments in the sales comparison approach, the applicability of the data available for analysis, and the data that is applied in the income approach.

» *Of all the broad forces, economic forces may be most likely to cause sporadic volatility in property values—either quickly or gradually* «

Governmental Forces

Government forces reflect the federal, state, or local jurisdictional right to impose laws, regulations, or taxes that affect property. Some of elements considered as government forces include:

- Property taxes
- Special assessments
- Government services, such as fire and police protection
- Zoning
- Building codes
- Safety standards
- Environmental regulations
- Historic preservation codes and regulations
- Development standards or regulations
- Public transportation

Competency in an appraisal assignment requires the appraiser to be aware of the governmental issues that affect a market and/or a property. Many of the elements considered as government forces can impact the legal permissibility in the highest and best use analysis, the supply and demand analysis, and/or the suitability of data that might be used in the sales comparison or income analysis.

» *It is important for appraisers to be aware of the governmental issues that affect a market or property. This is a requirement of competency in an appraisal assignment* «

Social Forces

The composition of people, their preferences, their attitudes, and their habits are all part of the **social forces** influencing a market area. Of course, these judgments and determinations must be made without bias or unsupported conclusions regarding protected class characteristics. Social forces include where people want to live, what they want to live in, what they find desirable, and what they do not. In general, one could simply define social forces as "what is in and what is out." Social forces that an appraiser examines might include:

- Population growth or diminishment
- Buyer tastes and requirements
- Geographic trends and preferences
- Lifestyle requirements and choices

» *When forming opinions regarding social forces, appraisers must not be biased or use unsupported conclusions regarding protected class characteristics of the property, the region, the market area, or the neighborhood* «

- Age of population and demographic categories (i.e., Baby Boomers, Generation X, etc.)
- Housing preferences

The social forces often present themselves in supply and (especially) demand trends for a market area or particular property type. While some of this information can be interpreted from demographic information, the appraiser's analysis of market data for use in the sales comparison and income approaches will usually reveal the affect of social forces.

> ***For Example:*** A demographic trend of having smaller households might demonstrate a trend for purchasing properties with fewer bedrooms, or not paying more (or much more) for a property that has a finished basement vs. one that is not finished. Or, an aging housing market might pay more rent for apartments conveniently located near services such as restaurants, drug stores, and shopping.

Again, appraisers must be careful about making unsupported, or subjective, conclusions when considering any perceived social force. They should rely on objective data evidenced by the market.

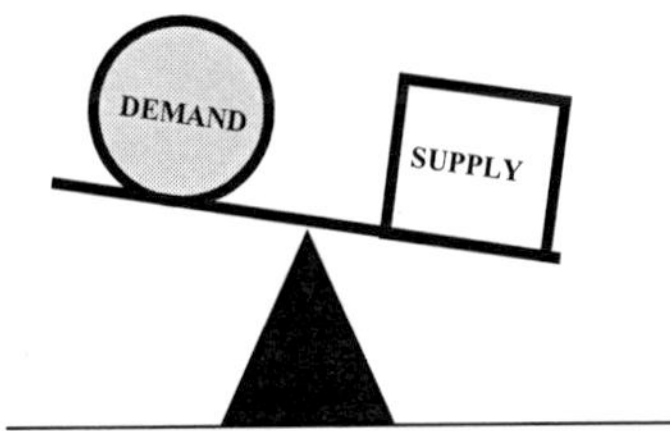

Market in Balance
SUPPLY SLIGHTLY OUTWEIGHS DEMAND

Seller's Market
DEMAND OUTWEIGHS SUPPLY

Buyer's Market
SUPPLY OUTWEIGHS DEMAND

Figure 1.1

Balance

Balance is a condition of supply and demand that exists in the real estate market when there are *slightly more properties available than buyers.* The principle of supply and demand suggests that when supply exceeds demand, prices will fall and when demand exceeds supply, prices will rise. In other words, if there are more buyers than properties, there is the potential for prices to rise. This is known as a **seller's market**. If there are more properties than buyers, property values diminish. This condition is known as a **buyer's market**.

Seller's Markets

A **seller's market** is *a circumstance in a real estate market where sellers can choose from a large number of buyers who are looking for property in a particular area or of a particular property type.* This may be due to people moving into an area, sparse new construction of housing, high construction costs for labor or materials, favorable economic conditions (like a new factory opening), or lower interest rates. When fewer properties are available, the lower supply (relative to the demand) tends to keep property values higher. Often in this situation, a seller is in a position to stay closer to the original asking price or negotiate favorable terms in the seller's best interest.

Buyer's Markets

A **buyer's market** is *a situation in the real estate market where buyers have a large selection of properties to choose from.* This may be due to population shifts away from an area, overbuilding of new housing, or bad economic conditions (such as a factory closing that causes unemployment or people to leaving an area). When more properties are available, the increased supply tends to keep property values lower. In this situation, a buyer is often in a position to negotiate for a lower price or more favorable terms in the buyer's best interest.

Because real estate markets are by nature inefficient, they typically respond to supply and demand more slowly than markets for other products or services. This slower response time is the result of the time it takes for property to be bought, sold, developed, or built. If people lose their jobs today, they cannot all expect to sell their homes readily. Or, if builders realize a need for housing, it takes time to build houses; and when that need diminishes, often there are houses started that still must be finished. Because of the inefficiencies of real estate markets, supply and demand are rarely in balance. When balance occurs in a market, the state of the market can change; often quickly.

» *Supply and demand are rarely in balance due to the inefficiencies of real estate markets. And when balance occurs in a market, it can change quickly* «

Conformity

The principle of **conformity,** sometimes called **homogeneity,** suggests that *a property's value is achieved and maintained when surrounded by properties that are similar in style, function, and utility.* A neighborhood itself can be affected by a lack of conformity. For instance, a very visible house in a subdivision that is of somewhat peculiar design or of poorer quality or condition could negatively affect the property value of the other homes in the subdivision.

Conformity, though, should not always be associated with "sameness." Conformity is in the eye of the beholder, or in the case of market value, the typical buyer. An example might be that in a small rural or suburban village or town, a mix of property uses and styles might be expected and acceptable. Some older historic areas might have a mix, such as restaurants and shops blended with the residential housing, and be perfectly acceptable or conforming.

» *The principle of progression or regression is being realized when a particular property's value is affected due to conformity* «

Most commonly, variations of conformity might necessitate the appraiser to apply a location or similar adjustment in the sales comparison approach. The affects of conformity may also be evidenced in potential market rent for the income approach. The appraiser determines in his market analysis when conformity is an issue. In some cases, there might not be any affect on property values. But when value is affected either positively or negatively, the principle of either **progression** or **regression** is being realized.

Progression

Location, location, location—the principle of **progression** holds that *the value of the worst or inferior home in a good area can benefit from being among other homes that are superior.* There are occasions in which neighborhoods can experience an increase in property values overall, due to things like new construction or revitalization of properties occurring within the neighborhood.

Regression

The principle of **regression** suggests that *the value of a superior home is negatively affected by an inferior home or homes in the neighborhood area,* or that an entire neighborhood is negatively impacted by a property or properties in the area.

Competition

Competition is *when two or more parties, such as a buyer or seller, or properties are trying to obtain the same thing.* When one considers competition affecting market value, it is simply acknowledged that available properties compete with

» *The appraiser needs to recognize the term "competition"—available properties competing with one another for the market's attention* «

one another in the marketplace for the market's attention. An informed buyer will consider other available properties before making a decision. A property that is priced higher must have some element that supports a higher value when compared with other competing properties in the marketplace. Without something to justify a higher value in the informed buyer's thinking, the limit of the property's value is likely to be no greater than the highest competing property in a given neighborhood or market area.

Contribution

Contribution and a feature's **contributory value** is a theory that suggests *a particular item or feature of a property is worth only what it actually contributes in value to the property as a whole when the type of value in the assignment is market value.* In the sales comparison approach, contribution is inherent in the comparable properties that are being analyzed and the specific adjustments that are applied to address the contribution. For the income approach, contribution is, again, reflected in the potential and/or net income, and sometimes in the rate or other factor being used for the analysis.

Within the principle of contribution, cost does not necessarily equate to value.

> ***For Example:*** If a five-bedroom home is not desired by the market, then putting an addition onto a four-bedroom house to add a fifth bedroom most likely will not increase the value of the home by more than the cost of the addition (and in some cases even less). A property owner may want or need a fifth bedroom, but he should not expect it to add value to the home, equal to the construction costs, when the home is sold.

The contributory value of an item or improvement is only equal to what the market indicates a typical buyer is willing to pay for it, rather than what it actually cost.

Contribution is more complex to analyze when it comes to repairs or replacement of items that are generally considered typical maintenance to a structure. Repairs may or may not add value to a property, depending on where the value started. A new roof that cost $5,000 may not contribute $5,000 to the price of the home when it is sold. Since the market typically expects a house to have a good roof and be in good repair, the typical buyer sometimes will not recognize a significantly greater value for a house that has a new roof when compared to another house that has a good roof, or at least not equal to the cost. However, from the standpoint of marketability, the house with a new roof might sell more quickly than a house that does not.

Some features and characteristics of a structure will aid marketability and help the property sell faster, but may not be a feature or characteristic with an identifiable specific contributory value. On the other hand, if a home is in serious need of exterior painting, $4,000 spent on new siding could add significantly more value than just $4,000. This is especially true when the surrounding properties are of superior exterior condition.

Many times appraisers are asked by a property owner, "How much will the value of my home increase if I say...remodel the kitchen?" Of course, as we will discuss later in this chapter, if the question is answered specifically, the appraiser is bound by USPAP to consider the request as an appraisal assignment and follow the diligence required in Standard 1 in developing an opinion. However, in order to respond to such an inquiry, the appraiser must analyze the marketability of the present kitchen. Is the present kitchen perfectly acceptable to the market, but the owner just wants a different look? Or, is the present kitchen deteriorated and/or suffering from functional issues (obsolescence)? The appraiser's response may be quite different for each scenario. This is why appraisers must understand the **law of diminishing returns** and the **law of increasing returns**.

» *In a market value assignment, an improvement or feature contributes only to the extent that the typical market participant (buyer or renter) would recognize the improvement or feature in dollars* «

Law of Diminishing Returns

The **law of diminishing returns** implies that beyond a certain point, *the added value of another feature, addition, repair, etc., is less than the actual cost.* Sometimes, this is also referred to as the **law of decreasing returns**. In other words, too much can be done or added to a property—such that the value will not increase enough to recoup the money invested. Certainly, property owners can do things to their property for their own enjoyment or use, but they should not expect to get the full cost of the labor and materials returned when market value of the property is considered.

Law of Increasing Returns

The **law of increasing returns** suggests that *the added value of an additional feature, repair, etc., is more than the actual cost.* This goes back to the example where the exterior of the house was in a poor state and that doing something would have a dramatic increase in its market value. Of course, beyond a certain point, one can go too far and result in the law of diminishing returns.

USPAP Standard 1—Real Property Appraisal Development

Standard 1 of USPAP is the appraiser's compass for developing a value opinion of real property using any of the methods of valuation. The real property appraiser should not only be familiar with the spirit and overall message of Standard 1, but also the Standards Rules and USPAP Advisory Opinions relating to the development of a value opinion.

Throughout this course, we will look more specifically at the direction and guidance provided by USPAP for developing an opinion of value using the sales comparison approach and/or the income approach. But for now, we will look at the general content of Standard 1.

In general, Standard 1 requires the appraiser to:

- Identify the problem to be solved
- Determine the scope of work necessary to solve the problem
- Correctly complete the research and analysis necessary to produce credible results

These three requirements establish the basis for this course. Each of these requirements is discussed at greater detail later in this chapter. Throughout the text, examples and challenges will be presented to assist with understanding the thought process and steps that must be taken to adequately satisfy these fundamental requirements.

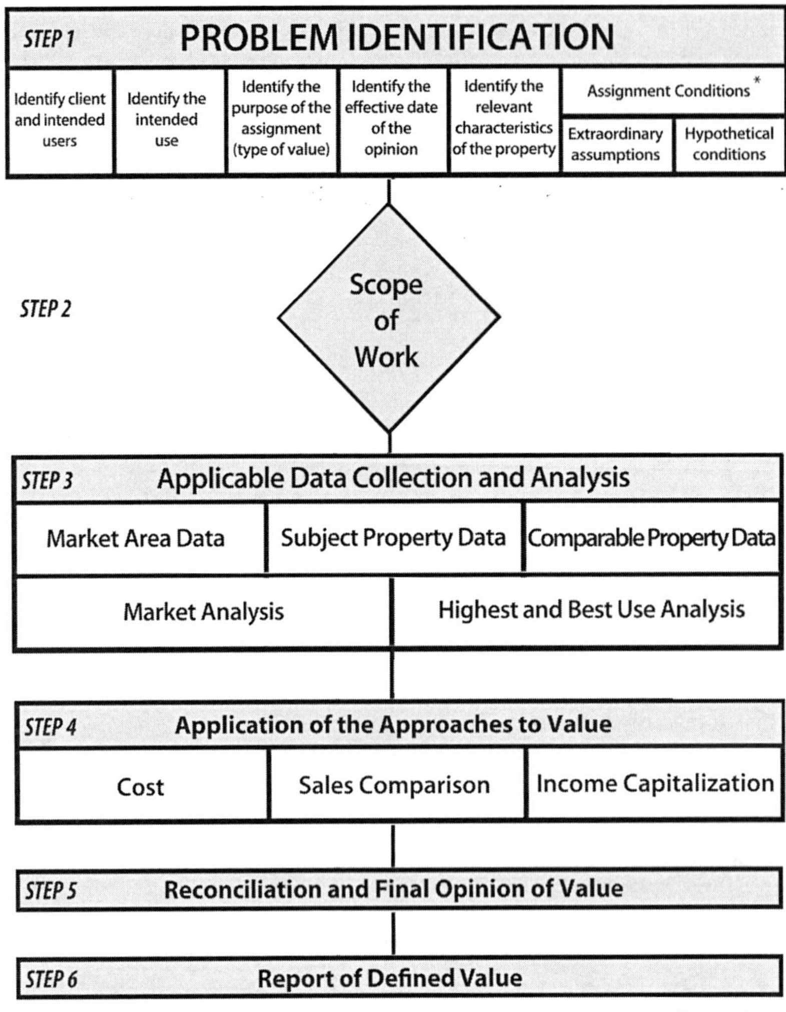

Figure 1.2

* *Assignment conditions also include assumptions, laws and regulations, jurisdictional exceptions, and other conditions that affect the scope of work.*

Standards Rules

The Standards Rules of Standard 1 elaborate on principle topics of the general Rules of USPAP (Ethics, Competency, and Scope of Work) as they apply specifically to the development of a real property appraisal. Standards Rule 1-1 conveys the general requirements for the appraiser to:

- Correctly employ recognized methods and techniques that are necessary to produce a credible appraisal
- Not commit a substantial error that significantly affects an appraisal
- Not render services in a careless or negligent manner

Standards Rules 1-2 through 1-6 create a flow or "checklist" of the development steps that an appraiser must undertake in a real property appraisal. Each of these Standards Rules coincides with a specific function within the development process, as is illustrated in figure 1.2 on page 11.

» *Standard 1 of USPAP sets the three foundational requirements for a real property appraisal: 1. identify the problem, 2. determine the necessary scope of work, and 3. correctly complete the research and analysis necessary to produce credible results* «

Problem Identification

Problem identification consists of identifying information the appraiser uses to determine the scope of work in an assignment. This step is also referred to as identifying the problem or defining the problem. Here, the appraiser identifies several elements:

- Client and intended users
- Intended use
- Type and definition of value
- Date of value opinion
- Relevant property characteristics
- Assignment conditions

» *In problem identification, the appraiser identifies information he then uses to determine the scope of work in an assignment* «

The appropriate valuation methods and techniques (such as whether the sales comparison and/or income approach will be applicable, meaningful, and produce **credible**—*worthy of belief*—results) are realized from what the appraiser learns during problem identification. Therefore, the appraiser should not abbreviate this process and must consider problem identification as being significant in his development. Communication with the client will be necessary to determine most of the elements that must be identified. The exception is identifying the relevant property characteristics, for which the appraiser has the sole responsibility to determine. Let's briefly review the elements of problem identification.

Identify the Client and Any Other Intended Users

The **client** is *the party who engages the appraiser in an appraisal assignment, and with whom the appraiser has an appraiser-client relationship*. An **intended user** is a party *identified by the client* at the time of the assignment. The *client is always an intended user* in an assignment. Additional intended users may be specified by the client when the appraiser is engaged.

√ ***Note:*** An additional intended user may or may not have the same need or use as the client. For instance, the sales comparison approach may best satisfy the intended use of the client, but would be of little value to an additional intended user for a different intended use for which the income approach might produce the most credible assignment results.

Identify the Intended Use

» *The client is always an intended user in an assignment—additional intended users may be specified by the client at the time of the assignment* «

An appraisal is the basis for some type of a decision. What that decision will be, or the *intended use* of the conclusions, is a primary driver of the research and analysis that is performed during the appraisal's development. The **intended use** is *the use or uses of an appraiser's reported appraisal or appraisal review assignment opinions and conclusions, as identified by the appraiser based on communication with the client at the time of the assignment.*

√ **Note:** Similar to intended users, different intended uses might require different research and/or analysis, or at different levels. Which approach to use, and the techniques that should be applied, are strongly affected by the intended use.

Identify the Type and Definition of Value

» *The research and analysis that is performed during the appraisal's development is primarily driven by the intended use of the appraiser's opinions and conclusions* «

The **type and definition of value** are sometimes referred to as the *purpose of the appraisal*. Care must be taken not to confuse the *purpose of the appraisal* with *intended use*. The **purpose of an appraisal** is always to determine a value opinion for a defined type of value.

Identifying the type and definition of value specific to an assignment prompts the appraiser to utilize the valuation method(s) that will produce the most credible result. It also alerts the appraiser of transaction characteristics to look for when choosing comparable data.

> ***For Example:*** The appraiser must be certain that the sale price of the comparable data being analyzed is reflective of the same type of transaction for which the data is being applied.

» *The purpose of an appraisal is always to determine a value opinion for a defined type of value and must not be confused with the intended use* «

In a market value assignment, the appraiser must be certain that the comparable data is being extracted from a transaction that represents an arms-length or market value transaction. As we will discuss in greater detail later, some elements of an arms-length or market value transaction can be addressed by adjustments in the sales comparison approach, such as financing concessions. Other adjustments may be difficult, if not impossible, to isolate (such as for haste or duress).

Market value is the value conclusion most frequently specified in an appraisal. However, other types of value can be derived, based on the appraisal's use. The type and definition of value should always be appropriate for the appraisal's intended use.

√ **Note:** Both the sales comparison and income approach can be useful for developing a market value opinion. However, there are types of value for which one or both of these approaches will not be a good indicator and the cost approach is most useful. For example, insurance value and investment value are typically not developed using the sales comparison approach.

Identify the Effective Date of the Value Opinion

Two dates are required for every appraisal—the *effective date* and the *date of the report*. Standard 2 of USPAP references the **effective date** as *establishing the context for the value opinion;* and **date of the report** as *an indication of the perspective from which the appraiser is examining the market*. Intended use dictates the date of relevance to a value opinion. The *effective date* can be a *current date, a retrospective date*, or a *prospective date*. The effective date may or may not be the same as the date the appraiser inspects a property. In a current appraisal, the effective date and the date of the report are the same.

» *Intended use of the appraisal dictates the date of relevance to a value opinion—a current, retrospective, or prospective date* «

√ **Note:** For either the sales comparison or income approach, the appraiser should choose data for his analysis that is most current and reflective of the effective date of the value opinion that is being expressed in the specific assignment.

Identify the Relevant Characteristics of the Property

Relevant property characteristics have significant influence on the applicability of a specific approach(es) the appraiser will employ and also the relativity of the data that will be researched and analyzed. The appraiser has the sole responsibility to determine the relevant property characteristics, which include (but are not necessarily limited to):

» *Whether or not a specific approach(es) is applicable is significantly influenced by relevant property characteristics. These characteristics also influence the relativity of the data that will be researched and analyzed* «

- Interest to be appraised
- Type of property
- Location
- Legal characteristics
- Specific physical characteristics

Identify Assignment Conditions

Assignment conditions are other elements applicable in an appraisal assignment, including:

- **Assumptions**—*That which is taken to be true.*
- **Extraordinary assumptions**—*An assignment-specific assumption as of the effective date regarding uncertain information used in an analysis which, if found to be false, could alter the appraiser's opinions or conclusions.*
- **Hypothetical conditions**—*A condition, related to a specific assignment, which is contrary to what is known by the appraiser to exist on the effective date of the assignment results, but is used for the purpose of analysis.*
- **Jurisdictional exception**—*An assignment condition established by applicable law or regulation, which precludes an appraiser from complying with a part of USPAP.*
- Other laws, regulations, guidelines, or other conditions agreed to with the client.

We will be more specific as we move through the course, but for many residential appraisals, the elements that will most affect the development and reliance of the particular approach to value are the laws, regulations, and guidelines applicable to the assignment:

- Laws and regulations may come in the form of IRS Codes for the appraisal of real property for some intended uses, or specific state licensing and certification limitations and requirements, such as limitations based on the

» *Laws, regulations, guidelines, and other client requirements applicable to the assignment are what will most affect what the appraiser does going forward in many residential appraisals* «

appraiser's license/certification credential, or the requirement to follow USPAP. Guidelines most often present themselves as additional lender underwriting requirements or guidelines such as Fannie Mae, FHA, or other conditions.

- The COMPETENCY RULE of USPAP requires the appraiser to recognize and comply with any laws and regulations applying to the appraiser or the assignment. If compliance with the assignment condition cannot be met by the appraiser for some reason within the assignment, the appraiser must not accept the assignment with that condition.
- Many assignment conditions will affect the approach being developed, the extent of the analysis, and the reliance to be given by the appraiser to the particular approach(es).

Scope of Work

As we have just seen, there is quite a bit of specific information the appraiser must gather and sort through during problem identification. This information is then used in the next step of the appraisal process—deciding the **scope of work**. This is where the appraiser decides, among other things, *the type and extent of property identification or inspection, and the research and analysis to apply in the appraisal assignment*. In other words, which valuation approach(es) is/are applicable, meaningful, and reliable in the assignment.

Scope of work will be further discussed in this chapter as well as throughout this course. But, there are some fundamental issues regarding the scope of work that should be highlighted here:

- The scope of work determined by the appraiser is considered appropriate when it meets or exceeds the expectations of those who are regularly intended users in the same or similar assignment, and what the **appraiser's peers** (*other appraisers with expertise and competency in a similar type of assignment*) would do in the same or similar assignment.
- Determining the appropriate scope of work is an ongoing process and can change during the assignment based on information and conditions learned by the appraiser, which can lead to modification of the scope of work.
- The scope of work an appraiser performs should not be limited by the client or intended user to the extent that credible results cannot be obtained or results are biased.

» *The appraiser's scope of work decision includes the type and extent of property identification or inspection, and the research and analysis to apply in the appraisal assignment* «

Data Collection and Analysis

Again, the scope of work will determine the type of data necessary in a particular assignment and the extent to which it is analyzed. Whatever the scope, the process is generally categorized into three progressive steps:

1. Collect
2. Organize
3. Analyze

Data Collection

There are two sources from which data is collected in appraisal assignments, data from **primary sources** and data from **secondary sources.**

Information from **primary data sources** is *data that is discovered by the appraiser*, such as through a direct interview or through the appraiser's personal investigation. Data that might be collected through primary sources includes (but is not limited to):

- Comparable sale transaction details from a participant to the transaction.
- Gross living area calculations (of the comparable or the subject) that are taken from the appraiser's measurements and calculated by the appraiser.
- Physical characteristics and features of the comparable and/or subject property gathered through a personal inspection.
- Market condition trends gathered through a personal interview with individuals and entities.
- Income data gathered from landlords in the market.

Information from **secondary data sources** is *data that is compiled by other parties and used by the appraiser*. Just as an example, sources could include auditor or assessors records, other appraisers, public records, published data, **multiple listing services (MLS®)**, etc. Many times, the appraiser must rely on secondary data because gathering the information first hand is not practical or possible. Or, the data pertains to a topic that the appraiser would need special expertise in order to determine by themselves, such as flood elevation information. Secondary data might include (but is not limited to):

- Comparable sales and income data gathered from other sources.
- Physical information regarding the subject or the comparable sales obtained from outside sources, such as public records.
- Demographic and economic data published by others.
- Rates of capitalization supplied by national surveys.

This is a good time to discuss the reliability of the data the appraiser collects from other sources, especially secondary sources. Regarding the property characteristics, the comment to Standards Rule 1-2 (i)-(v) states (in part):

> ***"The information used by an appraiser to identify the property characteristics must be from sources the appraiser reasonably believes are reliable."***

Therefore, when the appraiser is relying on information provided by others, the appraiser must be reasonably certain that the information can be depended on to produce credible results.

Standards Rule 1-4 of USPAP requires the appraiser (in part) to,

> ***"...collect, verify, and analyze all information necessary for credible assignment results."***

> ***For Example:*** Verification might be confirming a comparable sales transaction reported in a multiple listing service with another source, such as public records or a participant of the transaction.

Often, the use of an extraordinary assumption regarding the use of some of the data should be considered, if using the data with the extraordinary assumption would still produce credible assignment results.

> ***For Example:*** An exterior inspection for the purpose of an "exterior only" appraisal may include an extraordinary assumption about physical characteristics of the interior of the property. Details about the physical characteristics of the property interior are often from other sources, such as the property owner, the client, tax records, multiple listing service, or even a past appraisal assignment workfile. If the appraiser could reasonably rely on these sources but did not examine them first-hand, an extraordinary assumption may need to be used.

Of course, the appraiser must ensure that the scope of work, including the use of the extraordinary assumption, would produce credible results.

While we are discussing property inspection, the level of the inspection is determined in the scope of work. An appraiser's personal inspection of a property will undoubtedly provide the greatest confidence in the data that is collected by him while he is on site. USPAP allows for any combination of a property inspection and other documents to identify the relevant property characteristics. Specific USPAP courses for appraisers provide more detail in all of these areas.

The data collected for an appraisal from primary and secondary sources consists of two types of data, **general data** and **specific data**. Both types of data are required in all appraisal assignments in order to comply with Standard 1 of USPAP. Sources of general and specific data can be primary or secondary sources.

General Data

General data is *information that has an affect on the subject property or the comparable sales, but is not singularly related to only the subject or the comparables* (for instance, the school district, tax rates of an area, utility providers, etc). Economic and market conditions are also considered general data. Appraisers must stay current on national interest rate trends, and must be familiar with business conditions affecting the economic base of an area. Changes in federal laws are important, as are changes in local laws—particularly zoning. Demographic changes, population shifts, and buyer tastes, on national and local levels, are all important. Physical and environmental changes and trends are also vital to the appraiser's conclusions. Typically, appraisers use general data to analyze trends.

» The appraiser will collect both general and specific data, which can come from either primary data sources or secondary data sources «

Specific Data

Specific data is *information that is specific to the subject property and the comparable sales*. Specific data includes things such as site features and improvements. Site characteristics such as size, shape, topography, landscaping, etc., of the subject property and the comparables would be one example. Physical characteristics, such as features, quality, condition, etc., would be another. If there is a specific restrictive deed condition applying only to the subject property or the comparable, this would also be considered specific in nature.

Data Organization

Here, **data organization** refers to how the appraiser arranges or lays out the collected data for his eventual analysis. Appraisers use a variety of methods depending on the type of data being analyzed and what it is being applied to. For the sales comparison approach, the comparable data is often presented for analysis by organizing the comparable data on grids. Market conditions are sometimes organized on charts or tables to best observe trends. In the final reconciliation for the sales comparison approach, one of the methods of analysis that could be employed is a ranking analysis. For a ranking analysis, the data would be organized, usually, in a declining fashion from most comparable to the least comparable, based on a number of factors. The appraiser may have several tables, graphs, or grids for a single assignment. Similar methods may be employed for the income approach. Several examples will be illustrated later in this text.

» *Data organization refers to how the appraiser arranges his collected data to aid in his eventual analysis—often in grids, tables, or charts* «

Data Analysis

Data analysis should not be thought of as a single process in a particular assignment. In actuality, once data is collected, every step of the appraisal process from here forth through reconciliation consists of a series of individual analyses that includes:

- Market analysis
- Highest and best use analysis
- Application of the approaches of value
- Reconciliation

Just as a reminder, information that the appraiser obtains during the course of collecting and analyzing data could call for further analysis, which might cause the appraiser's scope of work in the assignment to change.

Market Analysis

Standards Rule 1-3 (a) of USPAP tells us that:

> ***"When necessary for credible assignment results in developing a market value opinion, an appraiser must: identify and analyze the effect on use and value of existing land use regulations, reasonably probable modifications of such land use regulations, economic supply and demand, the physical adaptability of the real estate, and market area trends…"***

The term **market analysis** might seem to imply that the process consists primarily of the analysis of economic and market conditions for the subject market, which is partially true. However, **market analysis** is much broader and *includes consideration of national and regional conditions, as well as specific data regarding the subject site and improvements.* The elements considered in a market analysis, depending on the scope of work, could include (but are not limited to):

- National trends
- Regional trends
- Economic base

- Local area and neighborhood
- Site and improvements

The Comment to USPAP Standards Rule 1-3 (a) continues to advise:

> ***"An appraiser must avoid making an unsupported assumption or premise about market area trends, effective age, and remaining life."***

Highest and Best Use Analysis

According to Standard Rule 1-3 (b), an opinion of **highest and best use** must be developed, when it is necessary for credible assignment results, in an assignment where the type of value is market value. The subsequent USPAP Comment to this portion of the Standards Rule further expresses that the appraiser must analyze the relevant legal, physical, and economic factors to the extent necessary to support the appraiser's conclusions about highest and best use.

Here the appraiser is forming opinions relating to the subject property in the context of the **characteristics of value**: Demand, Utility, Scarcity, and Transferability (or **D-U-S-T**). **Highest and best use** particularly *addresses the value of the land, and if improved, the improvement's contribution to value.* The process of highest and best use analysis consists of three steps:

1. Value the land as vacant.

2. Value the property as improved.

3. Conclude on the highest and best use.

The appraiser should be cautious however, that the **principle of consistent use** is observed in forming opinions. The **principle of consistent use** *holds that land cannot be valued for one use, while the improvements are valued at another use.*

Application of the Approaches to Value

Many misconceptions circulate regarding USPAP compliance and the steps that must be taken in developing an opinion of value using the approaches to value. This is especially true when it comes to the sales comparison approach. Examples include that at least three comparables must be analyzed in every case, the comparables can never be over six months or one year old, or the comparable sales must be from the same neighborhood or market area. While this may be common and arguably the soundest practice in most assignments, USPAP does not address such issues. The examples are typical assignment conditions found in some assignments and, of course, must be observed if the assignment is accepted with those conditions. However, the best advice for appraisers from USPAP is that which was discussed earlier—for the appraiser to *use recognized methods and techniques.*

In the following chapters, we will further discuss the requirements of Standards Rule 1-4 and 1-5 as they pertain to development of a value opinion using the sales comparison and/or the income approach. Standards Rule 1-4 details the minimum benchmark that must be met for the development of any of the approaches.

Standards Rule 1-5 discusses additional diligence that the appraiser must undertake in some assignments. As it pertains to the development of an appraisal, Standards Rule 1-5 states:

> ***"When the value opinion to be developed is market value, an appraiser must, if such information is available to the appraiser in the normal course of business:***
>
> **(a)** ***analyze all agreements of sale, options, and listings of the subject property current as of the effective date of the appraisal; and***
>
> **(b)** ***analyze all sales of the subject property that occurred within the three (3) years prior to the effective date of the appraisal."***

Reconciliation

The final analysis in the process of developing an opinion of value is reconciliation. This is where the appraiser reflects on each approach that was developed in the assignment and, per Standards Rule 1-6, the quality and quantity of the data that was available and analyzed in each approach individually.

Standards Rule 1-6 also obligates the appraiser to then weigh the relevance of all the approaches that were developed and make decisions regarding their influence and their indication of the final opinion of value as concluded by the appraiser. We will look at these items more specifically in later chapters.

» *Data analysis consists of a series of several individual analyses—market analysis, highest and best use analysis, application of the approaches to value, and reconciliation* «

Application Case Study

A real property appraiser has accepted an appraisal assignment for a single-family residential property. The appraiser recognizes the subject of the assignment is located in a predominately (95%) owner-occupied subdivision in which the appraiser has recently completed several assignments of single-family properties involved in arms-length and market value transactions. The appraiser has already verified that all of the recent transactions were for owner-occupancy.

A local mortgage banker needs the appraisal in order to complete a loan for a sales transaction involving the subject property. The loan originator, who is the contact person for the mortgage banker, indicates that the loan will be held "in-house," and will not require compliance with Fannie Mae or other secondary market underwriting requirements. The borrower has a high credit score and is putting down 40% of the sale price of the property. The borrower intends to use the property as a rental unit. The originator simply wants "something current to put in the file to satisfy the company's auditors when they review the file," and indicates that he "doesn't need anything fancy." In other words, "just do the minimum." The originator further indicates that he has no preference as to whether the appraiser inspects the interior or not, and that a drive-by inspection would be acceptable.

According to the loan originator, the subject property is a one-story dwelling that has recently had a substantial renovation completed. The current owner of the property was relocated by his employer just as the addition was finished. The loan originator has no information about the details of the addition as he has never spoken to the current owner and the property is now vacant. The loan originator's only knowledge of the property is that the borrower has told him the subject property "puts everything else in the neighborhood to shame."

The appraiser plans to inspect the property the next day after receiving the appraisal order (Wednesday), and will complete and submit the appraisal to the client at the end of the week (Friday).

Using the information provided in the case scenario, consider the following problem identification issues. If a question or issue cannot be addressed, due to a lack of information, indicate that the item cannot be answered.

Who is the client?

Are there other intended users?

What is the intended use of the appraiser's opinions and conclusions?

What is the effective date of the appraiser's value opinion?

What is the date of the report?

What relevant characteristics of the property can be noted from the scenario?

From this point, the appraiser should be able to form a scope of work decision. Consider the following scope of work issues and questions that are important to that decision. If a question or issue cannot be addressed, due to a lack of information, indicate that the item cannot be answered.

What level of property inspection would most likely be warranted in the assignment?

Why?

In particular, from the information provided, what fundamental valuation principle should be a specific concern in this assignment?

Why?

Of the sales comparison and income approaches, what would be the appraiser's choices to develop as part of the valuation analysis?

Why?

Selected USPAP Illustrations and Guidance

The following USPAP Advisory Opinion (AO) and Frequently Asked Questions (FAQ) have been selected to illustrate the application of USPAP in specific circumstances discussed in this chapter.

AO 2—Inspection of the Subject Property

AO 16—Fair Housing Laws and Appraisal Report Content

AO 23—Identifying the Relevant Characteristics of the Subject Property of a Real Property Appraisal Assignment

AO 28—Scope of Work Decision, Performance, and Disclosure

AO 29—An Acceptable Scope of Work

FAQ 125—Identification of Intended Users

FAQ 136—Appraisal Dates

FAQ 151—What is Scope of Work?

FAQ 153—Responsibility for the Scope of Work

FAQ 154—Client Specifies Scope of Work

FAQ 158—How "Credible" Results are Measured

FAQ 163—Judging the Actions of an Appraiser's Peers

FAQ 178—Inspection of Subject Property

FAQ 215—Extraordinary Assumptions Compared to Hypothetical Conditions

Quiz

1. ***The premise that an informed buyer will not pay more for a property than they would be required to pay for an acceptable comparable property is known as***
   a. anticipation.
   b. balance.
   c. change.
   d. substitution.

2. ***Which is NOT one of the broad forces of value (P-E-G-S)?***
   a. economic
   b. general data
   c. physical
   d. social

3. ***In a buyer's market,***
   a. property values tend to be higher.
   b. there are more buyers than homes.
   c. there are more homes than buyers.
   d. there is sparse construction of housing.

4. ***Joey has been trying to sell his home for six months. On more than one occasion, prospective buyers had stated they would buy the home if it were not located in a neighborhood with less attractive properties. Joey's home is being affected by***
   a. change.
   b. the law of diminishing returns.
   c. progression.
   d. regression.

5. ***Danni bought her home in 2006 for $120,000. Danni spent $20,000 on an in-ground pool before selling it in 2008 for $130,000. This is an example of***
   a. the law of diminishing returns.
   b. the law of increasing returns.
   c. progression.
   d. regression.

6. ***Determining a value opinion for a defined type of value is the***
   a. intended use.
   b. problem identification.
   c. purpose of an appraisal.
   d. scope of work.

7. ***The effective date of an appraisal can be a***
   a. current date, a retrospective date, or a prospective date.
   b. current date, a retrospective date, a prospective date, or a set range of dates.
   c. current date, a retrospective date, or a range of dates.
   d. current date or a set range of dates.

8. ***Appraiser's peers are***
   a. the appraiser's clients.
   b. homeowners, lenders, etc., who are relying on the appraisal.
   c. the intended users of the appraisal.
   d. other appraisers with expertise and competency in a similar type of assignment.

9. ***What is an example of a secondary data source?***
   a. comparable sale transaction details from a participant to the transaction
   b. information gathered from landlords in the market
   c. physical characteristics and features of the comparable and/or subject property gathered through a personal inspection
   d. rates of capitalization supplied by national surveys

10. ***What would be considered general data?***
    a. plot map
    b. restrictive deed conditions
    c. topography
    d. utility providers

11. ***What are the four characteristics of value?***
    a. demand, uniqueness, supply, and topography
    b. demand, utility, scarcity, and transferability
    c. demand, utility, supply, and taxes
    d. demand, utility, supply, and transferability

Sales Comparison Analysis—*Data Identification and Analysis*

There are numerous types of data collected and analyzed prior to and in performance of the sales comparison analysis, or for that matter, any type of valuation method. Identification of the subject property characteristics is very similar, whether the appraiser is developing the sales comparison approach, the cost approach, or as we will discuss later in this text, the income approach. In this chapter of the course, we will discuss the appraiser's collection and examination of pertinent data regarding the relevant characteristics of the subject and then the gathering and initial reaction to the available relevant data that can be used in the sales comparison analysis.

Data Analysis of the Subject Property

At this point, we will focus our emphasis on data as it relates to the subject property. The extent and depth of this portion of the analysis is determined in the scope of work decision. But in most appraisal assignments, the process will entail an examination of the subject property's physical facts and an examination of the economic and legal issues relating to the property. Let's begin by discussing identification of the subject property characteristics.

Identification of the Subject Property Characteristics

Looking first to USPAP, the comment to Standards Rule 1-2 (e) (i-v) tells us (in part):

> ***"An appraiser may use any combination of a property inspection and documents, such as a physical legal description, address, map reference, copy of a survey or map, property sketch, or photographs, to identify the relevant characteristics of the subject property."***

» *While other types of data (e.g., legal characteristics) can be gathered throughout review and analysis, physical characteristics are best noted during the property inspection* «

In the typical everyday residential appraisal, the scope of work most likely includes a personal inspection of the subject property, be it only an exterior observation or a complete exterior and interior inspection. In addition, the appraiser should, and usually does, collect a variety of other documentation to adequately identify and support the appraiser's conclusions about the property characteristics of the subject.

Physical characteristics are usually best noted during the property inspection, while identification of other characteristics, such as the legal characteristics, can be best accomplished through review and analysis of other types of data.

Inspection of the Subject Property

The purpose of inspecting the subject property is to collect data. Just as a practical note however, non-appraisers do not always necessarily understand this function and often think or refer to the inspection process as "the appraisal." Those misunderstanding the purpose of the inspection may comment that the appraiser spent only an hour or less and "earned all of that money," when, in fact, the appraiser spent hours or, in some cases, days completing the steps necessary to develop a value opinion once returning to his office. Even more dangerous are the parties who misinterpret the term "inspection" as being synonymous with the function and job description of a home, structural, or other inspector. Therefore, the appraiser should always make clear to all parties involved (clients and property owners) the purpose of the inspection, and refer to the process as an opportunity for data collection. This will help the appraiser avoid being misunderstood and potentially misleading.

For most experienced appraisers, the inspection process often begins as they approach and arrive at a subject property. Location and physical neighborhood characteristics can be observed from that vantage point. Additionally, and probably most importantly, the appraiser can form a first impression of the overall appeal of the property. This can be important, especially in market value assignments, as typical buyers are usually influenced to a certain degree by the property's street appeal, also known as curb appeal, and their first impression of the property.

During the property inspection, the appraiser will gather various types of information regarding the site and improvements. Some appraisers use checklists and/or other data collection methods that are available, or have been specially devised. However it is collected, the appraiser should be certain the information gathered is thorough and adequate for use in future analysis and reporting.

Even though some of this information may not be reported in certain reporting options (which is discussed in other courses), USPAP requires the appraiser's **workfile** to contain the necessary elements to produce *at least* an Appraisal Report. An appraiser's **workfile** is *the documentation necessary to support the appraiser's analyses, opinions, and conclusions.* The workfile also shows compliance with USPAP. Therefore, it is certainly better to over-collect information rather than under-collect it.

Specifically, listed on the following pages are some of the subject property characteristics that the appraiser may note during the inspection process—of course, these may not be all inclusive or applicable in every assignment.

» *To make sure that all parties involved (clients and property owners) do not confuse an appraiser with a professional inspector, the appraiser should make clear the purpose of the inspection, and refer to the process as an opportunity for data collection* «

» *The appraiser should be diligent in his information gathering (regarding the subject) because it will need to be thorough and adequate enough for use in future analysis and reporting* «

KEY TERMS

Competitive Property Those that compete head to head. A potential buyer for one property would also be interested in the competitive property.

Decline The third stage a neighborhood goes through in its life cycle, when property values begin to fall as demand falls.

Deed An instrument that conveys the grantor's interest in real property.

District The narrowest of definitions of a market area. A district is an area consisting of one particular land use, such as multi-family residential, commercial, industrial, etc.

Functional Utility When a building has the adequate design and features to be used as intended.

Gentrification The process of rapid revitalization of properties in a neighborhood, which causes current residents to be displaced.

Growth The first stage a neighborhood goes through in its life cycle, when property values rise as development activity begins and continues.

Market Area The broadest of all terms identifying the boundaries of a particular area. Market area takes into account the land uses and characteristics of typical market participants within the defined area.

Neighborhood Any constant, contiguous area that may be identified by similar characteristics of physical boundaries.

Revitalization The final stage a neighborhood goes through in its life cycle, when property values rise again as demand increases, resulting in increased renovation and rehabilitation. *See:* **Gentrification.**

Stability The second stage a neighborhood goes through in its life cycle, when the area is built up to the point where there is little, if any, vacant property. Also called **equilibrium**.

Workfile The documentation necessary to support the appraiser's analyses, opinions, and conclusions.*

** Definitions reference most current edition of USPAP.*

Site Characteristics

Utilities	• Are utilities public or private? • What is the general location of on-site provisions, such as wells, septic systems, etc.? • Is the electric service/cable/phone underground? • Who are the utility providers?
Off-site Improvements	• Are there sidewalks, curbs, and storm gutters? • Is there street lighting? If so, what type? • Are there fire hydrants?
Apparent Adverse Site Conditions	• Are there steep drop-offs that would be hazardous? • Are there areas that promote standing or ponding water? • Are there apparent environmental site issues? • Are easements adverse to value? • Are there any apparent encroachments?
Topographical Characteristics	• Is the site generally level, rolling, steep, etc.?
Landscaping	• Is the landscaping minimal, mature, etc.? • Does the landscaping meet market standards and conform to the surrounding properties? • Is any portion of the site wooded? • What is the overall maintenance and condition of landscaping?
View	• What are the immediate or adjacent property uses? • What is the view from the front, rear, and each side?
Street	• Is the street or access private? • What is the street surface? • How many lanes? • Is it a through street, cul-de-sac, primary artery, etc.? • Are there high traffic or noise issues?
Alley	• If there is an alley, is it private or public? • What is the alley surface? • Is the alley at the rear or side?
Driveway/Parking	• What is the driveway surface? • What is the number of vehicles?* • Are there additional parking areas or parking pads? • Are there any special driveway features (such as circular, heated, etc.)? * Typically, number of vehicles references how many vehicles can be stored/parked without stack parking, or requiring that one or more be moved to remove another.
Miscellaneous Structures/ Improvements	• Are there additional structures (e.g., storage shed, barn, gazebo, greenhouse, pool, pool house, patio, basketball court, tennis court, affixed children's play equipment, etc.)?
General Appearance/ Condition	• What is the market acceptability of the general site and any miscellaneous structures or site improvements? • What is the general level of site maintenance and condition of any miscellaneous structures or site improvements? • How does the site and any miscellaneous structures or site improvements conform to surrounding properties?

Dwelling Characteristics—Exterior

Number of Units	• How many units (e.g., single-family, two-, three-, four-unit, etc.)?
Number of Stories	• How many stories (e.g., one-story, one and one-half story, two-story, etc.)?
Detached/Attached	• Is the dwelling detached (free standing) or attached (with a common wall, such as a townhouse)?
Design/Style	• Is the dwelling a traditional, Colonial, ranch, Cape Cod, contemporary, bi-level, tri-level, split-level, etc.?* * Local traditions usually suggest the terminology associated with particular housing designs and styles. It is important whatever term is used by the appraiser that intended users will understand the term's meaning.
Exterior Dimensions	• What are the exterior dimensions of the dwelling that will be used to calculate the gross living area?
Actual Age	• What is the actual age or the year the primary dwelling was built? • If built in phases, what was the year each phase was built?
Exterior Construction/ Finish	• What is the exterior wall construction (e.g., block, concrete, wood framing, steel framing, solid brick, etc.)? • What is the exterior wall finish (e.g., brick veneer, vinyl or aluminum siding, wood siding, composition siding, stucco or synthetic stucco product, etc.)?
Foundation/Foundation Type	• Is the foundation poured concrete, concrete block, pier and beam, wood timber, etc? • What is the foundation type (e.g., basement, crawl space, slab, etc.)? • Is the visible exterior of the foundation finished (such as with a brick veneer)?
Trim	• Are there soffits, fascias, eaves, dormers, shutters, etc.? • What are the finish materials?
Gutters/Downspouts	• What are the construction materials of the gutters and downspouts (e.g., aluminum, vinyl, PVC, galvanized, etc,)?
Windows	• What is the window type (e.g., single-hung, double-hung, casement, sliding, fixed-bay, fixed-bow, etc.)? • Is the window insulated (e.g., single-pane, double-pane, triple-pane, etc.) or are there storm windows? • What is the window construction (e.g., wood, vinyl clad wood, metal, etc.)? • Are there screens for the windows? • Any security bars or special security equipment? • Do the windows operate properly?
Doors	• How would you describe the door type, materials, and construction?
Chimney(s)	• How many chimneys and what type of construction? • Are the chimneys capped or uncapped?
Insulation	• What type of insulation? • Where is it located? • What is the "R" rating?
General Appearance/ Condition	• What is the general appearance, appeal, and condition of the subject property? • How do these characteristics compare to other properties in the area?

Dwelling Characteristics—Interior

Number and Type of Rooms	• How many total rooms, bedrooms, and bathrooms does the subject property have?* * Rooms of a general utility nature are typically not included in the total room count, such as foyers, hallways, baths, utility rooms, pantry rooms, some laundry rooms, etc.
Wall/Ceiling Type and Finish	• What are the wall and ceiling materials (e.g., plaster, drywall, panel, masonry, etc.)? • How high are the ceilings? • Are any of the ceilings multi-story, vaulted, cathedral, beamed, etc.? • What are the ceiling and wall finishes?
Floor and Floor Coverings	• What is the basic floor construction (e.g., concrete, wood underlayment, tongue and groove wood, wood plank, etc)? • What is the description of floor covering or finish materials?
Door and Trim	• What is the style, material, and finish of woodwork and interior doors?
Kitchen Finishes and Features	• How would you describe the cabinetry, storage and work areas? How adequate are they? • What are the kitchen features (e.g., dishwasher, disposal, trash compactor, etc.)? • Are the appliances built-in or considered personal property?
Bath Finishes and Features	• How would you describe the cabinetry and storage areas and their adequacy? • What are the fixtures, wall, and wainscot like? • What are the bath features (e.g., exhaust fan, whirlpool or garden tubs, etc.)?
Functional Utility	• Are the floor plan and livability features acceptable to the current market?
Special Features	• Are there fireplaces, central vacuum and intercom/audio systems, security and fire systems, integrated technology provisions and devices, skylights, etc.?* *Here, the possibilities could be many; the above list is not all inclusive.
Market Acceptability of Décor	• Would the typical buyer (in a market value assignment) find the décor to be acceptable (usually neutral)? • Are there personalized décor features?
Basement Size and Features	• If any, what portions and percent of the dwelling have a basement under it? • What and where is the basement access, and is it adequate? • Is the basement a walk-out? If not, does it have egress (especially in a bedroom)? • Are any portions of the basement finished? • How is the basement finished, and what are the finishes (e.g., walls, floors, ceilings, etc.)? • Are there finished areas where the appraiser could not observe the structural components (e.g., outer basement walls, understructure of dwelling, etc.)?
General Appearance/ Condition	• What are the general appearance, appeal, and condition of the interior of the subject property? • How do these characteristics compare to other properties in the area?

Mechanical Systems

HVAC	• What is the type and fuel source for the heating and cooling systems? • Is there an integrated humidifier, dehumidifier, air-cleaner, etc.?
Electrical	• What is the capacity and type of service (e.g., 100 amp, 200 amp, circuit breaker, or fuse box)?* *Appraisers should take great care in this area. Electrical service boxes are often labeled for their maximum capacity; however, this may not represent the actual service capacity.
Plumbing	• What are the plumbing materials for service, drain, and waste lines (e.g., PVC, copper, galvanized iron, lead pipe, etc.)? • What type and capacity is the water heater, and what is the fuel source (e.g., gas, electric, etc.)?* • Is there a water conditioning or water filtration/purification system?* *In some areas, it is common for these components to be leased rather than owned and may or may not be considered fixtures.
Adequacy	• Is there anything **apparent** that would cause the appraiser to consider that an inspection would be warranted or recommended (e.g., minimal electric service with significant electrical components)?
General Observed Condition	• What is the general observed condition of the mechanical system components (e.g., obvious deterioration, etc.)? • Specifically, which mechanical components did the appraiser observe in operation?

Garage/Vehicle Storage

Number of Vehicles	• How many vehicles will the area accommodate?
Type	• Is the area a carport or a garage? • Is the garage attached, detached, or built-in?
Garage Access	• Is the garage front-load, rear-load, or side-load? • Is there a service door or is the garage accessed from the dwelling?
Finishes	• Is the garage interior finished? • Are there any storage areas, shelving, etc.?
Door Opener(s)	• How many garage door openers? • What type?
Adequacy and Functional Utility	• Is the car storage typical for the market, and similar to the properties around it? • Are there any function issues with the car storage?* * The functional utility of a garage is often related to the layout and if vehicles must be stacked (one vehicle in front of the other) or if all vehicles can enter and exit without moving another.

Of course, an appraiser will usually sketch the floor plan of the subject property and sometimes the site itself with the positioning of the various improvements. For most appraisals, a series of photographs illustrating the street view(s), views of one or more exterior sides of the subject dwelling, miscellaneous site improvements, and in some assignments, interior photographs may be included. USPAP does not require any of these items, but rather their inclusion is determined by the scope of work in the assignment. These items are an example of client requirements that might be specified by the client at the time of the assignment.

» *A series of photographs illustrating the street view(s), views of one or more exterior sides of the subject dwelling, miscellaneous site improvements, and in some assignments, interior photographs may be included in an appraisal as a result of assignment conditions. However, USPAP does not require any of these items* «

As a practical note, even if photographs, an interior sketch, etc., are not an assignment condition, it may be advisable for appraisers to consider their inclusion in the workfile. The sketch will assist in supporting the appraiser's conclusion regarding **functional utility** (*when a building has adequate design and features to be used as intended)*, while interior and exterior photographs may assist in supporting the opinions and conclusions regarding the property condition, quality, special features, etc. Interior photographs are strongly recommended, even when not required by regulation and agreement, to evidence the physical state of the property on the effective date of the assignment. Photographs can help protect the appraiser if questions arise regarding features, especially in foreclosure and REO properties.

» *Even if not required by assignment conditions, interior photographs are strongly recommended because they help to support the physical state of the property at the time of the inspection/ assignment* «

There are many other types of information that the appraiser might investigate that could be helpful or important to have knowledge of. Here are some questions an appraiser might ask of the property owner (or representative, depending on the circumstance):

- Have there been any recent improvements, additions, or alterations made to the property?
- Were building permits obtained for any work performed, and was the work performed by licensed contractors and in compliance with any building (or in some cases, zoning) codes?

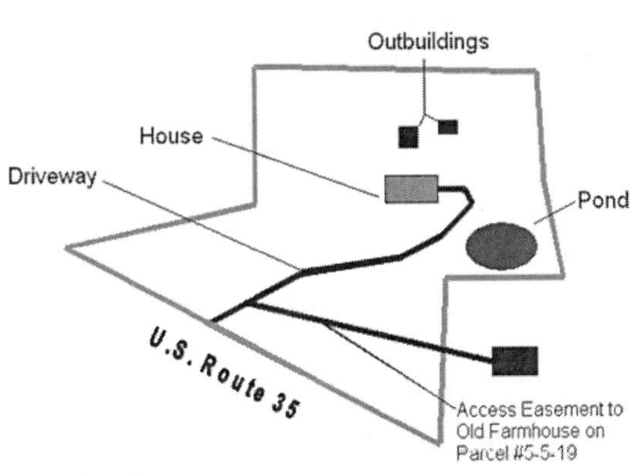

Site Sketch

This site sketch indicates the primary dwelling, the barn, the pond, and the driveway. Notice that it also illustrates the location of the driveway easement running through this property to access the property next door.

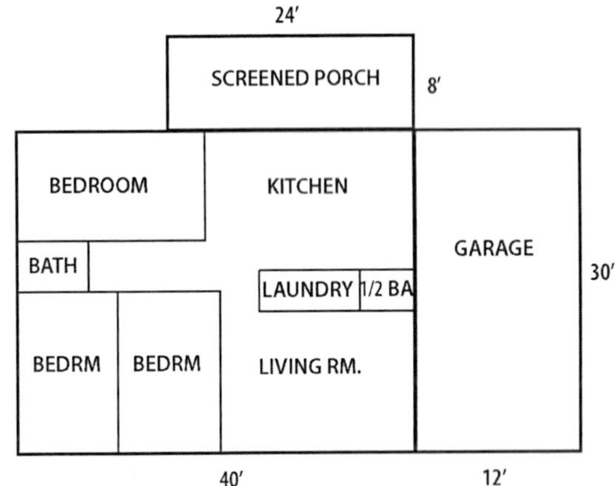

Floor Plan Sketch

In the above example, the house has 1,200 square feet, 5 rooms, 3 bedrooms, and 1½ baths. The 1-car garage and the screened porch are not counted in the gross living area. The laundry room is considered a utility area and is not included in the room count.

- Has the property been rezoned or had a variance granted?
- Is the property currently (or has been in the past) offered for sale, and if so, at what price?

Review of other Specific Data for the Subject Property

In addition to the specific data gathered during the inspection of the subject property, the appraiser will gather and analyze documents, maps, and other data obtained from other sources in order to identify the subject property. Most of these items are discussed in greater length within other courses but we will review some of them here. Depending on the particular property, the following types of data might be included.

Deed

A **deed** is *an instrument that conveys the grantor's interest in real property.* The deed to the subject property is an important document for the appraiser to review in the course of identifying the subject property. The deed will note (or refer to) any restrictive conditions or covenants, and possibly other information that will assist the appraiser, such as whether or not the property is part of a subdivision, easements that affect the subject property, etc.

Auditor's/Assessor's Property (Tax) Record

The **auditor's/assessor's property record** provides a great deal of information that is helpful to the appraiser. Property records vary broadly from area to area but most include:

- Legal description
- Sales history and sale prices
- Building size
- Tax information

Subdivision Plat Map

Subdivision plat maps are filed in public records and best illustrate the characteristics of a platted lot described by lot and block description. The map will illustrate the lot boundaries, dimensions, shape, easements, and building lines.

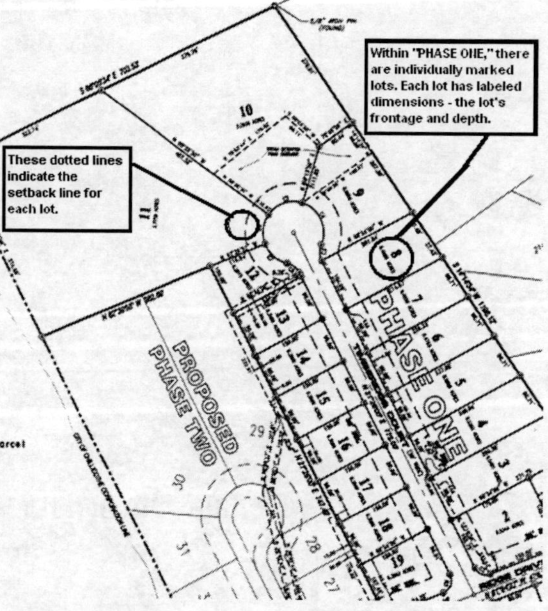

Subdivision Plat Map

Here we see a typical subdivision plat that is put on record when the subdivision is dedicated. This particular map represents one phase in a subdivision. Notice that the dimensions of each numbered lot are on the plat, as are the building set-back boundaries, utility easements, etc. For a lot and block description, the appraiser may need to refer to a subdivision plat map.

Subdivision Covenants and Restrictions

Subdivision covenants and restrictions assist the appraiser with determining legal compliance issues regarding the subject property and are also important in the highest and best use analysis.

> √ ***Note:*** This is particularly important if the appraiser has noticed, during inspection, something that appears unique to the subject property (such as a two-tiered deck). Is it allowed by the covenants and restrictions? If not, it should be noted in the report.

WARRANTY DEED 2922 PAGE 561 — COLUMBUS BLANK BOOK CO., COL., O. FORM NO. L12-9

FUTURE TAX BILLS TO THE CALHRGA P. ... CO.

Know all Men by these Presents

That Ralph B. S. Mowery, Widower 19096

of the City of Columbus, County of Franklin and State of Ohio Grantor, in consideration of the sum of One Dollar ($1.00) and other good and valuable considerations to him paid by William A. Thompson and Helen Thompson

of the City of Columbus, County of Franklin and State of Ohio Grantees, the receipt whereof is hereby acknowledged, does hereby **grant, bargain, sell and convey** to the said Grantees William A. Thompson and Helen Thompson

their heirs and assigns forever, the following **Real Estate** situated in the County of Franklin in the State of Ohio, and in the City of Columbus and bounded and described as follows:

Being Lot Number Eighty-five (85) of CHARLES R. CORNELL'S SUBDIVISION in the said City of Columbus, Ohio, as the same is numbered and delineated upon the recorded plat thereof, of record in Plat Book No. 5, page 48, Recorder's Office, Franklin County, Ohio.

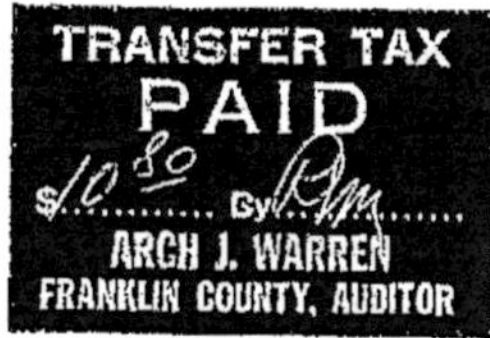

Last Transfer: Deed Record Volume 734, Page 67

To have and to hold said premises, with all the privileges and appurtenances thereunto belonging, to the said Grantees their heirs and assigns forever.

And the said Grantor for himself and his heirs, does hereby covenant with the said Grantees their heirs and assigns, that he is lawfully seized of the premises aforesaid; that the said premises are **Free and Clear from all Incumbrances whatsoever** Except taxes and assessments due and payable hereafter and all conditions, easements and restrictions of record.

Legal Description

The circled area in this General Warranty Deed identifies the legal description for the property. This property, in this case, is described by lot and block description. With a lot and block description, the plat and restrictions on record should be reviewed by the appraiser. The Plat Book reference indicates where in the public records the information is located.

Subdivision Covenants and Restrictions

1. APPROVAL

No building shall be erected, placed, or altered until the building plans, specifications, and elevations have been approved by the developer in writing.

Quality of materials, workmanship, and harmony of exterior design with existing structures must also be approved by the developer in writing.

2. USE

Each and every lot will be used for residential purposes only.

Each lot must be improved with a residential structure not to exceed two and one-half stories and must have an attached garage of not less than two cars and not more than four cars.

No temporary structure, trailer, basement, tent, shack, garage, barn, or other outbuilding shall be used at any time as a residence either temporarily or permanently.

No lot may be split to create another building lot.

No animals, livestock, or poultry of any kind shall be raised, bred, or kept on any lot, except that dogs, cats, or other household pets may be kept provided they are not bred or maintained for commercial purposes.

No noxious or offensive activity shall be carried on upon any lot, nor shall anything be done thereon which may become an annoyance of nuisance to the neighborhood.

No commercial vehicles, recreational vehicles, boats, trailers, construction equipment, or trucks over ¾ ton capacity shall be on any lot or street, except if in a garage; completely enclosed.

3. BUILDING REQUIREMENTS

The ground floor of any dwelling shall have a minimum living area of:

one-story – 1,400 square feet

one and one-half story - 1,200 square feet

two story – 900 square feet

split - level and tri – level – 1,100 square feet on the upper floor

bi-level – 1,300 square feet on the upper floor

All dwellings must be constructed of brick, stone, or cedar siding with the color approved by the developer in writing.

No building materials may be on-site for more than 60 days prior to construction or 15 days after completion, and construction must be completed within 6 months after commencement.

No outside sheds shall be erected.

4. LANDSCAPING

All lots shall be kept mowed and free from obnoxious weeds and grasses.

Shrubs, trees, bushes, and plantings of any kind shall be kept well maintained and free of unsightly material.

Initial landscaping design must be approved by the developer.

5. MAINTENANCE

No lot, building, or other improvement shall be permitted to become overgrown, unsightly, or fall into disrepair. All improvements shall be kept in good condition at all times.

6. SWIMMING POOLS

Above-ground pools are prohibited.

7. FENCES

No fence, wall, or barrier of any kind (including shrubbery or hedges) may be erected, except underground dog fences, which are subject to the approval of the developer.

8. ANTENNA

No antenna or dish for transmission or reception of television signals, radio signals shall be erected on any lot.

9. FUEL TANKS

No above-ground fuel tanks shall be permitted.

10. SIGNS

No sign of any kind shall be displayed to the public view on any lot, except one sign of not more than 6 square feet to advertise the sale of the property.

11. LIGHTING

No house may be erected on any lot unless there is an outdoor post yard light of either gas or electric power. The owner shall keep said light in good working order and properly maintained.

12. MAILBOXES

To insure conformity with the subdivision, all mail boxes shall be of a construction compatible with the subdivision, and is subject to the approval of the developer.

13. LIMIT OF RESTRICTIONS

These covenants are to run with the land and shall be binding for a period of thirty days from the date of these covenants, and shall be extended for successive periods of 10 years unless the majority of the owners of the lots file an instrument with the recorder agreeing to change the covenants in whole or in part.

14. ENFORCEMENT

In the event of a violation of any of the covenants or restrictions, it shall be lawful for any owner of any of the lots to prosecute any proceedings of law or in equity against the person or persons violating or attempting to violate any of these covenants or restrictions and either prevent such violations or recover damages for such violations.

Subdivision Regulations

The subdivision regulations are placed on record at a subdivision's dedication along with the subdivision plat. Here, we see examples typical restrictive covenants in this sample subdivision covenants and restrictions.

Tax Map

A **tax map** (or **plat map**) is especially important for subject properties that are described by metes and bounds (or some other) descriptions. Armed with this data, the appraiser can view the property's boundaries and shape, road frontage, and how the property is situated in relation to surrounding properties.

Other Data

Other data the appraiser might need to collect and examine in order to identify the characteristics of the subject property might include (but not be limited to) a plot map, zoning map, zoning regulations, topographical map, and census tract map.

Determining Market Conditions

When considering the boundaries of a market area for the purpose of analysis for determining market conditions, an appraiser must identify characteristics of the area that affect property values. The depth of the analysis will be determined by the scope of work. However, there are three terms that should be understood related to the analysis:

1. Market Area—A **market area** is *the broadest of all terms identifying the boundaries of a particular area.* When describing a market area, the appraiser is providing *an account of the land uses and characteristics of typical market participants within the defined area.*

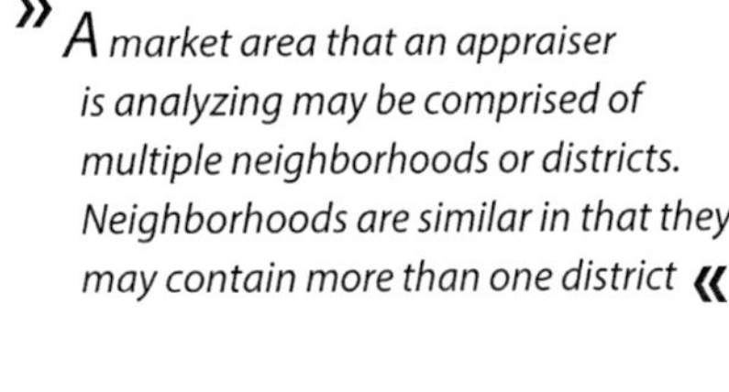

2. Neighborhood—A **neighborhood** is *any constant, contiguous area that may be identified by similar characteristics or physical boundaries.* When describing a neighborhood, which is *a compilation or a group of complimentary uses,* the appraiser is looking at all of the uses, even though varied, which create the overall environment impacting the subject. The complementary uses could be a mix of residential, commercial, service, as well as other amenities.
3. District—The term **district** is *the narrowest of definitions of a market area. A district is an area consisting of one particular land use* such as multi-family residential, commercial, industrial, etc.

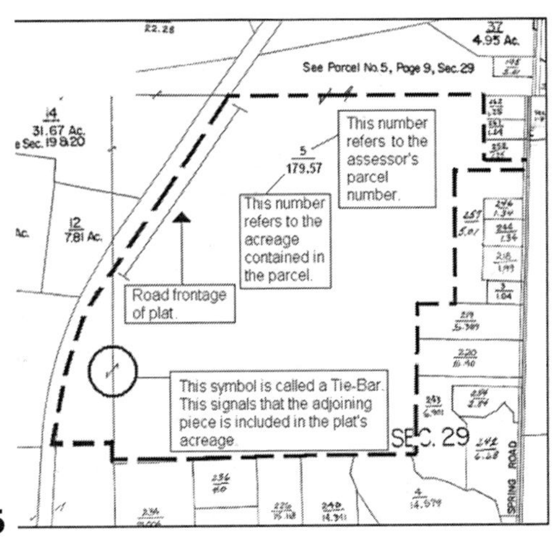

Plat Map

This is an assessor's, or tax, map and is available from local authorities. Its appearance can vary from area to area. It is used by the appraiser to obtain various elements of data, some of which are labeled.

When an appraiser analyzes and describes a market area, there could be more than one neighborhood or district included in the process, and likewise, a neighborhood could consist of more than one district.

Defining the Subject Neighborhood

For residential appraising, the term neighborhood is most commonly used for analysis of market conditions and defining the boundaries of that area. The properties in the neighborhood could share physical characteristics (e.g., similar style or age) or physical boundaries. Neighborhoods can also be defined by other characteristics, such as similar uses, zoning, price ranges, or income levels. Even shared shopping, social, civic, or recreational facilities can create a neighborhood. Almost any distinguishing characteristic can define a neighborhood—except those things protected by civil rights, fair housing, and other such laws and acts. Neighborhoods do not necessarily define the area encompassed by the comparables.

Prior to analyzing market conditions and other external characteristics relating to and affecting the subject property, the appraiser must determine the neighborhood that will be used for the purpose of analysis. This will assist the appraiser in recognizing data that is truly comparable for the purpose of developing an opinion of value by applying comparable data.

The appraiser will often start to define a neighborhood by looking at the natural and man-made geographic boundaries of an area. Natural boundaries include the obvious waterways, mountains, or valleys. Man-made boundaries include man-made items such as streets, highways, and railroads, and may also be drawn along a school district, a corporation boundary, or other jurisdiction (such as a township or county line).

Neighborhood Analysis

The appraiser should be familiar with the area to determine if there is currently any change occurring in the defined neighborhood or indications that change or transition could be on the horizon. The appraiser is also looking for similarity of land usage and types of improvements, as well as consistency of building style, landscaping, and general maintenance levels.

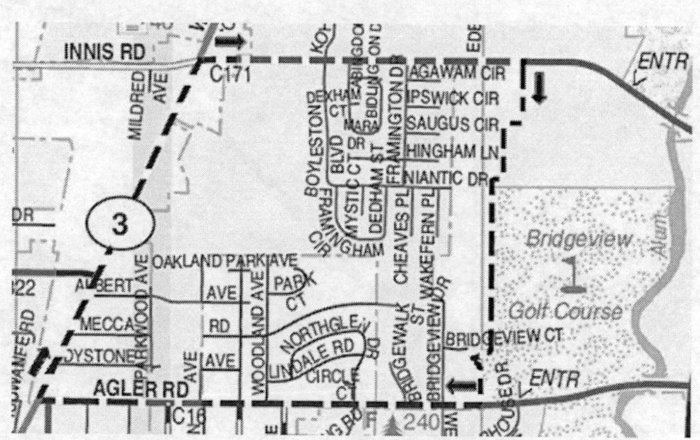

Defined Neighborhood

In this example, the appraiser has defined the neighborhood as being Innis Road to the north, Bridgeview Golf Course to the east, Agler Road to the south, and Route 3 to the west.

» *It is important that an appraiser be knowledgeable about the area in which he is appraising because he needs to be able to determine if there is any change occurring in the defined neighborhood—either currently or the possibility of it in the future* «

Change is most related to the broad forces of value, or P-E-G-S, which were discussed in Chapter 1. Outwardly, many of these changes can be observed by determining what stage of the neighborhood life cycle the subject neighborhood is experiencing.

Growth is *the first stage a neighborhood goes through in its life cycle. In this stage, property values tend to rise as development activity begins and continues.* Buyers fuel this growth by continuing to demand and purchase property in the area. This demand translates acceptance of the area and causes the area to grow.

Stability (also called **equilibrium)** is *the second stage a neighborhood goes through in its life cycle. In this stage, property values are at their highest level and the area is considered built up.* Demand typically remains high, as buyers continue to demonstrate preference for this neighborhood and there is little, if any, vacant property. Prices usually remain stable to increasing during this period.

√ ***Note:*** Some neighborhoods remain stable for indefinite periods of time.

Decline is *the third stage a neighborhood goes through in its life cycle. In this stage, property values begin to fall as demand falls.* Decline in a neighborhood is typically observable through deterioration. This, in turn, leads to the area becoming even less desirable, and the cycle feeds upon itself.

For Example: A less-desirable area where properties exhibit deferred maintenance translates into lower prices. Lower prices mean that lower-income residents with less money to spend on repairs will be attracted to the homes, with some or many properties converted physically, or in predominant occupancy, as rental units which could lead to lower maintenance. This may, in turn, accelerate the decline.

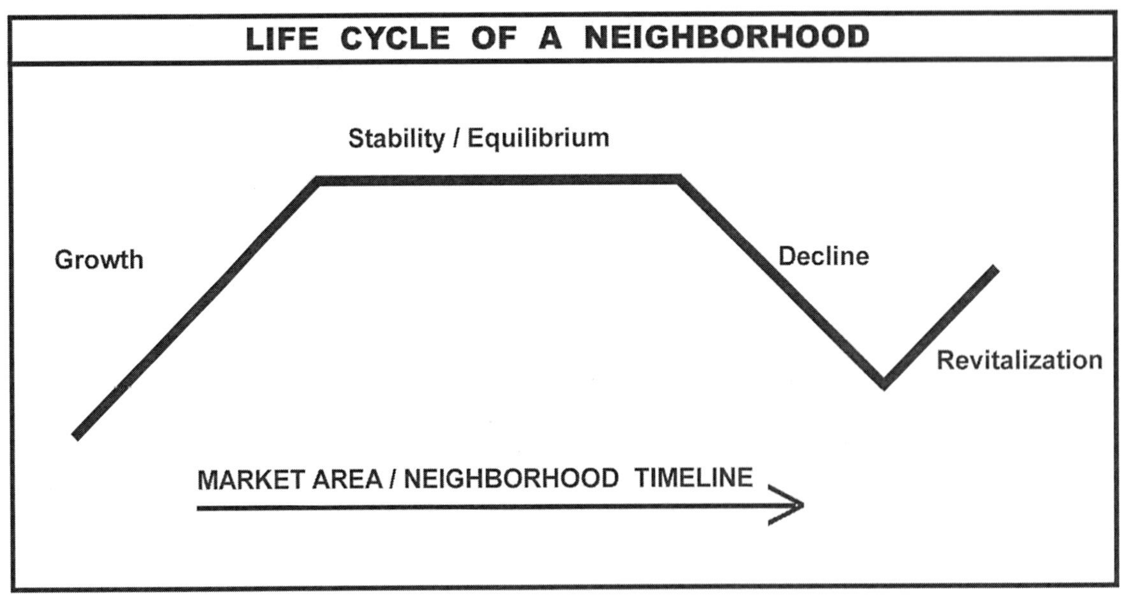

Revitalization is *the fourth and final stage a neighborhood goes through in its life cycle. In this stage, property values begin to rise again as demand increases, resulting in (or resulting from) a change in property condition levels due to increased restoration, renovation, modernization, or rehabilitation.* After a complete revitalization stage, the neighborhood returns to stability/equilibrium, and the cycle *could* begin again. Revitalization occurs when properties are again seen as attractive for their location, architectural features, or maybe even investment potential. Whatever the reason, people begin to spend money to improve these properties, and they become desirable again. Revitalization can be generally a slow process or one that occurs rather rapidly. *The process of rapid property revitalization, where current residents are displaced,* is called **gentrification.**

Analysis of Offering and Sale History of the Subject Property

Sales contracts, past and current listings, and any past or current agreements of sale are important components of the appraiser's subject property analysis. In Chapter 1, USPAP Standards Rule 1-5 was introduced, which discusses (in part) the appraiser's obligation in a market value assignment when it is available in the normal course of business to

> ***"analyze agreements of sale, options, and listings of the subject property, current as of the effective date of the appraisal."***

The Standards Rule also requires the analysis of

> ***"all sales of the subject property that occurred within three years prior to the effective date of the appraisal."***

The current or past listing of the subject property may well evidence a "test" of the property on the market and how the market responded to the offering. Analysis of any past or current agreement, such as a sales contract or an option, demonstrates an action by a particular party. The appraiser should analyze these agreements to determine if they reflect a typical market reaction.

While this analysis may not be part of the property inspection process specifically, vital information can often be gathered or evidenced during the subject property inspection. If the property owners are present during the property inspection, appraisers routinely will inquire about any past listing or agreement history of the subject property. Some evidence of past listings could include stray "For Sale" signs stored in or on the property. As well, most multiple listing services allow for the appraiser to research a particular property's listing history for insight.

If a property has (or had) been listed and offered to the open market at a particular price, the price for which the property was offered usually sets the limit for what the property's market value could be. This is true only given there is no upward trend in the market or the property's physical state. In fact, provided there is no evidence of change, the property is probably worth somewhere below this listing or offering price in a market value assignment.

> ***For Example:*** During a property inspection as part of an appraisal for a mortgage refinance transaction, the appraiser notes a "For Sale" sign leaning against the back of the garage on the subject property. Upon inquiry, the property owner discloses that the property had been listed for sale through a local real estate broker with an asking price of $190,000. The broker had not returned to pick up the sign. Further inquiry revealed that the property had been offered on the market for six months, which resulted in several showings to prospective buyers, but no offers were received.
>
> Provided that six months is a reasonable period of exposure for the particular market and that common marketing steps were taken by the broker, the appraiser could make a valuable observation. From the perspective of the most common definition of market value, it the appraiser could interpret that the market would not pay $190,000.

Using the most common definition of market value, the same could be said for a property subject to a sale transaction. If a sales agreement indicates a transaction price greater than the listing or offering price, there must be a reason. Typical buyers do not, by nature, offer more for a property than its asking price without some incentive, such as favorable financing terms or sale conditions which often makes the transaction something other than arm's length.

> ***For Example:*** An exception might be a property that is located in a seller's market where the listing price can represent a starting point for negotiations to go upward. However, in order for the list price to ***possibly*** represent market value, more than one interested buyer would have to negotiate or at least express strong intent to make an offer on the property for the eventual sales agreement price. The property's list price alone may not provide a valuable indication as to market value. The appraiser must take great care in such an analysis that the actions represent what a typical buyer in a market value transaction would do.

Analyzing a current purchase agreement can also yield any atypical terms of the transaction, such as seller financing, concessions, allowances, terms, or personal property items being included.

The practice of analyzing the subject property's prior sales for the immediate three years prior to the effective date of the appraisal serves to reveal any prior transfer and mortgage history that could be evidence of illegal flipping. Illegal flipping occurs when successive transfer and mortgage transactions are facilitated in a short time period for fraudulent and criminally profitable purposes. The past sales history also prompts the appraiser to further investigate a past sales transfer and if the terms of the transaction were arm's length. When the subject property historically has been the subject of multiple arm's-length transactions, the appraiser is often able to interpret change in market conditions over that period of time.

Data Analysis Conclusions

It is very important to note that the data research and analysis in an assignment can be, depending on the scope of work, a much broader and more complex process than we have discussed here. In summary, the data collected, and ultimately analyzed, would also include national and regional trends, economic base analysis, and other local and neighborhood market conditions. Other courses concentrating on market analysis will expand greatly on this topic area.

Once the appraiser has collected, verified, and analyzed the numerous data applying either generally or specifically to the subject property, he begins forming conclusions that will assist him in forming an opinion of highest and best use (in a market value assignment) and developing the particular valuation approach. In other words, once the appraiser forms conclusions of the subject property based on its physical, legal, and economic characteristics, he can go forward with identifying market data that can be used for his valuation analysis and how comparable the data is.

As we concentrate our study of the sales comparison approach from this point through the next section, it should be made clear that many, if not most, of the same data research and analysis steps will be applicable when we discuss the income approach later in this text. As well, the assumption is being made, as we move forward, that the highest and best use of the subject property is "as-improved." Highest and best use is discussed and expanded upon in other courses dedicated to the topic.

Data Collection for Comparable Analysis

Ultimately, this portion of the analysis could result in being one of the most time consuming aspects when developing the sales comparison approach, or as we will discuss later in this text, the income approach as well. But, in some cases, this process can go rather smoothly depending on several variables—most often the quantity and quality of data available, the resources the appraiser has and utilizes, and the appraiser's experience in that particular market.

As a general practice, the appraiser usually employs sold and closed transactions as comparable data when developing and supporting the conclusions reached in the sales comparison approach. However, it is common that the appraiser will also gather and analyze pending transactions and current listings. Some regulations and client requirements (discussed in Chapter 7 restrict the inclusion of pending sales data in the sales comparison analysis to be limited to additional data over and above a specified number of closed transactions (e.g., as a fourth analyzed comparable). Current listings assist in illustrating the competition present in the market and usually suggest a "top end" that can be supported in the market, and how the subject is positioned with that competition.

» *Generally, sold and closed transactions are used as comparable data. There may be times when the appraiser utilizes pending transactions and current listings, as well* «

To summarize, comparable data can represent sold properties, pending transactions, or active listings. To truly gain insight into the comparable analysis process, it is important to define the term "comparable."

Concepts of Comparable and Competitive Properties

One of the most potentially difficult steps for many appraisers in the sales comparison approach is choosing data for analysis that is "most comparable" to the subject property. This process requires competency, which relies heavily on the appraiser's experience, judgment skills, and knowledge of the market and/or neighborhood. This leads us to a sometimes complex question: What is a comparable property?

Comparable properties, or comparables, generically can be categorized as *properties that share great, or sometimes subtle, similarities with the subject property.* These similarities could be the location, design, or features. The similarity might

» *Choosing data for analysis that is "most comparable" to the subject property can be challenging for appraisers in some assignments. Thus, the appraiser must possess competency in the market* «

also be the typical buyer for these properties—similar buyer mindset and profile. Comparability can be translated to a very broad or a narrowly defined basis. Therefore, it must be recognized that there are comparable properties, competitive properties, and properties that are both comparable and competitive.

Comparable Properties

Comparable properties possess many of the same appeal factors. The similarities may be physical in nature, or the property may have a similar locational appeal. However, *the buyer for one property may not necessarily be interested in the comparable property.*

> ***For Example:*** A local builder has built two identical homes. One home is on the east side of the county, and the other home is on the west side of the county, nearly 30 miles apart. Let's go one step further and suppose that one of the properties is the subject of an appraisal assignment and the other property sold nine months ago. Is the sold property useful as a comparable for the subject? It probably is—if the buyer in the sale transaction purchased the property because of the home's design, features, quality, etc, there is nothing to say that this property would not be useful as a comparable. Obviously, locational differences as well as differences in market conditions would need to be addressed. We will discuss those later in this chapter.
>
> Another example of a comparable property could be a completely dissimilar house located in a very similar, but far away area. Take recreational waterfront properties for example. Here, the appeal is in the locational characteristics—view, water access, etc. The subject of an appraisal might be an "A- frame" design cottage, which is primarily used for recreational purposes. One comparable sale has been identified at another recreational lake in another market. The comparable sale is improved with a different (ranch style) cottage. However, water frontage is nearly identical, as are the dock rights and the dock itself. The two lakes are a similar distance from a comparable incorporated area. If the physical differences can be identified and equated to a dollar amount as well as any differences between the two areas, they are probably comparable. A similar buyer action was represented—purchase of a recreational property with similar locational amenities.

Of course, it may be very possible, in either example, that the buyer for one property would not be interested in the other property—thus, while the properties might be comparable, they would likely not be competitive.

Competitive Properties

Competitive properties are *those that compete head to head.* In other words, *a potential buyer for one property would also be interested in the competitive property.* These properties are not necessarily physically identical. A buyer might be interested in many styles and ages of houses as long as they are located in a particular area.

> ***For Example:*** Consider a subject property located in a particular subdivision where there are various styles and designs of houses—one-story, two-story, split-level, etc. A two-story house may be considered competitive because it would attract the same (not similar) buyer who desired, or limited his choices to, this particular subdivision for whatever reason (the motivation could be schools, proximity to services, etc.). But, a competitive property does not necessarily need to be located in the same development or on the same street. A property could be considered competitive anytime it would be considered attractive to the *same* buyer.

Comparable and Competitive Properties

There would be very little argument that the ideal data to be used for comparable analysis would represent properties that are both *comparable to* and *competitive with* the subject property—properties that are as similar physically, locationally, and/or legally as possible, and would attract the same buyer.

When relevant comparable and competitive data is plentiful, there is little need for the appraiser to venture outside of the market area for his analysis or to instead use a one and one-half story house to compare with a two-story subject. In some assignments, there may be readily available comparable *and* competitive data for subject properties and markets. Even more ideal is when the subject can be compared to a property that is physically identical and located next door with no differences what-so-ever. What a perfect world that would be!

To summarize this discussion, appraisers will select and evaluate comparable data by employing the following rationale:

- Identify properties that are both comparable and competitive.
- Identify properties that are competitive (but not comparable).
- Identify properties that are comparable (but not competitive).

An argument could be made as to which of the latter two should be identified and evaluated first—competitive or comparable properties? Since most analysis focuses on location, it is very common and logical that the appraiser will evaluate competitive properties from the subject market before going out in distance to identify comparable but not particularly competitive properties. Ideally, the data chosen will reflect the most recent, nearest, and physically similar when compared to the subject property. But, the quality and quantity of the data available, as well as any assignment conditions, will dictate this rationale. Client requirements, such as Fannie Mae requirements and guidelines, will be discussed in Chapter 7.

» *Location is an important aspect of an appraiser's analysis. For this reason, competitive properties within the subject's market are first evaluated. As a next step, appraisers may then go outside the subject's market to identify comparable properties that may not be necessarily competitive* «

The initial choice of data to be used in the sales comparison approach analysis is a decision that requires the appraiser's sound judgment skill. Experience is required to develop this skill. In many assignments, the appraiser will select several properties for his analysis. Depending on the assignment and the quantity of data available, the initial gathering of data could exceed that which will eventually be used in his valuation analysis. Once the data has been identified, it can be organized in a manner where the relevance and differences between the properties and the subject can be more easily recognized.

Data Array

The data array, or data array grid, is a popular and helpful method of data organization. With the subject and comparable data arranged and displayed in this manner, the appraiser can more easily observe the amount of data that has been collected and, foremost, the comparability and quality of the data. The data array grid should not be misunderstood as a method of adjusting comparable properties; that comes later. The process is purely for the purpose of displaying the data in a way that allows the appraiser to determine quantity and quality. As a starting point to the analysis process, the data array can reveal areas of differences where analysis must later take place for the necessity of adjustments.

» *The use of data array grids helps appraisers recognize the quantity and quality of the collected data—it is not meant as a method of adjusting comparable properties* «

In some assignments, relevant data can be plentiful and the data collection and organization process is rather simple. Of course, this also requires the appraiser to be fairly familiar with the particular market and the transactions that have taken place. USPAP does not place an obligation on the appraiser to use and analyze a specific number of comparables. Standards Rule 1-4 (a) of USPAP simply requires the appraiser to

"analyze such comparable sales data as are available."

A minimum of three comparables are most usually gathered, analyzed, and presented in keeping with the regulations and requirements of many clients and intended users (which will be further discussed in Chapter 7).

Data Array Grid Example 1

Consider the first scenario illustrated here. The appraiser has identified three comparable properties that are also competitive to the subject. All sales are from the subject's subdivision, are 1-story ranch style houses located on cul-de-sacs, and sold with no unusual sale conditions.

1. 232 Poplar Court sold 1 month ago for $337,000. The buyer paid cash. It was located 1 block from the subject and had 1,872 square feet. The property had 4 bedrooms and 3 full baths.

2. 621 Willow Court sold 2 months ago for $332,000. Conventional financing was used in the transaction and there were no financing concessions paid by the seller. This property was located 3 blocks away from the subject, had 1,798 square feet with 4 bedrooms and 2 full baths.

3. 441 Birch Circle sold 1 week ago for $338,000. This property also sold with conventional financing and no seller-paid financing concessions. It was located 2 doors from the subject and had an identical design and floor plan, having 1,832 square feet, 4 bedrooms, and 2 ½ baths.

When the data is organized in a data array grid by price, location, and sale date, it looks like the chart below.

	Subject	441 Birch Circle	232 Poplar Court	621 Willow Court
Sale Price	--	$338,000	$337,000	$332,000
Date of Sale	--	1 week ago	1 month ago	2 months ago
Location	Cul-de-sac	Cul-de-sac 2 doors away Same subdivision	Cul-de-sac 1 block away Same subdivision	Cul-de-sac 3 blocks away Same subdivision
Sale Terms	Assumed Cash Equivalent	Conventional No seller concessions	Cash	Conventional No seller concessions
Sale Conditions	Assumed Typical	No Atypical	No Atypical	No Atypical
Style/Design	1-story ranch	1-story ranch	1-story ranch	1-story ranch
GLA	1,832 SF	1,832 SF	1,872 SF	1,798 SF
Bedrooms/Baths	4/2 ½	4/2 ½	4/3	4/2

Arranged in this manner, it can be clearly seen that the appraiser would have most confidence in the Birch Circle sale as it is the most recent, nearest, and physically similar. Also evident is that an analysis of market conditions over the past two months will be required, as well as an analysis of the market reaction to the location, differences in gross living area, and bath characteristics.

The preceding scenario would represent the ideal preliminary result for the appraiser, and could be the norm in some markets, for some properties. However, it is more likely that the appraiser will not locate data that is quite as similar and relevant as has been illustrated here in all, or many, assignments.

Data Array Grid Example 2

Suppose the appraiser has fully investigated the sales in the subdivision and found only three sales occurring within the past year or so. Let's look at an example where the appraiser's initial data gathering did not produce the clear results that we previously illustrated. Here is the sales data that the appraiser has been able to find from the subject's subdivision within the past 18 months:

1. 627 Elm Lane sold for $337,000 4 months ago in a cash transaction. It was located on a through street (as opposed to the subject's cul-de-sac location) one block away from the subject. It, like the subject, was a 1-story ranch style and contained 1,972 square feet, 4 bedrooms, and 3 full baths. Financing was via conventional loan with no seller concessions or atypical conditions.
2. 532 Oak Drive sold for $309,000 2 months ago. The seller accepted the first offer he received on the property in order to expedite his pending relocation. It was located three blocks away on a cul-de-sac similar to the subject. Financing was conventional and there were no seller concessions. The 1-story ranch style house contained 1,758 square feet and had 4 bedrooms and 2 ½ baths.
3. 451 Birch Circle was located three doors away from the subject and sold for $385,000 3 weeks ago. It was in a similar cul-de-sac location like the subject. The sale included an additional building lot next to the house that was declared to have a transaction value of $40,000. The house contained 2,156 square feet with 4 bedrooms and 3 full baths. However, this house was a 1½-story, Cape Cod design. The financing was by conventional loan and there were no financing concessions paid by the seller.

When arranged by location, the data array is illustrated as in the chart on the next page.

	Subject	451 Birch Circle	627 Elm Lane	532 Oak Drive
Sale Price	--	$385,000	$337,000	$309,000
Date of Sale	--	3 weeks ago	4 months ago	2 months ago
Location	Cul-de-sac	Cul-de-sac 3 doors away Same subdivision	Through street 1 block away Same subdivision	Cul-de-sac 3 blocks away Same subdivision
Sale Terms	Assumed Cash Equivalent	Conventional No seller concessions	Cash	Conventional No seller concessions
Sale Conditions	Assumed Typical	The transaction included an additional building lot next door with a value of $40,000	No Atypical	Sold with 1st offer to expedite the owner's relocation
Style/Design	1-story ranch	1½-story Cape Cod	1-story ranch	1-story ranch
GLA	1,832 SF	2,156 SF	1,972 SF	1,758 SF
Bedrooms/Baths	4/2 ½	4/3	4/3	4/2 ½

As can easily be seen, the data illustrated in this manner is somewhat chaotic.

- The Elm Lane sale appears to be fairly usable. However the locational (through street vs. cul-de-sac) and slight physical differences (GLA and bath count) will have to be considered in our later analysis.
- The Birch Circle sale is very near the subject but includes an additional building site, is of a different design, and is significantly larger.
- The Oak Drive sale possesses many of the subject's locational and physical characteristics. However, the sale may represent a transaction that reflects liquidation rather than one that is arm's-length due to the motivation of the seller and the limited time the property was exposed to the market.

When the initial data identification does not produce enough reliable data that can be later used in the sales comparison analysis from the most immediate subject neighborhood, the appraiser must do further research. It will be necessary to go out geographically and/or in time to identify data to be used in the analysis.

Data Array Grid Example 3

As the appraiser continues his diligence, he identifies the following data which can be added to the data array, or arrayed separately from that which has already been identified.

1. 32 Mohican Trail was located 6 blocks away on a through street in an adjacent subdivision and sold for $319,000 three months ago. It was a 3-bedroom ranch containing 1,729 square feet and had 2 full baths. There were no atypical sale conditions; however, the seller paid 3% of the buyer's closing costs in a conventional loan arrangement.

2. 398 Seal Drive sold 1 month ago for $342,500 in a conventional loan transaction in which the seller paid no concessions. There were no unusual sale conditions. Although it was located 16 blocks from the subject in a completely different market, the house was a mirror to the subject (style, GLA, room count, etc.), having been built by the same builder. However, this property was located on a through street.

3. 69 Forrest Circle is located 7 blocks away in an adjacent subdivision. It too, was a mirror of the subject in all physical and locational characteristics, being located on a cul-de-sac and built by the same builder as the subject. The property sold for cash 2 weeks ago; however, the sale was via a Sheriff's foreclosure auction with the buyer being the mortgagee, who was bidding to regain title to the property. Any atypical sale conditions could not be determined as the buying entity was exempt from declaration by the jurisdiction.

When the data is arrayed on a grid, the following can be observed in the chart below.

	Subject	32 Mohican Trail	398 Seal Drive	69 Forrest Circle
Sale Price	--	$319,000	$342,500	$298,000
Date of Sale	--	3 months ago	1 month ago	2 weeks ago
Location	Cul-de-sac	Through street 6 blocks away Adjacent subdivision	Through street 16 blocks away Different market	Cul-de-sac 7 blocks away Adjacent subdivision
Sale Terms	Assumed Cash Equivalent	Conventional Seller paid 3% of buyers closing costs	Conventional No seller concessions	Cash
Sale Conditions	Assumed Typical	No Atypical	No Atypical	Not declared
Style/Design	1-story ranch	1-story ranch	1-story ranch	1-story ranch
GLA	1,832 SF	1,729 SF	1,832 SF	1,832 SF
Bedrooms/Baths	4/2½	3/2	4/2½	4/2½
Other		--	House was mirror to subject. Built by same builder.	House was mirror to subject. Built by same builder. Transaction was via Sheriff's Auction—bought back by mortgagee.

- The Seal Drive sale may lend good support for the appraiser's conclusions, given the locational differences can be accounted for, which is most likely possible.
- The Mohican Trail sale has some locational differences as well, but also has significant physical differences. At this point, we will leave this property in the mix and decide in the later analysis if it should be discarded or simply given a diminished weight.
- The Forrest Circle sale, though physically and somewhat locationally similar, appears to represent something other than an arms-length or market value transaction. Since this transaction may be additionally difficult to verify, it should probably be discarded as the conclusions could prove to be misleading.

Final Array of the Selected Comparable Data

To review what has been concluded so far, five comparable sales have been identified that can be used in the later sales comparison analysis. The data collected represents everything that could be found by the appraiser that would be considered relevant to the assignment. Granted, one or more of the sales may be slightly weak or need to be discarded. Due to the quantity of data that has been located, we won't eliminate the sales data that is questionable at this point with the exception of the latter Forrest Circle transaction, which would be extremely difficult to confirm as being arms-length or representing market value.

Whether or not the data array grids are included in the appraisal report is determined by whether or not they will be useful for understanding what the appraiser undertook in the process of data collection. The intended use and the intended user will guide the appraiser as to what will be appropriate and helpful. If not integrated into the report, the data array grids are useful for documentation contained in the appraiser's workfile to document the appraiser's data collection effort.

	Subject	447 Birch Circle	627 Elm Lane	532 Oak Drive	32 Mohican Trail	398 Seal Drive
Sale Price	--	$385,000	$337,000	$309,000	$319,000	$342,500
Date of Sale	--	3 weeks ago	4 months ago	2 months ago	3 months ago	1 month ago
Location	Cul-de-sac	Cul-de-sac 3 doors away Same subdivision	Through street 1 block away Same subdivision	Cul-de-sac 3 blocks away Same subdivision	Through street 6 blocks away Adjacent subdivision	Through street 16 blocks away Different market
Sale Terms	Assumed Cash Equivalent	Conventional No seller concessions	Cash	Conventional No seller concessions	Conventional Seller paid 3% of buyers closing costs	Conventional No seller concessions
Sale Conditions	Assumed Typical	The transaction included an additional building lot next door with a value of $40,000	No Atypical	Sold with 1st offer to expedite the owner's relocation	No Atypical	No Atypical
Style/Design	1-story ranch	1½-story Cape Cod	1-story ranch	1-story ranch	1-story ranch	1-story ranch
GLA	1,832 SF	2,156 SF	1,972 SF	1,758 SF	1,729 SF	1,832 SF
Bedrooms/Baths	4/2½	4/3	4/3	4/2½	3/2	4/2½
Other	--	--	--	--	--	House was mirror to subject Built by same builder

Application Case Study

Subject Property

The subject of the appraisal assignment is a 2-story colonial style residential dwelling located on a through street in a subdivision. The dwelling contains 2,169 square feet and has 4 bedrooms and 2½ baths. The intended use of the appraisal report is to assist in facilitation of a mortgage refinance transaction. Thus, all sale terms are assumed to be cash equivalent and sale conditions typical. The subject property features a 2-car garage, patio, and a fireplace.

Possible Comparable Data from the Subject's Subdivision

629 Logan Avenue sold for $279,400 7 weeks ago. Conditions of sale were typical and financing was via a conventional loan with no seller concessions. The dwelling was a similar 2-story Colonial that had 4 bedrooms, 3 baths, and 2,248 square feet of gross living area. The property was located 3 blocks from the subject on a through street and had a 2-car garage, deck, and fireplace.

427 Evergreen Court was located 2 blocks from the subject, but on a cul-de-sac lot. The 2-story Colonial sold for $310,000. The dwelling had 2,356 square feet, 5 bedrooms, 3 full baths, and 1 half bath. There were no atypical sale conditions, however the seller paid $3,000 of the buyer's closing costs in the conventional finance transaction 1 month ago. In addition to an in-ground pool, the property had a 3-car garage, deck, and 2 fireplaces.

432 Washington Drive sold for $265,000 9 months ago in a transaction that was facilitated by seller financing, where the seller paid all of the buyer's costs. Some furnishings were included in the sale. The property was located 1 block away from the subject on a through street. The dwelling had 1,879 square feet, 3 bedrooms, 2½ baths and was a 1½-story Cape Cod design. Other features included a 2-car garage and a patio.

299 Peachtree Court was a 1½-story Cape Cod dwelling located on a cul-de-sac 2 blocks away from the subject. It sold for $266,900 5 months ago via conventional financing with no seller concessions and typical sale conditions. The dwelling had 2,038 square feet, 4 bedrooms, 2½ baths, a 1-car garage, and a deck.

Possible Comparable Data from Outside of the Subject's Subdivision

152 Goodson Drive sold 2 weeks ago for $269,000. Financing was by conventional loan and there were no seller financing concessions or atypical sale conditions. Location was on a through street, 12 blocks from the subject, in a different market. The 2-story, Colonial design dwelling had 2,112 square feet, 4 bedrooms, and 3 full baths. Other features included a 2-car garage and a deck.

861 Cranberry Drive was located on a through street, 5 blocks from the subject in an adjacent subdivision. It sold for $271,500, 1 week ago, via a conventional loan where the seller paid $2,000 of the buyer's costs. There were no unusual sale conditions. This property was a 2-story Colonial design with 2,089 square feet, 4 bedrooms, 2½ baths, a 2-car garage, deck, and a fireplace.

591 Apollo Lane was located in a private community with a golf course view that had gated street access. It was situated 11 blocks from the subject in a different market. Sale price was $315,000 in the cash transaction with no financing involved, 3 months ago. No atypical sale conditions were reported. The 4-bedroom, 3½-bath, 2-story contemporary dwelling had 2,457 square feet and featured a 3-car garage, patio, and 3 fireplaces.

Other than the information given, the lot sizes and site utility are considered to be similar. Actual age, quality, and condition are similar, as is appeal. Using the data array grids provided, organize the data and determine what data appears relevant and what data that should be discarded.

Possible Comparable Data from the Subject's Subdivision:

	Subject				
Sale Price					
Date of Sale					
Location					
Sale Terms					
Sale Conditions					
Style/Design					
GLA					
Bedrooms/ Baths					
Other Features					

Possible Comparable Data from Outside of the Subject's Subdivision

	Subject			
Sale Price				
Date of Sale				
Location				
Sale Terms				
Sale Conditions				
Style/Design				
GLA				
Bedrooms/ Baths				
Other Features				

Selected USPAP Illustrations and Guidance

The following USPAP Advisory Opinion (AO) and Frequently Asked Questions (FAQ) have been selected to illustrate the application of USPAP in specific circumstances discussed in this chapter.

FAQ 169—Measuring Single Family Residences Using the ANSI Standard

FAQ 228—Pending Sales as Comparables

FAQ 229—Subject Property as a Comparable Sale

FAQ 280—Legal Description

Quiz

1. ***Gathering of what data is the appraiser's primary focus during a property inspection?***
   a. legal characteristics
   b. photographs
   c. physical characteristics
   d. property sketch

2. ***What type of room generally is NOT included in the total room count?***
   a. bathrooms
   b. bedrooms
   c. kitchens
   d. living rooms

3. ***Photographs of the subject property and its views are***
   a. considered an invasion of the property owner's privacy.
   b. included in the appraisal report if the scope of work in the assignment determines they should be.
   c. never necessary.
   b. required by USPAP to be included in the workfile.

4. ***What document contains tax information, building size, sales history and prices, and a legal description?***
   a. auditor's/assessor's property tax record
   b. deed
   c. subdivision plat map
   d. tax map

5. ***A neighborhood***
   a. consists of one particular land use.
   b. is an account of the land uses and characteristics of typical market participants within the defined area.
   c. is any constant, contiguous area that may be identified by similar characteristics or physical boundaries.
   d. is the narrowest of definitions of a market area.

6. ***What is an example of a natural boundary?***
   a. highway
   b. railroad
   c. school district
   d. waterway

7. ***A neighborhood is currently experiencing very high values and has only one vacant property. In what stage of the life cycle is this neighborhood?***
   a. decline
   b. growth
   c. revitalization
   d. stability

8. ***A neighborhood's property values are starting to fall and properties are taking a little longer to sell. In what stage of the life cycle is this neighborhood?***
   a. decline
   b. growth
   c. revitalization
   d. stability

9. ***The process of rapid property revitalization, where current residents are displaced is called***
   a. a buyer's market.
   b. gentrification.
   c. progression.
   d. regression.

10. ***USPAP requires appraisers to gather, analyze, and present a minimum of how many comparables in an appraisal report?***
    a. 1
    b. 2
    c. 3
    d. There is no minimum.

Sales Comparison Analysis—*Adjustments and Reconciliation*

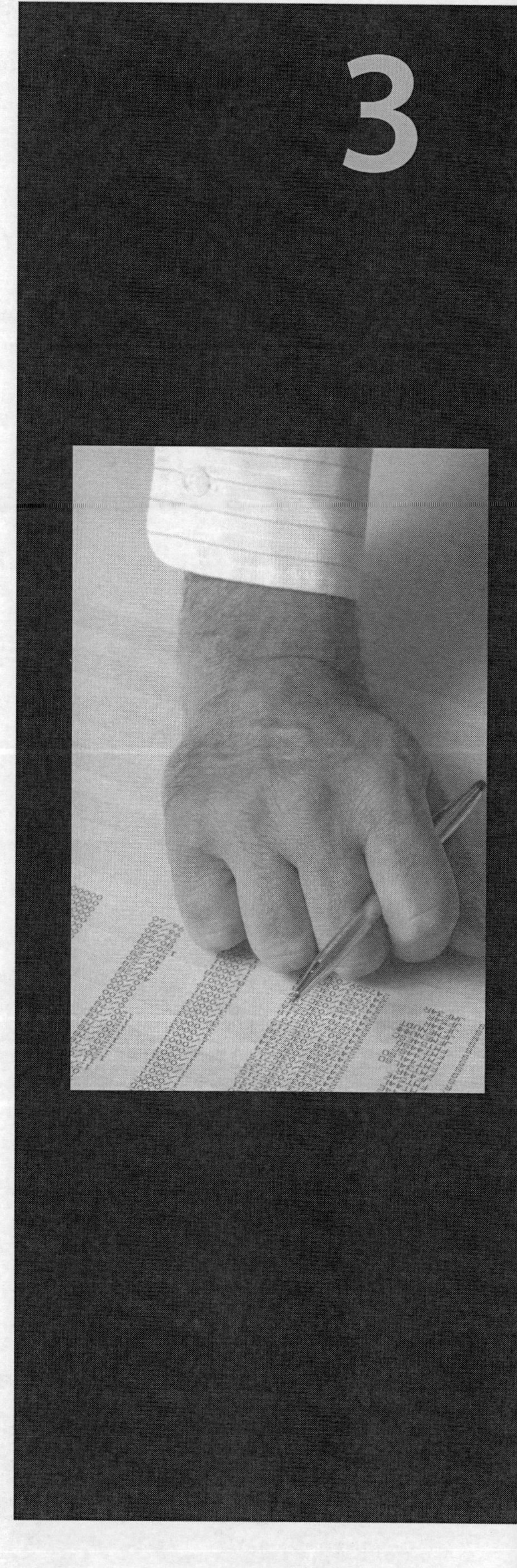

3

This chapter will cover what the appraiser does once the comparable data to be used in the sales comparison analysis is identified. The next course of action for the appraiser is to produce a value indication from the analysis. The value indication the appraiser produces in the sales comparison approach must be developed through a series of carefully performed comparisons and analyses. Again, the necessity and depth of each analysis is determined by the appraiser's scope of work decision. In this chapter, we will discuss the progression of analyses usually applied in the development of the sales comparison approach in most residential assignments where an opinion of market value is being sought. In most cases, the steps the appraiser will take include:

1. Determining the appropriate unit of comparison,
2. Examining the elements of comparison,
3. Identifying and supporting adjustments,
4. Applying the adjustments, and
5. Reconciling the conclusions.

Units of Comparison

In each assignment, appraisers select an appropriate *unit of comparison* for which to perform their analysis of the comparable data. The **unit of comparison** is *the context in which the sale price is stated.* In most residential assignments, the unit of comparison is typically the total sale price of the property. However, depending on the scope of work decided in the assignment, the sale price could be considered in other ways, as well.

For Example:

- Sale prices of residential properties can be unitized on a per square foot basis of gross living area:

  Sale price $400,000 ÷ 2,000 square feet = $200 sale price per square foot

- Residential apartment buildings can be stated as based on a price per apartment unit:

  Sale price $400,000 ÷ 4 apartment units = $100,000 per apartment

- Or, on a price per room:

  Sale price $400,000 ÷ 16 rooms = $25,000 per room

- Or, as with the earlier example for single-family properties, on per square foot of total gross living area.

Vacant land can be considered several different ways, as well. The sale price of smaller residential building lots is often stated in units of square feet. Larger residential tracts may be considered on a per-acre basis. Units of front feet are common when the land parcel's sale price is most influenced by what the parcel fronts on (e.g., a golf course, water). This is similar to how commercial land is considered when its sale price is dependent on the parcel's amount of street frontage.

KEY TERMS

Discount Points An amount paid to a lender (1% of loan amount) when a loan is made to make up the difference between the current market interest rate and the rate a lender gives a borrower on a note. Discount points increase a lender's yield on a note, allowing the lender to give a borrower a lower interest rate.

Elements of Comparison Characteristics of a property or a transaction that can be used to explain differences in the price paid in a transaction.

Excess Site A site that is not needed to support the existing improvements or highest and best use. Could have sell-off potential or be needed for future expansion of the existing or anticipated improvements.

Gross Adjustments The overall total of all adjustments applied regardless of whether the adjustment is applied as a positive or a negative. (For example, a +$1,000 and a -$1,000 adjustment would result in $2,000 gross adjustments.)

Linkages The proximity of property to common destinations and conveniences, and the time required to reach those places.

Net Adjustments The sum of the adjustments taking into account whether the adjustment was a positive or a negative. (For example, a +$1,000 and a -$1,000 adjustment would result in $0 net adjustments.)

For Example:

- A 100′x 200′ residential building lot sold for $40,000. Based on a per square foot unit, the sale price was $2.00 per square foot:

100′x 200′ = 20,000 square feet

$40,000 ÷ 20,000 = $2.00

- A 10-acre residential tract sold for $150,000. Using a per-acre unit of measure, the sale price per acre was $15,000 per acre:

$150,000 ÷ 10 acres = $15,000

- A 150′x 100′ waterfront parcel sold for $150,000. If front foot was the unit of measure, the unit sale price would be $1,000:

$150,000 ÷ 150 = $1,000

When size-related unit prices are used, the appraiser can apply the unit price to comparables of different sizes without making an adjustment for the size difference. However, the appraiser should strive to apply the unit price to comparable data that is the most similar in size as possible. Significantly larger or smaller sized data may need to be adjusted higher or lower due to the economics of scale.

For Example: Based on the economics of scale, the per square foot price of a 1,500 square foot house may be greater than the per square foot price of a 3,000 square foot house. And, therefore, the per square foot price unit derived may require an economics of scale adjustment.

Also, sometimes units of comparison are confused with other units used in the comparison process. Sometimes elements of comparison are broken down into primary units used in the selection of comparable data, such as the number of bedrooms, style, location, etc. While this is not theoretically incorrect, the term and concept should not be confused with units of comparison for stating sale price.

» *Depending on the type of property in the appraisal assignment, sale prices for units of comparison can be based per square foot, apartment, room, acre, front foot, etc.* «

KEY TERMS

Paired Data Analysis The process of determining the value of specific property characteristics or features by comparing pairs of similar properties. Also called **Matched Pair Analysis**.

Partial Interest Any interest in real estate that one may have, other than the full bundle of rights.

Qualitative Analysis A method used after any quantitative adjustments have been applied that employs the appraiser's judgment in forming opinions relying on such methods as relative comparison analysis (bracketing), ranking analysis, and/or personal interviews. The method requires good judgment and reasoning skills of the appraiser.

Quantitative Adjustments A method that requires the recognition of the differences between the comparable data and the subject property and assigning either a market derived dollar or percentage amount as an adjustment.

Reconciliation Analyzing the values derived from the different appraisal approaches to arrive at a final opinion of value.

Regression Analysis A statistical measure that attempts to ascertain the source of change in variables.

Scatter Diagram Graphs used to study the relationship between two variables.

Surplus Site A site that is not needed for the highest and best use of the subject and does not have potential for sell-off or an autonomous highest and best use.

Unit of Comparison A component with which a property can be divided for the purpose of comparison such as square foot, living unit, etc.

Elements of Comparison

In Chapter 2, you will recall several properties were chosen in the data array that represented properties that shared the most commonality. During our discussion, it was easily recognized that there were some fundamental differences between the properties chosen and the subject.

Examining the **elements of comparison** (*characteristics of a property or a transaction that can be used to explain differences in the price paid in a transaction*) provides the appraiser deeper insight about the similarity of the subject and the properties that have been chosen for comparison. During the course of this analysis, the appraiser will not only recognize the differences, but also determine how those differences will be perceived by the typical buyer in a market value transaction. If the perception results in either a negative or positive reaction, what will the monetary effect be of that difference?

√ ***In Other Words:*** The appraiser identifies the differences and decides whether or not an adjustment is warranted.

Appraisers take into account several elements when considering the comparability of a particular property and whether or not to make an adjustment. The elements of comparison reflect similarities of the legal interests, cash equivalency, market conditions, and physical factors between the subject and the comparable data. The basic elements of comparison that are examined in most transactions are:

- Property rights conveyed.
- Financing terms.
- Conditions of sale.
- Market conditions.
- Expenditures made after the sale.*
- Location.
- Physical characteristics.

**Note:* Expenditures made after the sale may be considered as an element in some assignments immediately following or as part of conditions of sale. This concept will be discussed later in this chapter.

There are certainly variations of these elements depending on the property and the scope of work in the assignment. However, it is important for the appraiser to be consistent with all comparisons throughout the sales comparison analysis.

When the type of value in an appraisal assignment is market value, and if the information is available to the appraiser in the normal course of business, Standards Rule 1-5(a) of USPAP requires the appraiser to

> ***"analyze all agreements of sale, options, and listings of the subject property current as of the effective date of the appraisal..."***

We will revisit this Standards Rule again later in this chapter, but for now let's focus on why it is important to analyze these agreements and offerings at this point in the process.

Some may question why appraisers are provided with the current agreement of sale, the details of a pending transaction, or certain listing information. The purpose is fairly simple and directly related to the elements of comparison. Important information regarding key elements can be gained from examining, first hand, what was being offered in a listing or what was agreed upon by the parties to a transaction. Sale contracts specifically alert the appraiser to property rights that are or are not being conveyed. As well, the agreement likely spells out any special financing terms, concessions, and items of value (such as personal property) that are included in the transaction. There could be other considerations noted that have a significant impact as well, such as extended possession periods for the seller or fixtures that the seller is taking with them and not including as part of the transaction.

Of course, appraisers must be independent and not allow the information to bias the assignment results. Here, the appraiser should be particularly sensitive and cautious. However, when the elements of a transaction are inconsistent with the data being used for comparison in the sales comparison approach, the appraiser must analyze and consider the potential for adjustments. Let's look at the basic elements a little further.

» *When the appraiser examines the elements of comparison, he is able to observe the similarities of the subject and the comparable properties* «

Property Rights Conveyed

The appraiser must make certain that the property rights of the subject in the assignment are consistent with the comparable data being used to compare it to. If the subject of the appraisal is being valued in fee simple and the property rights conveyed are something different than fee simple (e.g., being subject to an existing lease or other similar limitation), this would lead to something less than an apples-to-apples comparison.

Another example of a conundrum with property rights conveyed would be when only a fractional interest was the subject of the comparable sale. Consider a transaction where one or more co-owners were acquiring an interest in a property held by another co-owner or co-owners. The purchase price represented most likely would not represent what 100% of the fee simple interest in the property would be worth. It would be dangerous to simply try to assign a value to the entire interest in the property by using the transaction amount of the fractional interest.

For example, the appraiser has located a transaction for a particular property where the sale price was confirmed to be $100,000. However, that price represented only what one co-owner paid to buy the other co-owner's undivided one-half interest in the property—a *partial interest.* A **partial interest** is *any interest in real estate that one may have, other than the full bundle of rights.* The appraiser could not simply assume that the $100,000 sale price of the undivided one-half interest would equate to the fee simple interest of the entire ownership being worth $200,000. There are many things to consider here. The purchaser, by buying the co-owner's interest, gained full ownership and control of the property, which could make the $100,000 more than what one-half of the property interest actually may be worth, using the most common definition of market value of an open and competitive market. The $100,000 figure represented, somewhat, the purchaser's motivation to gain control of the ownership. In such case, if the 100% fee simple interest were offered to the open and competitive market, the value would probably be less than $200,000. Therefore, simply multiplying the sale price of $100,000, under such circumstances, by two would not prove reliable. The same would be true if the property interest being appraised in an assignment is a one-half interest. The appraiser should not simply divide the sale price of a 100% fee simple interest in a comparable transaction to arrive at a value opinion for a one-half ownership interest of the subject property.

In some cases, the inclusion of personal property might also be examined as part of the property rights conveyed, rather than as a condition of sale. The appraiser should recognize from the personal inspection and examination of the agreement to sell (and/or listing) whether or not personal property items (chattels) are being included with the sale. It is common for some personal property to be conveyed with residential real property, such as a refrigerator or draperies. Often, the appraiser determines that the item(s) have no significant impact on a transaction. Of course, that decision should be based on market evidence identified during the appraiser's analysis. If the comparable sale data included personal property that is not typically conveyed with real property, the transaction is not likely arm's length and should probably be omitted from the analysis, provided there is other data to use.

If the subject of the assignment includes personal property items, the appraiser must determine how the item(s) have affected the transaction. If the items are significant or relevant to the purchase price, the appraiser must consider competency in appraising the personal items (or accepting the assignment), possibly bring in an appraiser who does have competency in the assignment, or value the items separately. Standards Rule 1-4(g) of USPAP states

> ***"When personal property, trade fixtures, or intangible items are included in the appraisal, the appraiser must analyze the effect on value of such non-real property items."***

The comment to the Standards Rule addresses the appraiser's competency obligation:

> ***" When the scope of work includes an appraisal of personal property, trade fixtures or intangible items, competency in personal property appraisal or business appraisal is required."***

Personal property most often is, due to its potential as a strong motivator, considered during the examination of conditions of sale, which we will discuss next. How it is handled, and in what category it is considered, is less important than simply being consistent.

In reality, in most common residential appraisal assignments, examination of property rights conveyed is not usually performed after data has been selected, but rather as a primary consideration of the data's applicability in the initial selection process. In other words, the appraiser determined that the comparable data reflected the same property rights before he chose it for use in the analysis. Therefore, on some common appraisal forms, which we will cover in a future chapter, the appraiser may not actually see "Property Rights Conveyed" as a separate line item. The reasoning for this is that the guidelines and requirements of many clients and intended users of residential appraisals do not allow comparable data to be used where the property rights conveyed in a transaction are something different than the subject of the assignment.

In summary, comparable data that does not represent the same property interests are typically discarded and not used in direct market comparison. Sometimes adjustments can be supported and applied to such data; however, the process is complex and rarely applied in typical residential appraisal assignments. This topic is discussed in more advanced appraisal coursework.

» *When the subject of an assignment is a partial interest or includes rights in non-real property, the appraiser must consider competence for such an assignment* «

Financing Terms

The underlying premise of the most commonly used definition of market value assumes cash equivalency to the typical market. More simply, the assumption is that the subject is not part of a transaction that includes atypical financing terms or financing concessions when the definition of value is market value. Therefore, the effect of any unusual terms or concessions in the transaction of a comparable sale is not reflected by comparison to the subject, rather the amount in dollars, the terms, and concessions had on the comparable transaction in relationship to the market.

For Example: Consider the following sale—a subject property sold with the seller providing financing and contributing to the purchaser's closing costs:

	Subject	Comparable Sale
Sale Price	$390,000	$385,000
Financing Terms	Seller Financing Seller paying $2,500 of purchaser's closing costs	Cash No seller concessions

Based on this example, the comparable sale is cash equivalent as far as financing terms. The seller financing and concessions being paid by the seller are of no consequence other than possibly making the sale price of the subject not be the same as what the market value of the subject might be.

However, if that situation was reversed, as illustrated below, the comparable sale has financing terms with seller participation. In this case, it would indicate the appraiser must analyze the effect of the participation to the comparable transaction and whether an adjustment is warranted to address financing terms when reflected to the market:

	Subject	Comparable Sale
Sale Price	$385,000	$390,000
Financing Terms	Cash No seller concessions	Seller Financing Seller paid $2,500 of purchaser's closing costs

Unlike the other elements of comparison, financing terms and concessions affect only the comparable data in a market value assignment and have no relationship to the subject. We will see how the adjustments are identified and applied later in this chapter. The effect of financing terms should be analyzed to determine if an adjustment is warranted. In addition to seller participation in financing and seller-paid financing concessions, other examples of financing terms that might be considered include:

- Assumption of an existing mortgage.
- Buydowns and financial incentives offered by a builder or developer.
- Land or installment contracts with the seller retaining legal title until satisfied.
- Wraparound loans using existing mortgages.
- Program (financing) participation fees required to be paid by the seller.

It may be common, depending on the situation, that financing terms are distinguished using a separate analysis and adjustment for financing method and seller-paid fees and concessions.

Conditions of Sale

Usually, **conditions of sale** consider *atypical motivations of the parties of a transaction*. Most often, these non-market conditions will be elements that affect the sale price in a transaction that would not be considered arm's length, including, but not limited to:

- Related parties (materially or by natural relationship) in a transaction where the seller accepted less for the property due to the relationship.
- A seller facing hardship, a tight timeline, or other circumstance that could be interpreted as duress.
- A transaction of a property where the seller was not necessarily looking out for his own best interest, such as selling for less to a religious entity, or a non-profit or charitable organization.
- Property acquired for assemblage.

Some terms of a sales transaction that would need to be considered in conditions of sale will evidence themselves in the purchase contract. However, most of these transaction details can be determined only by communication with a party to, or familiar with, the comparable transaction.

Non-market conditions evidenced in an arm's-length transaction are often rarer, but could include circumstances arising out of an acquisition, eminent domain, or a lack of exposure to the open market. No matter what the condition is and what is causing it, the appraiser must carefully research and analyze market data before making an adjustment, because any adjustment for conditions of sale must be fully supported—and that is often very difficult to accomplish. In such a case, the comparable sale should probably not be used.

√ ***Note:*** Sometimes financing terms, concessions, and conditions of sale may arise, such as an allowance specified in the transaction because the seller and buyer were related. The appraiser must be careful not to double-count the adjustment in such cases.

Expenditures Made After the Sale

Expenditures made after the sale can be analyzed either as an independent element of comparison or as part of the conditions of sale. These items could include (but are not limited to) anticipated costs to cure property condition items, raze all or part of the improvements, or elimination of environmental issues. Most often these adjustments are addressed in terms of the actual dollars the purchaser anticipated at the time the purchase price was agreed upon.

Market Conditions

An appraiser may need to consider whether an adjustment may be warranted for market conditions when the conditions in which the transaction took place are different from the effective date of the value opinion in an assignment. The date of sale in the comparable transaction evidences to the appraiser the need for the analysis. However, appraisers should be cautious of immediately assuming that although the date of sale is different, even if the comparable data is months old, that an adjustment for market conditions is automatically warranted. In some cases, a few days may account for a measurable difference. In others, a period of several months may see very little change in market conditions.

Appraisers seldom locate data in which the comparable data transacted on the effective date in the appraiser's assignment. Thus, it is most likely that any affect between the market conditions in the comparable data and the subject property on the appraisal's effective date will always require analysis, but not always an adjustment.

» *An adjustment for market conditions addresses changes in market conditions, not simply the passing of time* «

Sometimes appraisers are directed by the client in an assignment to apply an adjustment to any comparable that exceeds a certain date (e.g., six months). The appraiser must be careful of accepting an assignment with such conditions. If an adjustment is not found to be warranted because market conditions in the comparable transaction are consistent with the effective date in the assignment, any adjustment applied likely could not be objectively supported and the assignment results could be misleading. We will look later at how market conditions are analyzed and adjustments are identified.

Location

Depending on the availability of data, it is possible that a location element could be found that is different between the comparable data and the subject property. When considering location, the appraiser is most concerned with the particular location's market preferences and external characteristics, and how the subject site compares with the data being analyzed. Certainly not all inclusive, these items could include things such as:

- Economic characteristics (including supply and demand)
- External influences
- **Linkages** *(the proximity of property to common destinations and conveniences, and the time required to reach those places)*
- Zoning
- Access
- View
- Position (e.g., corner vs. interior)

Physical Characteristics

It is said that no two properties are *exactly* the same. How the comparable data differs from the subject property and how the market will interpret those differences in dollars could result in a very broad analysis. Therefore, in most residential appraisal assignments, it is likely that there will be some degree of difference in the physical features and characteristics between the data being used for comparison and the subject property. These differences could be related to the style and design, condition or quality, size and room type, or features of the property.

While it is usually easy to recognize differences between properties, determining the necessity of an adjustment and the amount of the adjustment can often be much more painstaking.

Identifying and Supporting Adjustments

Standards Rule 1-1(a) of USPAP obligates an appraiser to

> "***be aware of, understand, and correctly employ those recognized methods and techniques that are necessary to produce a credible appraisal.***"

Once a difference or differences between the comparable data and the subject property are recognized, the next step is to determine if an adjustment is warranted—and if so, how much. There are several acceptable methods and techniques by which an appraiser can determine the necessity for, and the identification of, an adjustment. It is very important that the critical nature of this process be realized and not taken lightly. Failure to address or adequately support adjustments in the sales comparison approach ranks high in the reasons why an appraiser is sanctioned with disciplinary action. Appraisers must use great care in everything they do in developing any opinion of value. But, this is one area where the appraiser must be very thoughtful.

» *Failure to fully support an adjustment is a frequent cause of disciplinary action against appraisers* «

Determining the appropriateness and the amount of an adjustment requires competence that is gained through experience, diligent analytical process, and sound judgment and reasoning skills. Subjectivity has no place here. The results of the appraiser's analyses must be based on objective market evidence. Appraisers place themselves at great risk by deciding, without sound finding, whether or not an adjustment is warranted. Likewise, an appraiser cannot simply "rubber-stamp" adjustments based on an unsupported notion that a fireplace *always* contributes $500, or that *every* additional bedroom warrants a $1,000 adjustment. Such decisions can be made only when market evidence supports the conclusion.

Adjustments in the sales comparison approach are, for many elements of comparison, identified in the form of *quantitative adjustments*. Another type of analysis that appraisers employ during the valuation process is *qualitative analysis*.

Using Quantitative and Qualitative Techniques

Making **quantitative adjustments** is *a method that requires the recognition of the differences between the comparable data and the subject property and assigning either a dollar or percentage amount as an adjustment.* In the sales comparison approach for most residential appraisal assignments, adjustments are quantified through data analysis techniques such as **paired data analysis** or other quantitative techniques, some of which are more complex than those we will explore in this course.

Qualitative analysis is *a method used after any quantitative adjustments have been applied that employs the appraiser's judgment in forming opinions relying on such methods as relative comparison analysis (bracketing), ranking analysis, and/or personal interviews. The method requires the appraiser to have good judgment and reasoning skills.* This step is used during the reconciliation process (after any quantitative adjustments have been applied, as already stated) or when a quantitative adjustment cannot be reasonably determined. This concept will be discussed later.

Paired Data Analysis

Paired data analysis is *the process of determining the value of specific property characteristics or features by comparing pairs of similar properties.* This is also called a **matched pair analysis.** This process will provide the appraiser with an indication of the particular feature's dollar value. Ideally, there should be only one different characteristic between the pairs of properties being analyzed so the difference in sale price can be attributed directly to that feature. This will indicate the feature's contributory value.

Refer to the following chart for an example of the paired data analysis theory.

For Example: The following market data was gathered on recent sales in an area.

Note: These contributory values are examples only and may vary greatly in your area.

Comparable	Bedrooms	Baths	Square Feet	Garage	Basement	Price
#1	3	1.5	1,250	Yes	Yes	$77,000
#2	3	1.5	1,100	Yes	Yes	$74,000
#3	2	1.0	850	Yes	No	$63,500
#4	4	1.5	1,250	Yes	Yes	$79,000
#5	3	1.5	1,175	No	Yes	$69,500
#6	3	1.0	1,000	No	No	$65,000
#7	2	1.0	950	Yes	No	$65,500
#8	3	1.5	1,175	Yes	Yes	$72,500
#9	3	1.0	1,000	No	Yes	$67,500
#10	3	1.0	1,100	Yes	Yes	$72,500

In selecting paired data, look for comparables with the same features, except one. The following paired data sets were deduced from the given information. By finding the difference in price, the feature's contributory value can be determined.

	VALUE		
Matched Pairs:	Bedrooms	#1 and #4	$2,000
	Baths (Half)	#2 and #10	$1,500
	Square Feet	#3 and #7	$20/sq. ft.
	Garage	#5 and #8	$3,000
	Basement	#6 and #9	$2,500

The paired data analysis is one example of a quantitative adjustment—the dollar amounts revealed through the analysis have been quantified, or extracted as hard numbers, by using market data. The analysis supports the appraiser's action in applying the results in the sales comparison analysis of a subject property.

In reality, though, simply performing one paired data analysis to determine the contributory value of a property feature may not be sufficient. The appraiser's best conclusions and support will likely necessitate more than one analysis. For instance, it is unlikely that an appraiser will always find that the contributory value of an additional bedroom would consistently be $2,000 as was revealed in the previous example. Performing paired data analysis of several sets of data would likely yield varied results.

For Example: An appraiser has analyzed several paired data sets where the number of bedrooms was predominately the only difference in each analysis. Some houses had three bedrooms and some had four. The result of the analysis is as follows:

Paired Data Set	**1**	**2**	**3**	**4**
Extracted Contributory Value of a 4th Bedroom	$1,800	$2,100	$1,500	$2,400

As can be seen, the results presented are not conclusive and are, for the most part, rather broad. How the appraiser proceeds with this information is very much dependent on the scope of work in the particular assignment. Let's look at *some* acceptable techniques that the appraiser could choose to apply.

Statistical Measure of Central Tendency

The key measures for this application could be the mean (mathematical average) or the median (mid-point of the set). The mode (most frequently occurring number in the set) would not apply in this example as there is no common dollar amount presented.

- The mean would represent a $1,950 contributory value:

  ($1,800 + $2,100 + $1,500 + $2,400 = $7,800 ÷ 4)

- The median would also produce a result of $1,950:

  ($1,800 + $2,100 = $3,900 ÷ 2)

Since the mean and the median are both indicating the same conclusion, $1,950 is a fairly well supported adjustment for the contributory value of the fourth bedroom, given the data analyzed very closely mirrors the subject (e.g., the subject's total gross living area, location, etc.).

If, as may often be the case, the data presented has significant variables, the data might better be examined using other quantitative techniques.

Regression Analysis

A **regression analysis** is *a statistical measure that attempts to ascertain the source of change in variables.* A simple regression analysis can be used whenever there is a relationship between two characteristics of a property, such as a relationship between the sale price of a property and the property's gross living area (square feet). A multiple regression analysis is used when more than two variables are being examined. Regression analysis is simply an avenue for the appraiser to observe the relationship and to examine the subject property's relevance to the data, and is especially helpful when the data being analyzed is broad and not all of the data is closely comparable to the subject.

Let's look at how the data revealed by the paired data analysis could be more closely observed using a simple regression analysis— examining the total gross living area of the paired sales in relationship to the fourth bedroom's contributory value.

For Example: The appraiser has noted that as the paired sets' square footage increases, so does the contributory value of the fourth bedroom. While this may not be the case in every situation, or certainly not always as consistent as is presented here, this illustration of a simple regression analysis serves to introduce the methodology.

Paired Data Set	GLA	Extracted Contributory Value of a 4th Bedroom
3	1,800 SF	$1,500
1	2,000 SF	$1,800
2	2,200 SF	$2,100
4	2,400 SF	$2,400

If the subject property contains 2,300 square feet of gross living area, the indicated support is at the halfway point between the conclusions of paired data set #2 and #4, which contained 2,200 square feet and 2,400 square feet, respectively. Thus, the appraiser's conclusion for application to the subject could be bracketed between the $2,100 and $2,400 contributory value indication as $2,250. **Bracketing**, in this case, *is demonstrated by the value indications that are superior and inferior to the subject, with the subject's relevance positioned in between.*

One of the issues with effectively employing regression analysis has been the amount of data needed to result in a credible analysis. Depending on the source, most experts agree that between 20 and 30 properties must be analyzed in order for the results to be meaningful. This can become a tedious task if performed manually, and complicated if there is a limited amount of data available to analyze. Technology is playing a major role in removing these barriers.

The use of automated regression analysis is evolving the methodology to a new level of reliability and user friendliness. Many sources for automated regression analysis and adjustment data derived using the techniques are available to appraisers for their use. Fannie Mae, for example utilizes regression tools for quality control purposes from data derived from the thousands and thousands of appraisal reports used in the loans they process. Private firms also have amassed large quantities of comparable data, from which adjustment data can be harvested. These programs provide large amounts of data, suggested adjustments derived from the data, and even rationale and reconciliation commentary for inclusion in the appraisal report.

One of the more recent popular buzz-phrases in residential appraisal is hedonic regression analysis. Most would agree that there are virtually unlimited differences between one house and another – location, lot size, style, color, condition, various amenities, etc. In other words, buildings are heterogeneous, or not all the same. However, there are some key areas that are primary buying factors for most residential properties – location and gross living area are often the most frequently mentioned. Hedonic regression analysis might examine each those two variables to indicate a supported adjustment in each area. Other differences that could be difficult to specifically identify a dollar adjustment would be addressed within either of those two categories. For instance, do *most* buyers really recognize the difference between a 10 x 10 deck, and a 10 x 20 deck? Of course, it is still the appraiser's responsibility to address other items warranting an adjustment, either through quantitative or qualitative analysis.

Graphic Analysis

A graphic analysis is a simple method of displaying data so that it may be visually interpreted. There are several ways to present data graphically, but as an example, a **scatter diagram** is *a graph used to study the relationship between two variables.*

For Example: In the scatter diagram below, we see the relationship of the gross living area of the data sets and the contributory value of the fourth bedroom. As the total gross living area of the data increases, so does the contributory value of the fourth bedroom.

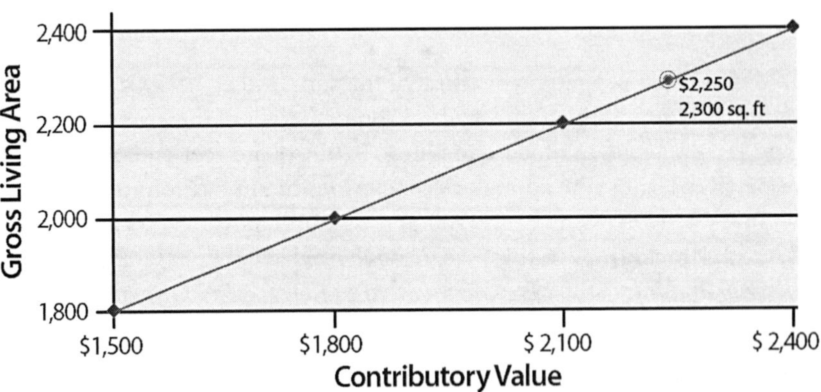

When the data is viewed two-dimensionally, as in this example, where the subject best fits within this data becomes obvious. Regression analysis and graphic analysis are discussed further in the ***Statistics, Modeling, and Finance*** course.

Data Collection and Storage

Before going further with the discussion of data analysis and application, it is important to look at where the appraiser's data is coming from and how the appraiser treats the data.

Comparable sales and listing data can come from a variety of sources. Most frequently, the appraiser subscribes to multiple listing services as well as other independent services that supply information on properties currently available and those that have sold or expired without selling. The availability of these services depends on the particular area of the assignment. The expectation for the sources to which an appraiser avails themselves is judged by what the appraiser's peers would use in a similar assignment.

Obtaining and Storing Comparable Data

One of the appraiser's best sources of relevant data comes from the appraiser's own files of past assignments. When an appraiser performs an appraisal where the subject of the assignment is part of a sale transaction, the subject's information is most often stored by the appraiser for potential use as comparable data in future assignments. Most residential appraisal computer software allows the appraiser to store not only the subject data, but also new comparable data as it is identified and verified into a comparable database for future reference and use. Most of the technology available provides flexibility to the appraiser to sort the data by date of sale, sale price, location, style, or other physical characteristics.

Public records, such as courthouse data, are also very useful to the appraiser and may reveal transaction data that was not made available to multiple listing services in private transactions. Using this data, however, may require the appraiser to broaden the scope of his verification process. When considering such data, the appraiser must identify if the transaction was arm's length. The characteristics of the property being transacted may not be as plainly (or accurately) stated in such records, making verification of that element more necessary and sometimes complex, as well. If the data being used is from a source not directly related to the transaction, a source that is familiar with the transaction and the property should be consulted. This more familiar source will help to provide the appraiser with critical elements in determining the transaction and property details.

Some parties who would be familiar with a specific transaction, such as a real estate agent, are often reluctant to provide information. Such individuals could also be prohibited by regulation or agreement from disclosing information about the transaction that is considered confidential in nature. In many areas, if not most, the sale price of a property is public record. However, details such as financing terms and concessions, and conditions of sale could be considered confidential. In such cases, the appraiser may need to verify directly with the buyer or seller the specifics of a particular transaction. If a transaction cannot be verified as being arm's length or other vital information cannot be reasonably obtained, the appraiser should consider whether the lack of such verification would satisfy the scope of work and whether the results would be credible.

USPAP does not specifically address verification of comparable data. The burden is placed on the appraiser to be consistent with what his peers would do and what the regularly intended users in a similar assignment would expect of the appraiser. The Scope of Work Rule of USPAP should be the appraiser's compass for what is appropriate in an assignment.

» *When the circumstances of a transaction cannot be verified, the appraiser should strongly consider whether the data could still be used and if credible assignment results could still be produced* «

Maintaining Adjustment Data

Individual adjustments identified by the appraiser and derived from analysis, such as those indicated by paired data, are also usually kept on file by the appraiser and used in future assignments. Appraisers do not perform a new paired data analysis for every element in each assignment. Once an adjustment has been identified for a particular element (such as a physical characteristic in one assignment), the adjustment can be applied in other similar assignments, when warranted. But, while the appraiser may not perform a paired data analysis for every assignment, it is very important that the appraiser consider in *each* assignment if an adjustment continues to reflect the current market and is appropriate for use in the assignment. A predetermined adjustment for which its relevance and applicability has not been considered for that particular assignment is not acceptable.

Adjustment data for common differences can become part of the appraiser's stored data and is often categorized for possible application in future assignments. Stored historic data can also be useful when the appraiser is developing a retrospective value opinion, or in an appraisal review assignment where the review appraiser is forming his own value conclusion as of the effective date in the original assignment or an effective date in the past. The appraiser, however, must monitor and check the data for market changes that have taken place which might indicate if the data still is indicative of a typical market reaction in a current assignment.

Identifying Adjustments for Specific Elements

Most adjustments for use in the sales comparison approach can be identified through one or more of the quantitative techniques. There will be some occasions, however, when the appraiser recognizes that a difference would be addressed in dollars paid by market participants. but cannot with any degree of confidence identify what the specific adjustment should be. When the amount of an adjustment cannot be clearly supported, an adjustment simply should not be made, as doing so could produce misleading results. However, in such cases, the appraiser should not dismiss the need to address the element, but rather consider using qualitative techniques to address the difference.

Now, we are ready to take a more specific look into each of the primary elements of comparison and illustrate by example how an adjustment can be identified and supported. Although no course can cover every scenario that an appraiser might encounter in a residential assignment, we will discuss some common application examples.

Property Rights Conveyed

The property rights conveyed in the comparable should always be the same as that of the subject property.

> ***For Example:*** If the subject's fee simple interest is being valued, the comparable transactions must also represent a fee simple interest. If a partial interest is the subject of an appraisal assignment, the comparable data should reflect the same interest.

As was expressed earlier, the property rights conveyed, in most residential appraisal assignments, are considered when the comparable data is initially selected—selecting comparables that match the same property interest as the subject. In most common residential appraisal assignments, sufficient comparable data is usually available where the property rights conveyed are not atypical or different from that of the subject.

However, if relevant comparable data is non-existent or scarce, appraisers can sometimes isolate adjustments for certain property rights differences. But, the process can be complex and may require a greater degree of competency than is usually possessed by many residential appraisers. Examples of possible adjustments might be for differences in a leased fee estate, which can sometimes be addressed using an income approach. Adjustments for certain property limitations, such as an easement, can be identified through paired data analysis and applied to the comparable data as a percentage adjustment.

Financing Terms

The purpose of applying adjustments for special, or non-market, financing terms is to bring the comparable data to cash equivalency. Sometimes this adjustment can also reflect items that could be considered conditions of sale. Financing terms could also be broken down into separate adjustments for the method of financing, such as seller financing, and costs paid by the seller related to financing, such as the payment of *discount points*. A **discount point** is *an amount paid to a lender when a loan is made to make up the difference between the current market interest rate and the rate a lender gives a borrower on a note. Discount points increase a lender's yield on a note, allowing the lender to give a borrower a lower interest rate. Each discount point equals 1 percent of the loan amount.*

Following is a very simple example of how an adjustment might be calculated, by discounting, when the property is financed at a below market interest rate.

For Example: The purchaser is buying a $120,000 home with a down payment of $20,000, with the seller offering to carry the $100,000 balance at 5% interest for a 20-year term. That mortgage has a payment of $659.96. Current market interest rates for a 20-year mortgage are 7%, which would have resulted in a payment of $775.30 on the $100,000 principle. Thus, the cash equivalency calculation is as follows:

$775.30 - $659.96 = $115.34 savings per month

The monthly savings, discounted at a market interest rate of 7% over the 20 year term, has a present value of $14,876.84. (Present value calculations will be illustrated in Chapter 4)

The cash equivalent sale price is $105,123.16
$85,123.16 ($100,000 - $14,876.84) + $20,000 (down payment)
= $105,123.16

Important considerations when using this calculation are that the seller interest rate and the market interest rate would remain consistent throughout the entire life of the loan and that homes in the market area are typically held for the full 20-year term. The present value calculation should always reflect the typical holding period. The same formula can be employed for loan assumptions.

Adjustments for financing concessions, which most commonly are financing-related costs being paid by the seller, should reflect the amount over and above what is typically paid by sellers in a particular market. There may be many markets in which it is *not* common for the seller to contribute to the purchaser's financing-related costs. If this is the case, the entire amount being paid by the seller would be deducted from the sale price of the comparable.

> ***For Example:*** A seller is paying 3 discount points in a transaction in which the purchaser is acquiring a $100,000 mortgage. The sale price of the property is $115,000. Each discount point is equal to 1% of the mortgage amount. So, in this example, the financing concession would be 3% of the $100,000 mortgage amount, or $3,000.
>
> **$115,000 sale price - $3,000 financing concession**
> **= $112,000 adjusted sale price**
>
> If it were found, however, that for this particular market, sellers usually pay 1 discount point as normal practice, the adjustment would be only $2,000 (2 discount points) and the sale price of the comparable, adjusted for cash equivalency, would be $113,000.

Depending on the particular market, the necessity of making adjustments for financing concessions may not be all that uncommon. Appraisers must be certain that any adjustment truly reflects typical market actions.

Conditions of Sale

In the previous discussion of the financing term elements, we cautioned that, for most residential transactions, comparable data in which the transaction included special financing terms should be discarded. The reasoning for this is not particularly because an appropriate adjustment cannot be identified, but, for the most part, because an appropriate adjustment for some aspects of the element would sometimes require a more complex analysis. Therefore, if sufficient relevant data is available that did not include special financing circumstances, this data may prove better as an apples-to-apples comparison that would not require an adjustment.

The advice for the element of **conditions of sale** (in most cases) is the same, except for a slightly different reason. Many atypical conditions of sale, especially in residential transactions, are based on actions of emotion, lack of knowledge, state of mind, or pressure charged conditions such as duress or haste. The problem with these issues in a comparable transaction is not that it is a complex procedure to identify an adjustment (as in financing terms); rather, it is often not possible to associate a dollar amount with what a market participant felt or was thinking during that transaction.

Personal interviews with transaction participants may prove to be insightful, but often the motivations and awareness of the participants cannot be aligned with a conclusive dollar adjustment. Such information may be helpful for qualitative analysis.

For Example: Both buyer and seller agree that the sale price of the transaction represented less than, or more than, market value. This might indicate whether the adjustment would be upward or downward, but likely little more than that. The appraiser could bracket the market value conclusion somewhere above or below what the comparable transaction sold for based on information gained from the transaction participants. But this practice will often not be acceptable in many residential appraisal assignments due to assignment conditions.

Considering the method by which the comparable property was offered and sold is also important. Appraisers will most often not use comparable data that sold via a sheriff's sale, or for that matter, by any type of auction. While selling property by auction is a popular and, in some markets for some properties, very effective method of generating a real estate transaction, it can often be problematic for the appraiser's analysis. The emotions, motivations, and influences surrounding the transaction, and if the transaction represented a typical market reaction, are difficult to interpret.

Usually, the residential appraiser will be able to locate enough arm's-length data in a market value assignment that will likely eliminate the need to use comparable data in which there have been atypical conditions of sale. Therefore, if arm's-length comparable sales are available to use, the appraiser should probably discard other comparable sales if they sold with one or more of the following conditions:

- Parties in the transaction were related—could include family members, landlord to tenant, employer to employee, etc.
- Personal property was included in sale
- One or both parties were atypically motivated
- Parties were not knowledgeable of market, property value, etc.
- Properties sold via a non-conventional marketing method

» When there is sufficient comparable data available from arms-length transactions for the appraiser to use, data in which there were atypical sale conditions probably should not be used «

There are, however, some sale conditions that can be addressed with a quantitative adjustment. They could present themselves as a concession not related to financing and might include repair allowances, decorating allowances, allowances for moving expenses, etc.—often as specific dollar amounts. If the particular concession is not common for the market, the amount of the allowance or other specified amount can be subtracted from the sale price as an adjustment.

In some markets, extended-possession periods negotiated between the purchaser and seller might also be quantified monetarily and might have resulted in the seller accepting less due to the sale condition. In this case, the adjustment is added to the sale price.

For Example: In a comparable transaction, the appraiser has noted that the purchaser and seller have negotiated a 60-day possession period. The purchaser is not receiving any rent payment from the seller during this period. In this particular market, it is most common for the purchaser to get possession on the date of closing. Upon contact with the seller in the transaction, the appraiser learns that the seller accepted the purchaser's offer only due to the extended possession without paying rent. The seller estimated if he were to rent the property from the purchaser for the 60-day period, he would have paid $1,500 for the total period. Likewise, verification with the purchaser revealed that he would have been willing to pay similarly more if possession had been granted at closing. Thus, the $1,500 would be added to the sale price as it reflects the sale participant's perception of the concession's value when the agreement was reached.

Expenditures Made After the Sale

Expenditures made after the sale can be analyzed either as an independent element of comparison or as part of the conditions of sale. When applied to comparable data, the cost anticipated by the new owner is applied as a positive adjustment to the sale price of the comparable. If the subject requires expenditures after the transaction, the anticipated cost is subtracted from the indicated value of the subject.

> ***For Example:*** A property in a comparable sale required installation of a heating system as the property was not equipped with one. The buyer anticipated, at the time of his offer, that the cost of installing the system would be $4,000. The agreed upon sale price was $30,000. Therefore, adjusted, the sale price would be $34,000. As a word of caution, double counting could occur if the lack of the heating system is considered in other areas within the analysis such as condition, quality, functional utility, etc.

Market Conditions

Change is constantly occurring in real estate markets and is driven by many factors. An adjustment for market conditions is also often referred to as a *date of sale* or *time adjustment*. Any adjustment identified here must address differing market conditions between the effective date of the value opinion in the appraisal assignment and the comparable data. A market condition adjustment should never be mechanically applied simply to address the passing of time, but rather a market condition change during that time.

When analyzing sold or pending comparable data, the appraiser must focus on market conditions at the time of the participant's decision—the date on which there was a meeting of the minds and an agreement was made. The agreement or contract date may or may not be available to the appraiser, depending on the particular area and service. Sometimes multiple listing services as well as other information sources will report the closing date of a transaction but provide no information regarding the date of the agreement.

When an appraiser cannot determine the date of the agreement, whether or not it is an issue would depend on market condition trends. Good judgment as well as competency in the particular market is necessary on the part of the appraiser. Has there been a long period of consistent market behavior and conditions using the closing date as the date of sale?

In many residential appraisal assignments, the time period between agreement and closing of a transaction could be minimal and little change may have occurred. However, if the market has demonstrated volatility, it is possible that market conditions at the time of the agreement and on the date of the closing were different. Therefore, in this case, knowledge of when the sale agreement was made between the parties to the transaction is vital to the appraiser's analysis.

An adjustment for market conditions can be quantified by analyzing comparable sales data that have a resale history. Consider the following example.

For Example: An appraiser has located a comparable sale within the subject market that sold in recent days for $315,000. That same property sold three years ago for $290,000. Both transactions were affirmed to be arm's length, and there were no significant physical changes in the property during that period.

To calculate the market change, the appraiser must recognize the amount of (in this case) appreciation—$25,000.

For application in the sales comparison approach, the amount of appreciation is interpreted as a percent. To calculate this, the appraiser must divide the amount appreciated by the amount it appreciated from:

$25,000 ÷ $290,000 = 0.08621, or 8.62%

Since this change was over a three year period, the change per month is figured as follows:

0.08621 ÷ 36 = 0.002395, or 0.2395% per month

Illustrating this pattern on a graph using a straight line, it looks like this:

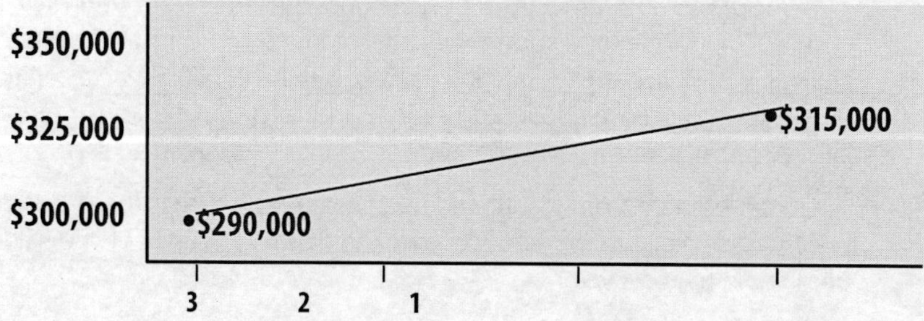

As can be seen, the adjustment could be safely applied to comparable data, if the appreciation was consistent.

Applying this factor to a comparable transaction, it would look something like this:

	627 Elm Lane		**532 Oak Drive**	
Sale Price		$337,000		$309,000
Date of Sale	4 months ago 4 x 0.2395% = 0.96% 0.0096 x $337,000 =	$3,235	2 months ago 2 x 0.2395% = 0.48% 0.0048 x $309,000 =	$1,483
Time Adjusted Sale Price		**$340,235**		**$310,483**

The appraiser must clearly understand, however, that market conditions do not always move in such a straight-line fashion. There actually may be steps, or up and down movements during this course. This is why it is very important that the appraiser looks at sales and resales in the shortest time frame possible.

Let's look now at another example in which the comparable sale has had multiple arm's-length transfers in the past several years.

For Example: Another comparable transaction has been located in the subject market which sold in the past few days for $326,000. The property transferred one year ago for $335,000, and three years ago for $295,000.

When we plot these sales on a graph, the following trend line is revealed:

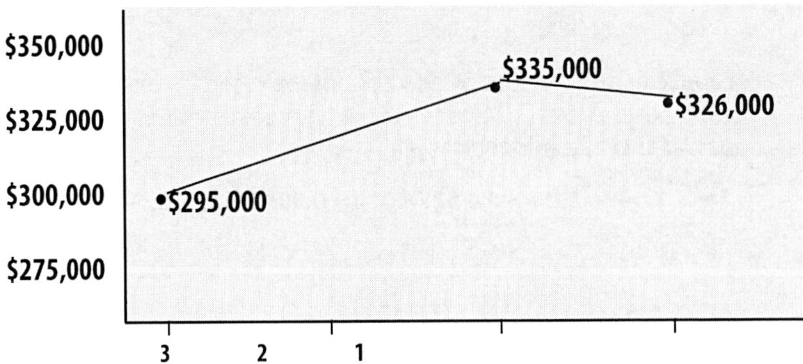

If the appraiser attempted to consider only the three-year trend ($295,000 - $326,000), a false indication would be produced. The result from such an analysis would appear to indicate slightly more than 10.5% appreciation, or 0.29% per month, which would result in an inappropriate adjustment when applied to sales transactions that took place in the last year.

What can be seen from the trend line on the graph is that the property sale price had significant appreciation over the first two years, but the sale price declined in the past year.

Looking now at the change in sale price for just the past year, the rate of decline in sale price is revealed as -2.69%.

To calculate the rate, divide the amount of the decrease in sale price during the last year ($335,000 - $326,000 = $9,000) by the amount it decreased from ($335,000).

- $9,000 ÷ $335,000 = - 2.69%, or - 0.2242% per month

If this downward factor were applied to the same comparable data that we used in the last example, the result would look like this:

	627 Elm Lane		**532 Oak Drive**	
Sale Price		$337,000		$309,000
Date of Sale	4 months ago 4 x - 0.2242% = -0.90% -0.0090 x $337,000 =	- $3,033	2 months ago 2 x - 0.2242% = - 0.45% -0.0045 x $309,000 =	- $1,391
Time Adjusted Sale Price		$333,967		$307,609

The two previous examples illustrate how sales and resales of the same property can be used to identify an adjustment for market conditions as well as the importance of carefully observing trends of change and the amount of change.

Another method that an appraiser could use to identify and support an adjustment for market conditions, though possibly not quite as reliable, is paired data of sales that are mirrored in all respects other than their sale date. Possible paired data might include:

- Mirrored (physically and locationally) homes in a subdivision
- Mirrored condominium units
- Mirrored residential building lots

When relying on mirrored data, it must be recognized that real estate markets are imperfect and even though the paired data may be outwardly similar or for the most part identical, market participants do not always recognize all properties the same.

√ ***In Other Words:*** The difference in selling price between different properties may be caused by factors other than purely market conditions. Therefore, several sets of data may need to be analyzed before reaching a conclusion.

When the appraiser does not have any of the aforementioned data available for analysis, the appraiser could look for indications of changing market conditions by examining other types of data, such as (but not limited to):

- Differences between listing prices and selling prices
- Trends in listing prices
- Rent trends
- Marketing and exposure time
- Number of offers and back-up contracts received
- Number of contracted properties that close
- Financing trends (such as rates, LTV ratios, and seller financing)
- New construction activity
- Number of foreclosures
- Changing demographics

While some of this information may not provide the appraiser with a conclusive dollar amount, it may provide the appraiser with the direction of the current market, which could be used for qualitative analysis.

Location

Location adjustments can be, and often are, analyzed as more than one component. The most common residential appraisal forms break down the element into two specific categories—location and view. However, in some assignments, location, as an element of comparison, may be classified even further, requiring individual analysis for the favorability of zoning, accessibility, etc.

In the majority of residential assignments, the most common method of identifying the necessity and amount of an adjustment is through paired data analysis.

> ***For Example:*** An appraiser has identified sales of two newly constructed homes in a subdivision. Both sales took place in similar market conditions. The properties shared the same design, floor plan, and features. One property was located on a corner lot and sold for $410,000, while the other property was located on an interior lot and sold for $425,000. Given the properties were similar in every other aspect, the location adjustment for corner vs. interior can easily be interpreted as $15,000.

The preceding example illustrates a very simple scenario where the view from both of the properties was comparable. In some residential assignments, however, there may be locational differences that require the view of the property be separately considered. Here is another simple scenario:

> ***For Example:*** The subject of a residential appraisal is a two-story dwelling backing to a golf course in the Gilford Greens subdivision. The appraiser has located one similar comparable sale in the same subdivision. It is located across the street from the subject but did not share the subject's golf course view. None of the other properties on the golf course in the subject's subdivision have transacted. The appraiser has, however, located a very similar subdivision across town, Langford Links, that has recent sales of a similar property on a golf course and one that is similar but not located on the golf course.
>
> The appraiser plans to use the property across the street as well as the two properties in the other subdivision as comparable sales in his sales comparison analysis. There are two locational components that require analysis:
>
> 1. Determine locational differences between the two subdivisions.
> 2. Identify the contributory value of the golf course view.
>
> Let's take a look at the data the appraiser has gathered.

	Comparable #1	**Comparable #2**	**Comparable #3**
	Subject Subdivision	Comparable Subdivision	Comparable Subdivision
Sale Price	$392,000	$398,000	$432,000
Location	Gilford Greens	Langford Links	Langford Links
View	Residential	Residential	Golf Course

- To determine a location adjustment, Comparable #1 and #2 can be compared.

  $392,000 vs. $398,000—location adjustment is $6,000

- Comparing #2 to #3 demonstrates the difference between a residential view and a golf course view.

  $398,000 vs. $432,000—view adjustment is $34,000

In some cases, especially when an adjustment is being derived from, or being applied to, data of a different price point (such as a $1,000,000 property), a percentage adjustment might be more appropriate.

For instance, to find the percentage adjustment for view, the appraiser would divide the amount of the derived adjustment ($34,000) by what it is superior to ($398,000) to conclude on a positive percentage adjustment of 8.54% ($34,000 ÷ $398,000).

Or, if the adjustment is being applied downwardly, the appraiser would divide the $34,000 by what it is inferior to ($432,000) to reveal a negative adjustment of 7.87% ($34,000 ÷ $432,000).

When using data from, or applying data to properties of different price points, locations, designs, etc., the appraiser should always be very careful to determine if a particular adjustment is relevant and applicable.

Physical Characteristics

It may be possible, and often very probable, in many assignments that an appraiser could locate data with no atypical financing terms, similar market conditions with no unusual conditions of sale, and very similar locational aspects. However, even if all of these elements of comparison align themselves when comparing the data to the subject property, it is very common for there to be one or several differences in the physical characteristics among them.

A compilation of all physical characteristics that an appraiser could consider in this analysis would be exhaustive and likely not include every conceivable difference that might be encountered. But, in summary, physical characteristics are all inclusive of the internal characteristics of a property and can be defined in a few broad categories:

- Site
- Improvements
- Quality
- Condition
- Functional Utility
- Appeal

In Chapter 2, a detailed listing of subject characteristics which the appraiser typically gathers during his inspection was illustrated. For the most part, this information becomes the benchmark for comparison to the comparable data that has been identified for application in the valuation process.

Similar to the appraiser's diligence when analyzing other elements of comparison, the appraiser must recognize the difference, consider the significance of the difference, determine if an adjustment is warranted, and address the component in the valuation process.

Most often in residential appraisal assignments, physical features are addressed using a quantitative adjustment. Earlier in this chapter, paired data analysis of several physical characteristics was illustrated. This illustration explained the process when there is one significant difference in the paired data set—a primary pairing. However, it is very possible that each and every difference will not be able to be identified through primary pairing since data is not always available through which to identify the necessity and amount of an adjustment. Sometimes, a secondary pairing is needed.

For Example: An appraiser needs to identify the necessity and amount of an adjustment for a greenhouse. Although he has not been able to find any data where a greenhouse was the only difference, he has been able to locate data that has two differences, one of which is a greenhouse. The other difference involves the size of the garages. Everything else about the paired properties is the same.

	630 Amherst Court	**570 Beechwood Drive**
Sale Price	$253,000	$250,000
Garage	2-Car Detached	1-Car Detached
Greenhouse	Yes	No

The difference between the sale prices of the two properties is $3,000. The appraiser has already identified, through a previous primary pairing, that the adjustment for a 2-car garage vs. a 1-car garage is $2,000. Thus, this secondary paring indicates that the greenhouse does warrant an adjustment in the amount of $1,000.

The appraiser must be *very* careful using paired data analysis. As we discussed earlier in this chapter, the appraiser usually will need to analyze several sets of data to support an adjustment due to the imperfect actions of buyers and sellers. Therefore, the appraiser must rely on good logic and judgment to determine if the numerical conclusion reached through such an analysis is actually meaningful and relevant to the typical actions of market participants. As the number of variables between data in a data set increases, the reliability of the indication reached can often be diminished. Therefore, the appraiser relies on his judgment and market intelligence to determine what is significant and what is not.

Admittedly, some physical characteristics are easier to analyze and determine the necessity and amount of a quantitative adjustment than others. Since the element of physical characteristics is so broad and can address many aspects of the physical property, the appraiser must be cautious not to double count an adjustment.

For Example: An appraiser is considering the necessity of an adjustment for differences between a comparable sale and the subject property. The comparable property has one additional bedroom which primarily accounts for additional gross living area. The question often arises: Should the appraiser make distinctions and adjust for each individually? There is no clear-cut answer for this question. The appraiser must use good judgment and be cautious with his determination and consistent with his application.

One of the ways that an appraiser could consider such a situation would be to survey where the contribution rests. Does the additional bedroom add utility to the property, and/or does the additional gross living area add livability to the property? If the living areas of the two properties are basically the same and the additional bedroom accounts for the additional gross living area, double counting could result by making an adjustment for each.

However, let's consider that the subject house had three large bedrooms and the comparable house had four smaller bedrooms. In total, the bedroom area of the two houses was basically the same. But, the four-bedroom house had a much larger kitchen and living areas. In that case, good logic might suggest that the four-bedroom house had increased utility due to the extra bedroom and increased livability due to the larger kitchen and living areas and an adjustment would be appropriate for bedroom count and gross living area. The appraiser must have knowledge of market preferences to make this decision.

A similar conundrum could result during the analysis of several different physical characteristics. In some cases, opportunities to double count could be when one item is affecting a property's value, but could sometimes be addressed by more than one adjustment. Some scenarios where the appraiser must be very careful due to the potential to double count *might* include:

- Age and condition to address the state of deterioration
- Functional utility and design/appeal to address market acceptability
- Quality and design/appeal to address market preference
- Adjustments for lack of a market-expected feature and functional utility

Many of the items the appraiser considers when analyzing physical characteristics can be difficult to quantify. Often, when conclusive evidence does not reveal that an adjustment is warranted for a certain feature or condition, that particular feature or condition may not be significant. However, if evidence indicates that the typical market participant would be influenced either positively or negatively due to the feature or condition, but an adjustment cannot be numerically applied, the element could be handled during reconciliation by qualitative analysis. That concept will be discussed later in this chapter.

Purely for the purpose of illustration, let's examine the major categories of physical characteristics for an improved residential property and some of the different ways that identification of adjustments to be applied in the sales comparison approach can be handled.

Site

Analyzing the site characteristics for potential adjustments can sometimes become a complex analysis in itself. Theoretically, no two sites are exactly the same and some differences may be recognized by the market and some may not. Not all inclusive, key site components might include:

- Size and shape
- Topography
- Landscaping
- Flood and environmental hazards
- Excess or surplus site
- Easements

Most adjustments for differences in site characteristics are identified through paired data analysis. Ideally, the comparable data should reflect properties that have similar size and shape, in context to the overall utility of the site. Small differences in site area often do not result in a market reaction as they usually do not affect the utility of the site. However, consider a site where utility of the site is influenced from it being larger. If evidence supports that the difference would be noted by the market, the appraiser must determine an adjustment for the larger, **surplus site** (*site that is not needed for the highest and best use of the subject and does not have potential for sell-off or a stand-alone highest and best use).*

One method the appraiser could use to identify an adjustment is to analyze sales of similar sites that are vacant.

For Example: An appraiser is trying to determine an adjustment for surplus site of a subject property. The subject site consists of a residential dwelling on a 0.69-acre lot. Most improved sales in the subject subdivision are 0.50 acre. The appraiser could use paired data of vacant lots to extract a square footage adjustment for the 0.19-acre difference between the comparable data and the subject.

The appraiser has found three lots in the subject subdivision that were 0.50 acre and all recently sold for $50,000. The appraiser has also located two lots that sold about the same time which had surplus site.

	Comparable Land — Sale #1	Comparable Land — Sale #2	Comparable Land — Sale #3
Sale Price	$50,000	$55,000	$57,000
Site area	0.50 acre	0.65 acre	0.72 acre

Let's look at what can be determined through the paired data analysis:

- The 0.65-acre lot sold for $5,000 more than the 0.50-acre lot and
- the 0.72-acre lot sold for $7,000 more than the 0.50-acre lot.

(Continued on next page)

For Example continued:

The calculation to derive the difference numerically would be as follows:

Comparable Land Sale #2

0.15 acre (0.65 - 0.50) x 43,560 = 6,534 sq ft

$5,000 ($55,000 - $50,000) ÷ 6,534 = $0.77 per sq ft contribution

Comparable Land Sale #3

0.22 acre (0.72 - 0.50) x 43,560 = 9,583 sq ft

$7,000 ($57,000 - $50,000) ÷ 9,583 = $0.73 per sq ft contribution

Demonstrated here is how the economy of scale works. It can be easily seen that as the surplus area of a site increases, the contributory value of the square foot unit decreases.

The subject site contains 0.19 acre, or 8,276 square feet of surplus site. The mid point of the revealed square foot sale price conclusions ($0.73 and $0.77) is $0.75. The mid point of the surplus site analyzed (6,534 and 9,583) is 8,059. Keeping the economy of scale in mind, the subject is slightly greater than the mid point (8,276 vs. 8,059), so a supported conclusion could be applied at $0.745 per square foot.

8,276 square feet x $0.745 = $6,166, or rounded, the appropriate adjustment to apply to an improved comparable for the site difference would be $6,200.

A common error would be for the appraiser to determine an adjustment by dividing the sale price of the of the 0.50 acre lot by the lot area:

0.50 x 43,560 = 21,780 sq ft

$50,000 ÷ 21,780 = $2.30 per sq ft

Calculating an adjustment in this manner would yield a misleading indication.

When *excess site* is present, the contributory value of the excess site could be identified using paired data, if comparable data is available. **Excess site** is *site that is not needed to support the existing improvements or highest and best use. Could have sell-off potential or be needed for future expansion of the existing or anticipated improvements.* However, when the excess site has sell-off potential, the contributory value of the excess portion could be its value for sell-off minus the associated costs (e.g., survey, legal fees, etc.). As a word of caution, valuing excess site in some assignments requires an elevated degree of competency and can often be considered complex. More is discussed about valuing excess site in other coursework.

Most other elements of physical site characteristics can be handled using a quantitative adjustment through a paired-data analysis, or may be considered qualitatively during reconciliation of the sales comparison approach.

Improvements

The broad category of improvements encompasses all the components that have been added to the site (the tangible physical items and characteristics of a property). In most residential appraisal assignments, these components (or primary comparative units) are classified as:

- Design and style of the dwelling
- Above grade room count
- Bedrooms and baths (above grade)
- Above grade gross living area (GLA)
- Basement and finished rooms below grade
- Heating and cooling systems
- Car storage
- Interior and exterior features (e.g., fireplaces, deck, pool, etc.)
- Other site improvements (e.g., driveway, walkways, on-site utilities, etc.)
- Auxiliary structures (e.g., shed, pole barn, etc.)

For some residential properties in some markets, the appraiser may only need to address two or three of these items. And, in some assignments, not all of these characteristics will be recognized by the market and may not require an adjustment. In other situations, the improvement characteristics that warrant an adjustment could be much more extensive than what has been presented here.

In most assignments, a quantitative adjustment for improvement characteristics can be isolated through paired-data analysis as we earlier discussed. But as the property presents more differences and greater numbers of characteristics to consider, such as a custom built or unique residential dwelling, qualitative analysis may need to be applied.

Functional Utility

Market knowledge and experience equip the appraiser with the perception to gauge when the functional utility of a property is acceptable or unacceptable to market participants. Functional utility relates to the acceptability and marketability of a property's design. There is no cookie-cutter definition of a good or poor functional utility and the acceptability may differ with different properties and in different markets.

The key to determining whether or not a design characteristic is acceptable to market participants is to know the market. Generally, the most common issues with functional utility are floor plan layout, access, market-expected features, and sometimes unfinished areas of a residential dwelling that are vital to the property's livability.

For Example:

- Tandem bedrooms—a bedroom accessed through another
- Bath access—baths that are located off a kitchen or sleeping area
- Exterior entrance— primary access into dining area, bedroom, garage, etc.
- Basement access—access from exterior, garage, bedroom, etc.
- Stairway location—upper level accessed though a bedroom or unusual location
- Heating sources—lack of central heating (or sometimes cooling) source
- Ceiling height—ceilings too low for typical livability
- Car storage—lack of garage or on-site parking

The preceding examples represent a few of the items that *could* lend to a poor functional utility; the possibilities could obviously go on and on. But, as was mentioned earlier, not all properties in every market would reject each of these items as being unacceptable. Consider an older historic dwelling—typical buyers for such properties may often dismiss tandem bedrooms or odd bath access. In some properties of a lower price point, the lack of a garage may be acceptable, while for a property in an upper price range, the lack of a garage would likely encounter significant market reaction. An unfinished basement designed primarily for storage might not suffer from poor functional utility if the basement access were through the garage. However, a finished basement with such access would probably yield a diminishing contribution for the finished areas.

The necessity and amount of an adjustment for functional utility is ideally and most commonly identified through paired-data analysis, examining properties that had similar functional issues with like properties that did not.

An alternative method sometimes used for supporting a functional utility adjustment is to develop a cost to cure. Determining the cost to cure requires a costing analysis. This will be discussed in a later chapter. The cost to cure is relevant and appropriate when the appraiser has determined the adjustment would reflect a typical buyer's thinking. In other words, the typical buyer would base his decision of the present value of the property with curing the functional utility issue and keeping the costs related to curing in mind. Personal interviews and communication with others, such as real estate agents, who interact with buyers for such properties is helpful when weighing the applicability of a cost to cure adjustment.

Quality, Condition, and Appeal

While quality, condition, and appeal previously were identified as individual categories, it is appropriate to handle them together at this point in the text. It is recognized that each of these physical components usually addresses different aspects of a property. However, the message of caution for the appraiser and the methods for handling the property's quality, condition, and appeal factors for the purpose of an adjustment are quite similar.

The determination of the condition of a property is made by comparing the property to other properties in the neighborhood. Quality of the property's overall appeal and components can be determined in much the same way. This may not be too daunting of a task, as common sense can usually dictate when one property is better than another in any of these categories. Good judgment skills are required.

However, there is a particular caution the appraiser must exercise when considering the quality, condition, and appeal—avoid subjectivity. (You, the appraiser, are not buying the property. Your subjective opinion is irrelevant.) As simple as it seems, this is sometimes difficult. Quality, condition, and appeal factors usually are rated as *fair, average, good*, etc. The appraiser should have and present a factual and reasonable basis for his determination and remain consistent throughout the rating process. Expertise in rating these areas is something that can be acquired only through experience and market competence. An acceptable alternative in some cases might be to use simple ratings of *inferior* or *superior*, although the more specific ratings could be specified as assignment conditions in some appraisals.

Adjustments for quality, condition, or appeal of a property can be identified through paired data analysis. Still, it is critical for good judgment to prevail in measuring the amount of any adjustment to be applied for these physical components. Any resulting adjustment must reflect typical market actions. When unsupported or subjective adjustments are applied, the result could be a poor quality appraisal. In some cases, a discriminatory appraisal could result, which would be unacceptable.

Sometimes, an adjustment for quality, condition, or appeal can be supported by a cost to cure *if* such an adjustment would reflect a typical market participant's reaction. If such an adjustment would be relevant and applicable, the opportunity for subjectivity can be reduced since the basis for the adjustment must be founded on factual costing.

» *When the appraiser is examining the elements of comparison, a difference may be illustrated in two different elements or components, such as age and condition. The appraiser must be careful not to double count* «

Another acceptable alternative, but only when assignment conditions allow, is to address differences in quality, condition, or appeal through qualitative analysis during the reconciliation process. Such technique, though, is often contradictory to many clients and intended users of appraisals for some mortgage purposes.

For income-producing properties, an adjustment based on the affect to the potential rent of a property could also be used as the basis for an adjustment for quality, condition, or appeal. This income technique could also be used for a location adjustment. The income technique for deriving an adjustment will be discussed in later.

As a final word of guidance, this particular area of analysis is especially susceptible to double counting.

> ***For Example:*** The appeal of a property may be strongly affected by the property's condition or quality. The appraiser must be cautious to carefully define each of these elements and any adjustment for them, separately.

Applying Adjustments

Once the necessity and amount of an adjustment has been determined, the next step for the appraiser is to apply the adjustments to the comparable properties selected for analysis in the sales comparison approach. Theoretically, the purpose of adjusting comparable properties is to express the differences of the comparable and the subject property as they would be perceived by the market. This portion of the chapter will focus on the types of adjustments that could be made, the proper methods of applying adjustments, and the order in which adjustments are applied.

Dollar Adjustments and Percentage Adjustments

In residential appraising, applying dollar adjustments to comparable properties is the most common practice when using the sales comparison approach. Most quantitative adjustments identified for physical characteristics are applied in this manner, as well as others, depending on the specifics of the assignment.

Percentage adjustments are applied more frequently for elements of comparison such as property rights conveyed, financing terms, conditions of sale, market conditions, and location. In many cases, the percentage may be converted back to a dollar amount for application to a particular comparable. The appraiser must use his judgment as to the appropriateness of the type of adjustment to apply in each assignment.

Direction of Adjustment—Ups and Downs

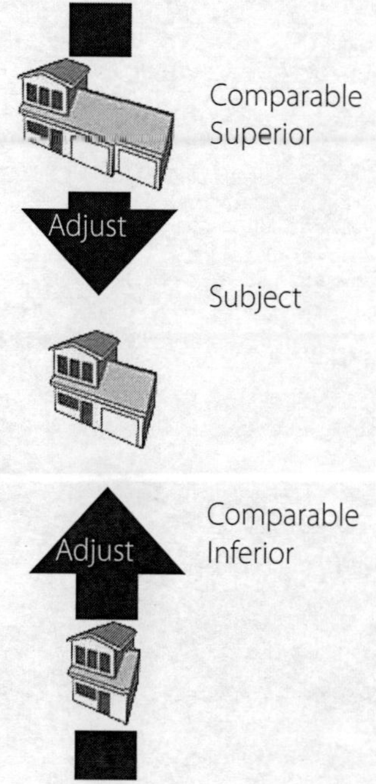

As was mentioned at the beginning of this section, the purpose of applying an adjustment is to make the comparable as similar to the subject as possible. The subject property is the benchmark for all adjustments; thus, *the subject property is never adjusted*! Adjustments are applied to only the comparable properties.

When the comparable property is inferior to the subject, an upward adjustment is applied to the comparable to align it with the subject. When the comparable property is superior to the subject, a downward adjustment is applied.

√ ***Note:*** Knowing when to apply an adjustment as a plus or a minus may seem to be a fairly simple topic. However, making the application in the wrong direction is a frequent and embarrassing error for appraisers.

Sequence of Adjustments

The order in which adjustments are applied in the sales comparison approach in most residential assignment is similar to the order in which we discussed the elements of comparison:

1. Property rights conveyed
2. Financing terms
3. Conditions of sale
4. Expenditures Made After the Sale*
5. Market conditions
6. Location
7. Physical characteristics

* In some assignments

In some instances, there could be variations in the order in which the appraiser applies adjustments. However, most residential appraisers will follow this progression and most state appraiser examinations use this sequence for testing purposes. Using this sequence allows the appraiser (assuming the data reflects the same property rights conveyed) to: First, adjust for cash equivalency; bring the comparable to the conditions found in an arm's-length transaction; then, bring the comparable data to the market conditions as of the effective date in the assignment; and, finally, mirror the comparable property to the location and physical characteristics if possible or warranted in the assignment. As will be seen in the forthcoming examples, adjusting properties in this sequence has a special significance when percentage adjustments are being applied.

Adjustment Application Examples

There are a number of ways that the appraiser can apply either dollar or percentage adjustments. Let's look at a couple of examples using a market data grid.

In the following scenario, we see how percentage adjustments are converted to dollar adjustments and how the dollar adjustments for other elements are applied either in a positive or negative manner. For property rights conveyed, financing terms, conditions of sale, and market conditions, the sale price of the comparable is adjusted after each percentage application as illustrated:

- Property rights conveyed is adjusted as a percent of the actual sale price
- Financing terms are addressed as a percent of the sale price adjusted for property rights conveyed
- Conditions of sale is expressed as a percentage of the adjusted sale price after property rights conveyed and financing terms have been addressed
- Market conditions are adjusted as a percent of the adjusted sale price after property rights conveyed, financing terms, and conditions of sale have been addressed

Once all of these adjustments have been applied, the adjusted price of the comparable is revealed. All other adjustments (in this case, location and physical characteristics) are then applied to the adjusted sale price to produce an indication for the price of the subject.

Element of Comparison	Adjustment %	Adjustment
Sale Price		**$400,000**
Property Rights Conveyed ($400,000 x 10%)	+10%	+$40,000
Adjusted Price		**$440,000**
Financing Terms ($440,000 x -5%)	-5%	-$22,000
Adjusted Price		**$418,000**
Conditions of Sale ($418,000 x -3%)	-3%	-$12,540
Adjusted Price		**$405,460**
Market Conditions ($405,460 x 9%)	+9%	+$36,491
Adjusted Price		**$441,951**

There may be times when the appraiser applies all adjustments as percentages, although this may be rare in residential assignments. Property rights conveyed, financing terms, conditions of sale, and market condition adjustments are applied as in the prior example. Location and physical characteristics are applied as a percentage of the price after adjustments for property rights conveyed, financing terms, conditions of sale, and market conditions have been applied.

Element of Comparison	Adjustment %	Adjustment
Sale Price		**$400,000**
Property Rights Conveyed	+10%	+$40,000
Adjusted Price		**$440,000**
Financing Terms	-5%	-$22,000
Adjusted Price		**$418,000**
Conditions of Sale	-3%	-$12,540
Adjusted Price		**$405,460**
Market Conditions	+9%	+$36,491
Adjusted Price		**$441,951**
Location (15% x $441,951)	+15%	+$66,293
Physical Characteristics (-10% x $441,951)	-10%	-$44,195
Adjusted Price		**$464,049**

Also rare in residential assignments, a unit of comparison, such as square feet, could be utilized in the sales comparison approach. In this case, the total sale price of the comparable is used for applying adjustments for property rights conveyed, financing terms, conditions of sale, and market conditions as we have seen in the previous examples. Typically, the adjusted price is then converted to the square foot unit and percentage adjustments are applied directly to the unit amount for location and physical characteristics, etc. The unit price (per square foot) is then applied to the subject's square feet to produce an indication of value for the subject. (It is also rare for expenditures made after the sale to be utilized as a point of adjustment in most residential assignments. For simplicity, that element is not included in the following discussion.)

Element of Comparison	Adjustment %	Adjustment
Sales Price		**$400,000**
Property Rights Conveyed	+10%	+$40,000
Adjusted Price		**$440,000**
Financing Terms	-5%	-$22,000
Adjusted Price		**$418,000**
Conditions of Sale	-3%	-$12,540
Adjusted Price		**$405,460**
Market Conditions	+9%	+$36,491
Adjusted Price		**$441,951**
Comparable SF = 3,597 ($441,951 ÷ 3,597 square feet) **Unit Price**		**$122.8666 Per SF**
Location (15% x $122.8666)	+15%	+$18.4300
Physical Characteristics (10% x $122.8666)	-10%	-$12.2867
Adjusted Unit Sale Price		**$129.0099 Per SF**
Subject SF = 3,362 ($129.0099 x 3,362) **Indicated Value of Subject**		**$433,731**

Reconciliation

In finalizing the development of the sales comparison approach, the appraiser has performed a series of analyses. However, after everything the appraiser has done, the results are without conclusion and somewhat meaningless unless the appraiser reflects on what the analyses revealed. The appraiser needs to perform a final step in order to make sense of the indications produced by the analysis. Thus, the final step in the development process of each valuation method is **reconciliation**—*analyzing the values derived from the different appraisal approaches to arrive at a final opinion of value.*

After all the individual adjustments are applied and the comparable sales are adjusted, a range of value is revealed. In the sales comparison approach, reconciliation consists of determining the relevance of each comparable and the indications produced. Where, in (or in some cases, outside) the value range, is the best value indication for the subject? Which comparable, or comparables, provide the best support? As can be seen, reconciliation is not purely premised on a mathematical process. The appraiser must use very good logic and reasoning skills when looking at the indications, which lead to sound judgment.

Sometimes, appraisers support a value opinion simply because that opinion is within the produced value range. However, in some cases, especially if the appraiser is being intentionally or unintentionally biased by a sale price or some other predetermined value, this practice would not be appropriate. Depending on the scope of work, appraisers can state the final value opinion as a range of value, a single-number, or a relationship to a numerical benchmark. Using the indicated value range to support a range of value ($100,000 to $105,000) or even a numerical benchmark (at least as much as…etc.) may be acceptable. However, concluding on a single-number opinion should include additional diligence. We will discuss several scenarios to illustrate the process.

» *Reconciliation in the sales comparison approach brings all the appraiser's analyses together and allows the appraiser to judge the quality and amount of the data examined, as well as the indications the analyses produce* «

"A Perfect Textbook Example"

Suppose that three comparable sales have been used and adjusted in development of the sale comparison analysis. Once adjusted, all of the comparable sales produce the same indication.

	Subject	Comp #1	Comp #2	Comp #3
Sale Price	------	$333,000	$347,000	$335,000
Absolute Adjustments		+$7,000	-$7,000	+$5,000
Adjusted Sale Price	-----	$340,000	$340,000	$340,000

In this scenario, there is little thought that needs to take place in the reconciliation process because the value indication produced in the sales comparison approach is precise.

The results shown in the previous "perfect textbook" example will seldom (if possibly ever) be seen in the real world. Occasionally, more by coincidence than precision, the appraiser might find that one or more comparable sales will produce the same adjusted value even when the same adjustments have been applied. But usually, the indications produced will not be this conclusive. Real estate markets are imperfect. Real estate markets and their participants simply do not typically function in such patterned harmony.

Reconciliation Examples

Looking now to a more common situation, three comparable sales have been processed revealing a range of value. The scope of work in the assignment requires the value opinion to be expressed as a single number. We will use this illustration to demonstrate several different conclusions that could be reached.

	Subject	Comp #1		Comp #2		Comp #3	
Sale Price	------		$325,000		$346,000		$332,000
Property Rights Conveyed	Fee simple	Same		Same		Same	
Financing Terms Concessions	-----	Conventional None		Conventional Yes	-$2,500	Conventional None	
Conditions of Sale	Typical	Typical		Typical			
Market Conditions (Date of Sale)	------	6 months	+$1,500	2 months	+$500	1 month	+$250
Location	Through street	Inferior	+$1,000	Same		Superior	-$1,000
GLA	2,200	2,000	+$4,000	2,300	-$2,000	2,225	-$500
Bedrooms Baths	4 3	4 2	+$2,000	4 3		4 3	
Fireplace	1	None	+$500	1		1	
Garage	2-car	2-car		2-car		3-car	-$2,000
Absolute Adjustments			**+$9,000**		**-$4,000**		**-$3,250**
Adjusted Sale Price			**$334,000**		**$342,000**		**$328,750**
Net Adjustments		+$9,000	+2.77%	-$4,000	-1.16%	-$3,250	-0.98%
Gross Adjustments		$9,000	2.77%	$5,000	1.45%	$3,750	1.13%

Net and Gross Adjustments

Observing the adjustment total helps the appraiser to recognize the relevance of the data analyzed in the sales comparison approach, given that all differences have been quantified and resulted with a corresponding adjustment. In general, the rationale demonstrated here is that the less a comparable must be adjusted, the more relevant and comparable the data is.

At one time many intended users of appraisals used for financing observed guidelines that preferred net adjustments not exceed 15% of the comparable's sale price and gross adjustments not exceed 25%. However, that preference was removed from Fannie Mae's guidelines, as it was believed to cause the appraiser to be guided by the preference and thus, limiting the amount of adjustments when a greater adjustment was actually warranted.

Gross adjustments are *the overall total of all adjustments applied regardless of whether the adjustment is applied as a positive or negative.* In comparison, **net adjustments** are *the sum of the adjustments taking into account whether the adjustment was a positive or negative.* Net adjustments reflect the percent of absolute adjustments when compared to the sale price of the comparable.

> ***For Example:*** If a comparable requires a +$500 adjustment and a -$500 adjustment, the absolute adjustments would be $0, and the net adjustments total would be 0% as the two adjustments cancel each other.
>
> Gross adjustments address the sum of all adjustments as a running total. So, the comparable that requires a +$500 adjustment and a -$500 adjustment would have $1,000 in gross adjustments. The dollar amount of gross adjustments would then be divided by the sale price of the comparable to determine the percent of gross adjustments.

Applying this concept to the chart of three comparables, both net and gross adjustments are minimal and demonstrate an excellent comparability to the subject property. Appraisers could, if appropriate to the assignment, place most confidence in the indications given by the comparable sale which has the least adjustments, which in this case would be Comparable #3. However, Comparable #3 has four adjustments applied and Comparable #2 has three. We will discuss this next.

Number of Adjustments

In the analysis illustrated, Comparable #1 has five adjustments, Comparable #2 has three adjustments, and Comparable #3 has four. In some assignments, the appraiser could find good reasoning in placing the most emphasis on the comparable sale that requires the least number of adjustments. Theoretically, we can say the greater the number of adjustments, the more dissimilar the comparable sale.

Also, there is validity to the thinking that the more adjustments that are applied, the greater the chance for error. Appraisers cannot judge the relevance of the comparable by simply applying this test, however. A comparable could have several small adjustments that do not particularly jeopardize the relevance to the subject in the analysis. On the other hand, a comparable might have only one or two sizable adjustments that could make the comparable significantly less reliable depending on what the adjustment is for and how well the adjustment is supported.

In our example, it should be noted that Comparable #2, with the least number of adjustments, did not produce the least adjustments in terms of dollars. Comparable #3 has the least dollar adjustments. The appraiser must use good judgment in determining the relevance of data based on the number of adjustments.

Location, Market Conditions, and Physical Characteristics

In many assignments, appraisers may reason that the comparable located nearest the subject, the most recent sale, or the physical similarities of the comparable to the subject are good reasoning for placing most emphasis on a particular comparable sale.

Since location is one of the most important influences of buyer, this reasoning may be very valid. Sales that took place during different market conditions or physically dissimilar comparables could be considered in the same way. Again, the appraiser must use good judgment when forming his conclusions based on the relevance of the comparable's proximity, how similar the market conditions were at the time of sale, and the comparable's physical characteristics.

Relative Comparison Analysis

Relative comparison analysis involves qualitative analysis. As we mentioned earlier in this section, qualitative analysis techniques require the appraiser's good judgment and reasoning skills. Qualitative analysis takes place in reconciliation after applying any quantitative adjustments. In relative comparison analysis, the comparable sales are ranked as to how they reflect to the subject property as superior, similar, or inferior. The appraiser then determines where in (or, perhaps, outside of) the value range the subject is best represented.

For Example: Let's go back to the bottom-line conclusions found in our previous illustration.

	Subject	Comp #1		Comp #2		Comp #3	
Adjusted Sale Price			$334,000		$342,000		$328,750

You may have noted that no quantitative adjustment was applied for the physical condition of the property. However, Comparable #1 was in inferior condition, as was Comparable #3. Comparable #2 was in superior condition to the subject. So, using qualitative analysis, the conclusions formed are demonstrating that an indicated value for the subject is somewhere above $334,000 (the higher of the inferior comparables), and somewhere below $342,000.

Ranking and Weighting

To summarize what the analysis revealed, the appraiser can rank and weight the data by considering the elements of comparison and the resulting adjustments. The data then could be ranked from those having the most relevance to the least relevance, or the most dependable to the least dependable. In weighting, the appraiser could assign a percentage to each comparable—signifying the confidence the appraiser has in that particular data.

For Example: In our illustration, we can surmise the following:

- Comparable #1 requires five individual adjustments and the greatest absolute adjustments (+$9,000). It also is the oldest of all the comparable sales (six months) and resulted in the greatest differences (three) in physical characteristics (GLA, baths, and fireplace). Location was inferior.
- Comparable #2 required three individual adjustments and the second highest number of absolute adjustments (-$4,000). The sale was the second oldest at two months. There was only one difference in physical characteristics (GLA). Location was similar.
- Comparable #3 required four individual adjustments but the least absolute adjustments (-$3,250) and the least gross adjustments of any of the data. There were two adjustments for physical characteristics, although one was for GLA which was nearly the same as the subject (it had only 25 sq. ft. more than subject), and the additional garage stall. Location was superior and the comparable sale transaction took place one month ago.

Obviously, Comparable #1 would be ranked least comparable. It will be ranked last. It could be argued whether Comparable #2 or #3 is the most comparable. Therefore, no distinction will be made.

Thus, the appraiser could assign a degree of confidence to each comparable sale and as a reconciled value indication:

Comparable	Adjusted Sale Price	Percent of Confidence	Weighted Value
#1	$334,000	20%	66,800
#2	$342,000	40%	136,800
#3	$328,750	40%	131,500
Total Weighted Value	-----	100%	$335,100

Statistical Measure

A final indication from the sales comparison analysis could also be supported, when appropriate, by using a statistical measure. Appraisers should not simply apply arithmetic averages, as this practice removes the appraiser's thought process from the methodology. However, if all data is of good quality and consistently reliable, the appraiser could logically conclude at, say, the mean or the median of the adjusted value range. When the mean or the median (or in cases where the same adjusted value is produced, the mode) of the value indications is used, the appraiser has analyzed the data and found that using the mean, median, or mode would produce credible results.

The adjusted value range of our illustration would produce a value indication using the mean of $334,900 (rounded), and a median value of $334,000.

Final Reconciliation

The appraiser, in the final step in reconciliation, could logically use the conclusions found through the various reconciliation analysis techniques that have been used. Let's summarize the products of using relative comparison, ranking and weighting, and statistical measure.

- Relative comparison analysis—more than $334,000 but less than $342,000
- Ranking and weighting—$335,100
- Statistical measure
    - Mean = $334,900
    - Median = $334,000

This summary reveals that the mean of the adjusted value range ($334,900) and the conclusion of the ranking and weighting analysis ($335,100) is $335,000. The relative comparison analysis indicates that the value conclusion should be somewhat more than $334,000. Thus, a logical and supported conclusion in the final reconciliation could be $335,000.

The final opinion of value is usually rounded, often to the nearest thousand in most cases. Stating value opinions in specific dollars such as $335,325 implies a precision that does not exist in an opinion.

As a final observance, the conclusion is bracketed in both the unadjusted range ($325,000 - $346,000) and the adjusted value range ($328,750 - $342,000). Many clients and intended users prefer that the final value opinion be bracketed.

Application Case Study #1
Comparable Properties versus Competitive Properties

Comparable Properties versus Competitive Properties

For a tract home in a developer's neighborhood with several builders offering many similar models, there may be many properties that are simply comparable; or both comparable and competitive.

For Example: If the subject is a "Heritage II" by Builtgood Homes, there may be several other "Heritage II" models that have recently sold, which would be truly competitive as well as comparable. There also could be several other homes of similar size and utility and with similar features that are comparable but not truly competitive because they are built by different builders and are not exactly like the Heritage II.

Subject Information: The subject is located at 1105 North Star Drive in Denville. It is a two-story traditional design with 2,350 square feet and contains eight rooms, four bedrooms, two full baths, and one half bath. It was built in 2003 by Well-Built Homes, sits on 1/2-acre site, and is in average condition. It abuts the Branch Elementary School to the west. Your research assistant collected some additional information that is included on the data sheet on the following page.

List the competitive properties:

List the comparable properties:

Data Grid

Address	Location	Sale Price	Rooms	Bed	Bath	Size	Style	Stories	Yr. Built	Research Comments
330 Segweg Ave	Denville	$213,500	8	4	2	2,400	Traditional	2	1999	4 blocks NE of Branch Elementary. Lot size 0.567 acre. Average condition.
1099 North Star Dr.	Denville	$211,000	8	4	2.5	2,350	Traditional	2	2002	2 houses east of Branch Elementary: same side of street. Lot size 0.575 acre. Average condition.
1943 Wontell	Litonburg	$148,750	7	3	1.5	1,450	Cape Cod	1.5	1994	Property abuts Seaside Elementary. Lot 0.675 acre. Average condition.
4343 Brampter Ct.	Denville	$216,500	8	4	2.5	2,480	Traditional	2	2001	2 blocks SW of Branch Elementary. Lot size 0.650 acre. Average condition.
593 Centinal Ave.	Denville	$108,700	6	2	1	1,250	Ranch	1	1967	Ranch on slab. No garage. Across the street from Baylor Elementary. Lot size 0.289 acre.
23 State Route 45	Denville	$198,000	6	3	1	1,800	Farm	2	1948	Older farm home located on 6 acres at the edge of Denville. 4 miles from Branch Elementary. Home in poor condition.
4896 Tomly Ave.	Bilton	$196,000	8	4	2	2,500	Contemporary	1	1997	1/2 block from Washington Elementary: same side of street. Average condition. Better than average landscaping. Lot size 0.505 acre.
438 Segweg Ave.	Denville	$215,000	8	4	2	2,420	Traditional	2	2000	5 blocks NE of Branch Elementary. Lot size 0.595 acre. Average condition.
6312 Cedarridge	Bilton	$194,200	8	4	2	2,500	Ranch	1	2000	Approximately 1.5 miles north of Washington Elementary. Average condition. Lot size 0.500 acre.
987 North Star Dr.	Denville	$211,500	8	4	2.5	2,400	Traditional	2	2004	2 houses west of Branch Elementary: same side of street. Lot size 0.599 acre.

Application Case Study #2
Deriving Adjustments Using Paired-Data

Paired Data

Using the information below, find the matched pairs for:

Fireplace #___ $______________

#___ $______________ Difference $______________

1/2 Bath #___ $______________

#___ $______________ Difference $______________

Family Room #___ $______________

#___ $______________ Difference $______________

Garage #___ $______________

#___ $______________ Difference $______________

Size #___ $______________

#___ $______________ Difference $______________

Per Sq Ft $______________

Sale	Rooms	Bedrooms	Baths	Size (sq. ft.)	Family Room	Fireplace	Garage	Price
#1	8	4	2	2,220	No	Yes	Yes	$262,800
#2	8	4	2	2,120	Yes	Yes	Yes	$260,500
#3	7	4	2.5	2,232	Yes	No	No	$263,400
#4	9	4	2.5	2,382	Yes	Yes	Yes	$264,500
#5	8	4	2.5	2,120	Yes	Yes	Yes	$262,500
#6	8	4	2	2,220	No	No	Yes	$259,400
#7	7	3	2	2,224	Yes	No	Yes	$259,000
#8	7	4	2.5	2,232	No	No	No	$253,100
#9	7	3	2	2,224	Yes	No	No	$256,000
#10	9	4	2.5	2,262	Yes	Yes	Yes	$259,500

Application Case Study #3
Applying Adjustments

Adjustments

Apply the following adjustments to a comparable sale that had a sale price of $272,000.

Market conditions:	+6.5%
Property rights conveyed:	+2%
Location:	-20%
Physical characteristics:	+12%
Financing terms:	-5%
Concessions:	-$1,500
Conditions of Sale:	-10%

Element of Comparison	Adjustment %	Adjustment
Sale Price		$272,000

What is the final adjusted sale price of the comparable sale?

What was the percent of net and gross adjustments?

Selected USPAP Illustrations and Guidance

The following USPAP Advisory Opinion (AO) and Frequently Asked Questions (FAQ) have been selected to illustrate the application of USPAP in specific circumstances discussed in this chapter.

AO 9—The Appraisal of Real Property That May Be Impacted by Environmental Contamination

AO 22—Scope of Work in Market Value Appraisal Assignments

AO 24—Normal Course of Business

FAQ 174—Range of Value

FAQ 198—Reconciliation of the Approaches to Value

FAQ 199—Adjustments in Sales Comparison Approach

FAQ 233—Analysis of Sales History for Comparable Sales

Quiz

1. ***A unit of comparison is a***
   a. component with which a property can be divided for the purpose of comparison, such as square foot, living unit, etc.
   b. demonstration of the proximity of the subject property to common destinations and conveniences.
   c. demonstration of the value by using superior and inferior indications to the subject.
   d. property feature that can be used to explain differences in the marketplace.

2. ***A vacant plot of land with dimensions of 200' x 150' sold for $75,000. Using front feet as the unit of comparison, what would the unit sale price be?***
   a. $150.00
   b. $214.00
   c. $375.00
   d. $500.00

3. ***An element of comparison is a***
   a. characteristic of a property or a transaction that can be used to explain differences in the price paid in a transaction.
   b. demonstration of the proximity of the subject property to common destinations and conveniences.
   c. demonstration of the value using superior and inferior indications to the subject.
   d. device used to compare the price paid for comparable properties of different sizes or with differing features.

4. ***Who would be an example of a person with a partial interest in an apartment building?***
   a. co-owner
   b. owner of restaurant on the same street
   c. property manager
   d. taxing authority

5. ***According to USPAP Standards Rule 1-4, when personal property, trade fixtures, or intangible items are included in the appraisal, the appraiser must***
   a. analyze the effect on value of such non-real property items.
   b. assign a value opinion to the individual items.
   c. ignore such items in the course of the appraisal.
   d. remove the items from the property during the inspection.

6. ***The comment to the USPAP Standards Rule 1-4 states that when the scope of work includes an appraisal of personal property, trade fixtures or intangible items,***
   a. the appraiser can disclose his lack of competency and carry on with the assignment.
   b. the appraiser can ignore the items and carry on with the assignment as usual.
   c. competency in personal property appraisal or business appraisal is required.
   d. competency in personal property appraisal or business appraisal is not required.

7. ***What scenario would be an example of an arm's-length transaction?***
   a. After winning the lottery, a man sells his home at a discounted price to a local college he attended that will use it for office space.
   b. A couple getting a divorce quickly sells their home.
   c. A man offers and sells his house to his friend at the appraised market value before he puts it on the market.
   d. A woman accepts the first offer on her house before she leaves the country for military service.

8. ***In terms of elements of comparison, a difference between the subject and comparable in zoning is an element of***
   a. location.
   b. market conditions.
   c. physical characteristics.
   d. property rights conveyed.

9. ***An adjustment derived through paired data analysis results in***
   a. a qualitative analysis.
   b. a quantitative adjustment.
   c. reconciliation.
   d. a regression analysis.

10. ***The following values have been identified as the extracted contributions of a third full bath: $4,000, $2,750, $3,500, $3,000. What is the median? (Round your answer to the nearest dollar.)***
    a. $3,250
    b. $3,313
    c. $3,500
    d. $3,375

11. ***The following values have been identified as the extracted contributions of a full finished basement: $10,000, $8,000, $9,500, $10,750, $9,000. What is the mean? (Round your answer to the nearest dollar.)***
    a. $9,000
    b. $9,375
    c. $9,450
    d. $9,500

12. ***A statistical measure that attempts to ascertain the source of change in variables is known as***
    a. bracketing.
    b. a regression analysis.
    c. a scatter diagram.
    d. a statistical measure of central tendency.

13. ***A home is found with the same floor plan as the subject but is in a different market and would not appeal to the same buyer. The home is***
    a. comparable to the subject.
    b. competitive with the subject.
    c. inferior to the subject.
    d. superior to the subject.

14. ***The condition of a property is considered within analysis of***
    a. conditions of sale.
    b. location.
    c. market conditions.
    d. physical characteristics.

15. ***In order for the correct application of percentage adjustments, what is the order in which adjustments are applied in the sales comparison approach?***
    a. financing terms, property rights conveyed, conditions of sale, location, market characteristics, and physical characteristics
    b. property rights conveyed, financing terms, conditions of sale, market conditions, location, and physical characteristics
    c. property rights conveyed, location, market conditions, financing terms, conditions of sale, and physical characteristics
    d. property rights conveyed, physical characteristics, financing terms, conditions of sale, market conditions, and location

Introduction to *Financial Calculators*

A financial calculator has become a necessary tool for today's real estate appraiser. Through the years, numerous manufacturers have developed various versions of financial calculators that, while different in design, allow an appraiser to perform complicated and time-intensive financial calculations quickly and with much greater ease.

While it is recognized that there are many fine financial calculators available on the market today, it becomes confusing to attempt to illustrate the functions of various makes and models within the learning process. It is not the intent of this course to promote one financial calculator over another. That being said, most appraisers acknowledge the Hewlett Packard HP 12c calculator as the standard of the appraisal industry. In fact, some states require coursework specifically addressing problem solving with the HP 12c. In addition, many advanced appraisal courses from a broad range of providers focus specifically on applications using the HP 12c.

This chapter is intended to provide a comfort level for using the HP 12c financial calculator in common calculations and to introduce the more basic functions that will be routine in everyday residential appraising. In some cases, there may be more than one method that can be used to solve a particular problem. As well, the HP 12c calculator is capable of many more functions than can be introduced within the constraints of this chapter. Many of the examples shown can admittedly be performed on a standard calculator. However, it is important to discuss basic math applications as they apply to the HP 12c, as most appraisers limit their mathematic calculations to a single calculator. Additional application examples, as appropriate, will be introduced in future chapters of this text.

Finally, the National Uniform Appraiser Examination will present mathematic problems that the examinee must solve using a financial calculator. Therefore, proficiency in the use of a financial calculator is no longer an option for the prospective examinee as examination providers are permitted to allow only one calculator to be brought into the testing area by the examinee.

KEY TERMS

Amortization Elimination of a debt with a series of equal payments (principle and interest) at regular time intervals.

Compound Interest Interest paid on previously earned interest based on the original principal amount. The more frequent the compounding period and the higher the effective interest rate, the greater the impact on the calculation.

Discounting The process, by some investors, that uses the principles of TVM to convert future income or cash flows into present value, at a specified interest rate.

Future Value Amount of money that an investment (either a single payment or an annuity) at a fixed interest rate, for a specified period of time, will grow to in the future.

Present Value An amount today that is equivalent to a future payment, or series of payments (annuity), based on a specified interest rate, for a specific period of time.

Reverse Polish Notation (RPN) A formal logic system used in the HP 12c calculator that allows mathematical equations to be expressed by pressing the arithmetic operations key (+, -, x, ÷) after the numbers, or variables, have been keyed.

Sinking Fund Factor Amount set aside on a periodic basis so that, when compounded at a given interest rate for a defined term, it will accumulate to a specified future sum.

Time Value of Money (TVM) The concept that a dollar today is usually worth more than receiving a dollar at some point in the future.

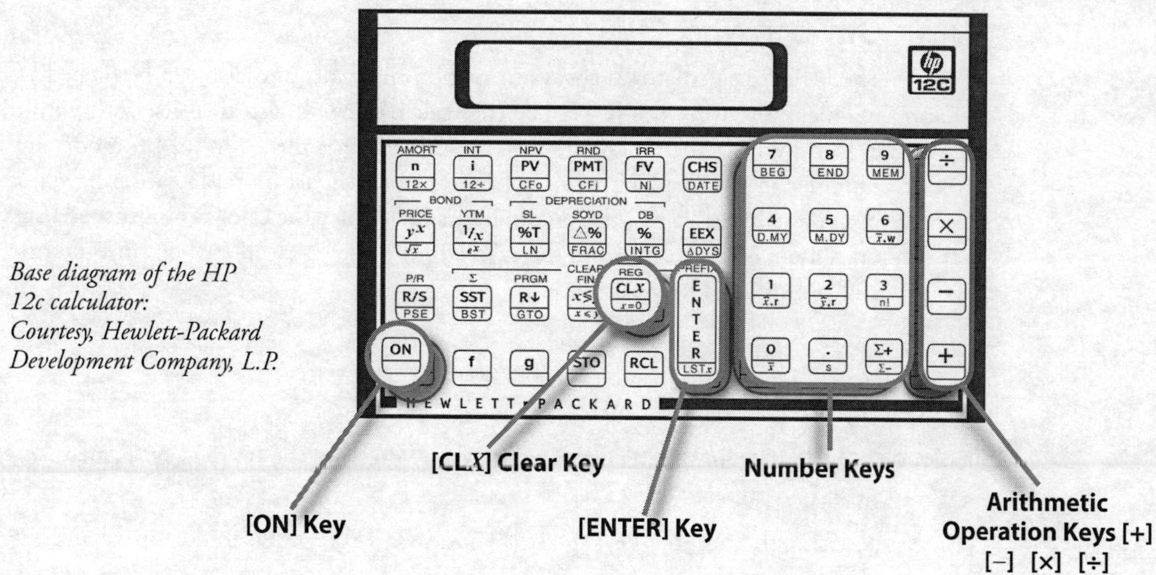

Base diagram of the HP 12c calculator: Courtesy, Hewlett-Packard Development Company, L.P.

The Basic HP 12c Keyboard

You will note that the keyboard of the HP 12c calculator is designed in a horizontal pattern as opposed to the vertical pattern found on most calculators. Before we introduce some of the more complex abilities of the calculator, let's begin by taking a look at the keyboard and some of the basic arithmetic functions.

The [ON] key is located in the lower left hand corner of the calculator keyboard. The HP 12c has no "off" key. When the calculator is on, simply press the [ON] key again to turn the calculator off. Also, the calculator will turn itself off after several minutes of non-use.

The arithmetic operation keys (+, -, x, and ÷) are located vertically to the far right of the keyboard.

The number keys and the decimal key are located immediately to the left of the arithmetic operation keys.

The [ENTER] key is a vertically-elongated key and is located at the lower part of the keyboard, just right of the keyboard's mid-point.

The [CL*X*] key clears the number in the display and, in simple arithmetic calculations, the entries for that calculation. Clearing the calculator using the [CL*X*] key can be used if a number is mistakenly entered during an arithmetic calculation to clear just that number or an entire calculation once it is completed. There are several more keys that clear other registers and memories. A more expanded discussion of "clear" keys will be found later.

Other keys will be introduced, as they are needed, throughout the chapter.

√ ***Note:*** The HP 12c has no equal [=] key.

On, Off, and Clear

The HP 12c calculator is always turned on manually and also can be turned off manually by using the [ON] key (the calculator will also turn itself off within 8-15 minutes of being idle.) When the calculator is placed in the off mode, any numbers in the display that have been entered as part of a calculation have not been erased; thus, a calculation can be resumed once the calculator is turned back on. Often, errors result from the calculator not being cleared when turning it on and beginning a new calculation.

1. Turn the calculator on by pressing the [ON] key.
2. Make certain the calculator is cleared by pressing the [CLX] key (display should appear with all 0's).
3. Using the number keys, press [2] and then [5] (25.00 should appear in the display).
4. Turn the calculator off by pressing the [ON] key.
5. Turn the calculator back on again by pressing the [ON] key (25.00 should appear in the display).
6. Press [CLX] to clear the display (display should now appear with all 0's).

» *What You Have Learned...*

- *How the calculator is turned on and off manually.*
- *Number(s) keyed into the calculator (or a part of a calculation or the solution result) remain in the display and/or memory even when the calculator is turned off and back on again.*
- *Clear function for the display and simple entry calculations.* «

Simple Arithmetic Functions

In simple arithmetic calculations, two numbers are always involved and are either added, subtracted, divided, or multiplied. Standard calculators and some other financial calculators use algebraic input for simple arithmetic problems.

> ***For Example:*** To find the total of five plus five, the algebraic calculator keystrokes are [5] [+] [5] [=]. The HP 12c financial calculator employs a method of inputting numbers for simple arithmetic problems known as Reverse Polish Notation, or RPN.

Reverse Polish Notation (RPN) is *a formal logic system used in the HP 12c calculator that allows mathematical equations to be expressed by pressing the arithmetic operation key (+, -, x, ÷) after the numbers or variables have been keyed.* This chapter will illustrate the advantage of RPN as we get into some longer mathematical calculations. Many appraisal industry users actually prefer the RPN method of input to the algebraic method, but it does take some practice.

At first, inputting numbers for simple math calculations may seem somewhat backwards. But soon, the input will become second nature and will especially be appreciated when working with longer calculations. Therefore, it is probably good advice to rely on the HP 12c for all math calculations, as going back and forth between a calculator using algebraic mode and the HP 12c can be confusing. Let's illustrate this concept with some simple arithmetic calculations.

Addition

As was just illustrated, using algebraic input, the keystrokes for five plus five on a standard calculator are [5] [+] [5] [=]. When adding two numbers using RPN on the HP 12c, the keystrokes are [5] [ENTER] [5] [+]. The solution to the calculation will be displayed immediately after pressing the [+] key. Let's try that calculation using the HP 12c. The keystrokes are:

√ ***Note:*** As mentioned previously, the HP 12c has no equal [=] key.

Try This...

[CLX] (always a good habit when starting a new calculation!)

[5]

[ENTER] (separates the input and tells the calculator that you have finished the first entry in the calculation.)

[5]

[+]

Result: If you have correctly followed this example, **10.00** should be displayed.

Subtraction

A simple subtraction problem is similar to the addition calculation except that the subtraction sign is used instead of the addition sign. Let's subtract 6 from 10. The keystrokes are:

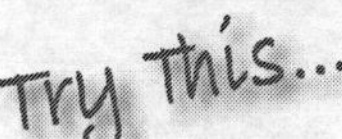

[CLX]

[10]

[ENTER]

[6]

[–]

Result: If you have correctly followed this example, **4.00** should be displayed.

Division

Again, just like before only using the division sign for solving the problem, for example, 60 divided by 20. The keystrokes are:

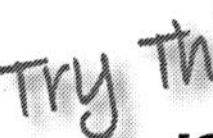

[CLX]

[60]

[ENTER]

[20]

[÷]

Result: If you have correctly followed this example**, 3.00** should be displayed.

Multiplication

Finally, we use the [x] key to solve the multiplication problem of 5 times 20. The keystrokes are:

[CLX]

[5]

[ENTER]

[20]

[x]

Result: If you have correctly followed this example**, 100.00** should be displayed.

» *What You Have Learned...*

- *How various simple arithmetic calculations are entered into the HP 12c using RPN.*
- *Clearing previous calculations using the [CLX] key.* «

Practice Problems

1. A one and one-half story residential dwelling has 1,400 square feet of GLA on the first floor and 546 square feet of GLA on the second floor. What is the total GLA of the dwelling?

2. A residential dwelling has a total gross area of 1,830 square feet. Included in the gross area is a porch that has 260 square feet of area that will not be included in the total gross living area. Excluding the porch, what is the total gross living area of the dwelling?

3. If a parcel of land contains 38,000 square feet and can be divided into three building lots of equal size, how many square feet will each building lot contain?

4. The fenced-in portion of a rear yard is 52' x 37'. How many square feet does the fenced-in yard contain?

Combined Arithmetic Methods

Frequently, appraisers must employ calculations that combine a series of input that use addition, subtraction, division, and/or multiplication. While many standard calculators also allow this in similar function, the keystrokes will be different.

To become comfortable with the keystrokes for various types of calculations, we will offer some simple examples that are relevant to a property description.

Lot Size Stated in Acres

To find the area of a building lot or parcel the formula is:

Frontage x Depth = Total square feet ÷ 43,560 (square feet in an acre)

The appraiser is trying to find the lot area, in acres, of a building lot that has 135 feet frontage and 220 feet depth. The keystrokes are (before you start, remember to clear the calculator):

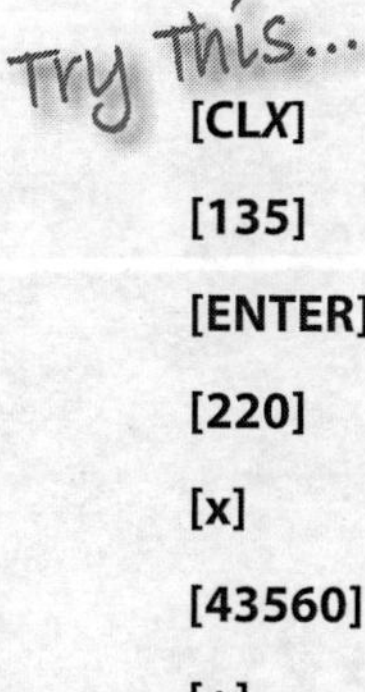

[CLX]

[135]

[ENTER]

[220]

[x]

[43560]

[÷]

Result: If you have correctly followed this example**, 0.68** should be displayed. This is the lot area in acres.

√ ***Important:*** Do **NOT** press [CLX] as we will use this result in the next calculation.

Usable Site Area by Percentage

When the appraiser determines the percent of a parcel that is usable, one additional calculation can determine the usable area. In this example, we will assume the appraiser has estimated that 75% of the parcel is usable.

In order to complete this calculation, we need to introduce another key on the HP 12c calculator, the percent key [%]. The percent key is located in the second row from the top, fifth key from the left.

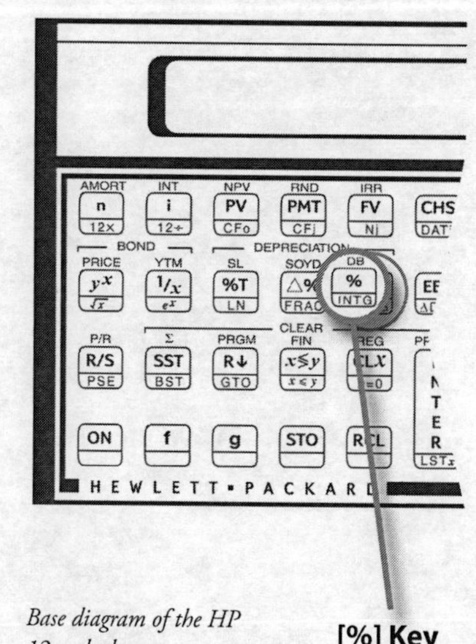

Base diagram of the HP 12c calculator: Courtesy, Hewlett-Packard Development Company, L.P.

With the answer to the previous example still on the display (0.68), the keystrokes are:

Try this...

[75]

[%]

Result: If you have correctly followed this example, **0.51** should be displayed. This is the usable area in acres.

Square Yards

In the income approach, for example, the appraiser may need to determine the amount of carpet for which replacement reserves must be estimated. Carpet is most often priced in increments of square yards. There are nine square feet in each square yard.

The calculation to determine square yards is:

Length x Width ÷ 9 = Square Yards

If the appraiser is determining the square yards of floor covering needed to carpet a room that is 12' x 14', the keystrokes are:

[CLX]

[12]

[ENTER]

[14]

[x]

[9]

[÷]

Result: If you have correctly followed this example, **18.67** should be displayed. This is how many square yards of carpet would be needed.

Cubic Feet

A cubic foot is a unit of volume. The interior space of a warehouse, for example, is often referenced in cubic feet of area. Cubic feet are calculated as:

Length x Width x Height (or, in some cases, depth) = Cubic Feet

If an appraiser is determining the cubic feet contained in a building that has ground dimensions of 100' x 75' and is 18' high, the keystrokes are:

Try this...

[CLX]

[100]

[ENTER]

[75]

[x]

[18]

[x]

Result: If you have correctly followed this example, **135,000.00** should be displayed. This is the number of cubic feet contained in the building.

Cubic Yards

There may be some occasions where the appraiser needs to determine cubic yards for certain aspects of appraising (e.g., when costing concrete). There are 27 cubic feet in each cubic yard. Cubic yards are calculated as:

Length x Width x Depth ÷ 27 = Cubic Yards

If an appraiser is determining the cubic yards of concrete needed to install a patio that will be 15' x 18' and 6" (0.50 foot) thick, the keystrokes are:

Try this...

[CLX]

[15]

[ENTER]

[18]

[x]

[0.50]

[x]

[27]

[÷]

Result: If you have correctly followed this example, **5.00** should be displayed. This is the number of cubic yards of concrete needed.

» *What You Have Learned...*

- *How various real estate calculations are entered into the HP 12c using RPN.*
- *The location and use of the [%] key.* «

Practice Problems

1. An appraiser is determining the total cost of carpeting a room that is 22' x 18.5'. If the carpet costs $38 per square yard installed, what is the total cost of the carpet?

2. How many acres are contained in a parcel that has dimensions of 366' x 407'?

3. A jurisdiction allows for 65% of a residential building lot to be covered by the primary dwelling. What is the square footage of the first floor of the dwelling if the lot dimensions are 110' x 165'?

4. A storage building is 25' x 30' and is 12' high. How many cubic feet are contained in the building?

Chain Calculations

A chain calculation results when an arithmetic problem using two numbers is extended into an additional calculation. Standard calculators are often cumbersome for such calculations and may require jotting down the results of one calculation and re-entering individual calculation results. The HP 12c is especially efficient with chain calculations and allows the results of two calculations to be combined into a final solution with a simple keystroke.

For Example: An appraiser needs to calculate the gross living area of a house that consists of a one-story dwelling measuring 38' x 52', with a one-story addition that is 18' x 22'.

Depending on the type of algebraic calculator being used, such a calculation could require the appraiser to first conclude that the larger portion of the dwelling consists of 1,976 square feet (38' x 52') and secondly, that the addition contains 396 square feet (18' x 22'). To arrive at the final total, the results would need to be at least partially re-entered and manually added together to arrive at the total gross living area for the dwelling of 2,372 square feet (1,976 + 396).

Adding the Results of Two Multiplication Calculations

Using the gross living area dimensions from the previous example, the keystrokes are:

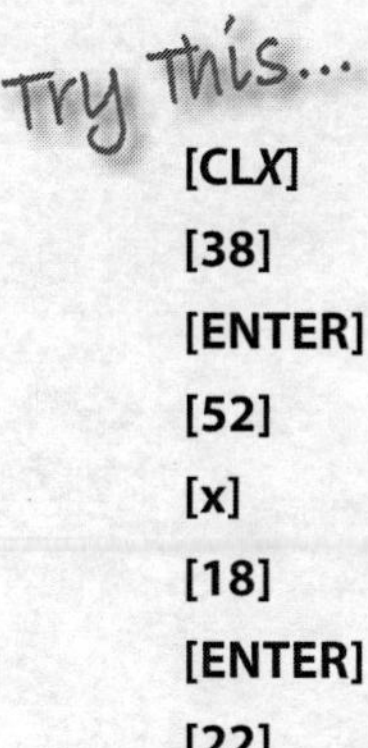

[CLX]

[38]

[ENTER]

[52]

[x]

[18]

[ENTER]

[22]

[x]

[+]

Result: If you have correctly followed this example**, 2,372.00** should be displayed. This is the total gross living area in square feet.

Subtracting the Results of Two Multiplication Calculations

Subtracting the result of one calculation from the result of a second calculation is achieved in much the same manner as our previous example, only this time, the final solution is derived by using the subtraction key [-] instead of the addition key [+].

Consider a ranch-style house with an attached garage that measures, in total, 56' x 28'. The garage portion is 14' x 28'. To find the gross living area of the house, the keystrokes are:

Try this...

[CLX]

[56]

[ENTER]

[28]

[x] (total square foot is displayed)

[14]

[ENTER]

[28]

[x] (garage square foot is displayed)

[-]

Result: If you have correctly followed this example**, 1,176.00** should be displayed. This is the total gross living area of the house in square feet.

Dividing the Sum of Two Multiplication Calculations

For our example here, the appraiser is seeking to find the total site area, in acres, of a subject that consists of two parcels that have been assembled. One parcel is 150' x 200' and the second parcel is 75' x 200'. The keystrokes are:

Try this...

[CLX]

[150]

[ENTER]

[200]

[x]

[75]

[ENTER]

[200]

[x]

[+] (total square feet is displayed)

[43560]

[÷]

Result: If you have correctly followed this example**, 1.03** should be displayed. This is the total site area in acres.

Stack Registers

There are numerous combinations of problem solving calculations that could use this method. The feature allowing the HP 12c to be so different that it can so easily perform these types of calculations is the registers. There are several registers integrated into the HP 12c calculator, including the *stack registers.*

The concept is a little more detailed than is appropriate for this introduction, but simply, the stack registers could be thought of as storage areas that are stacked, or layered, on top of each other.

T Register
Z Register
Y Register
X Register (Display)

When a calculation is keyed in into the HP 12c calculator, the information is displayed in the X Register. Each time a new calculation is input and the [ENTER] key is pressed, the previous calculation moves up to the register above it. For example, if [4] [+] [4] is calculated, the result (8) will be stored in the X Register. Immediately after, and without clearing anything, [5] [+] [5] is calculated. The

4 + 4 calculation and its result (8) will move up from the X Register to the Y Register and the 5 + 5 calculation with its result (10) is now in the X Register. When the addition key [+] is pressed to add the two results together (8 + 10), the results of the first calculation (4 + 4 = 8) will come back down to combine with the results that are currently in the X Register (5 + 5 = 10) to arrive at a total of 18, which will be displayed.

» *What You Have Learned...*

- *Various methods of performing a simple chain calculation.*
- *Basic function of the stack registers.* «

Practice Problems

1. The rear yard of a residence measures 50' x 40' and a 16' x 20' section of this area is fenced. What percent of the yard is fenced?
2. An L-shaped ranch dwelling, including a porch and a garage, consists of a portion that is 38' x 30' and a portion that is 18' x 20'. The appraiser has determined that 80% of the structure is considered living area. What is the gross living area?
3. Two building parcels have been assembled. Individually, the parcels have dimensions of 80' x 160' and 75' x 160'. In acres, what is the gross area of the assembled site?
4. Two rooms of a residential dwelling must be carpeted. One room is 12' x 12', and the carpet will cost $28 per square yard installed. The other room is 15' x 17', and the carpet will cost $34 per square yard installed. What is the total cost of the carpet?

Prefix Keys

By this point in surveying the keyboard of the HP 12c calculator, you may be curious about the gold and blue keys located in the bottom row toward the left side of the keyboard. The gold [f] key and the blue [g] key are prefix keys.

Likewise, you may have noticed that many keys have gold text above them and blue writing on their lower face..

The keys that have blue writing on their lower face have two functions. When there is gold writing above the keys, those keys have an additional third function. In order to engage the second or third function of a key, the matching prefix key is pressed and released first before the desired key is pressed.

√ ***Note:*** Anytime a prefix key is pressed, a small "f" or "g" will appear in the display.

There are many functions of the HP 12c and types of calculations that require the prefix keys—we will discuss these as we go forward. One exception to the function of a prefix key that is not associated with a key label is how to set the number of decimal places that will be displayed (or carried out) to the right of the decimal point.

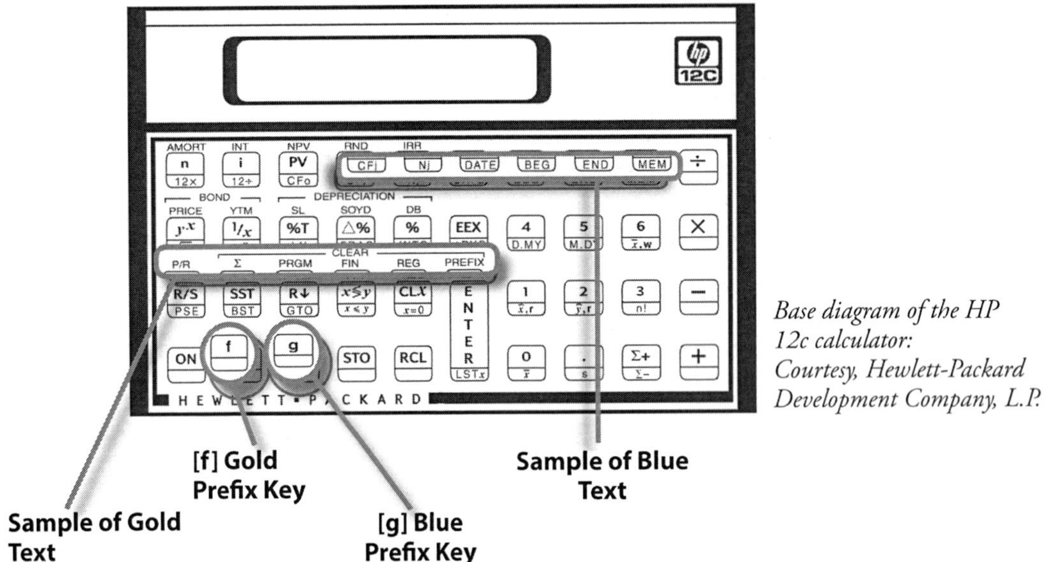

Base diagram of the HP 12c calculator: Courtesy, Hewlett-Packard Development Company, L.P.

Setting the Decimal Point

The factory setting for the HP 12c calculator is to display two places to the right of the decimal point. In other words, when turning the calculator on and using the factory setting, all calculation results displayed will be rounded to two places. It is simple to change the setting to display more or less places after the decimal point by pressing the gold [f] prefix key and then the corresponding number on the keyboard for the desired number of places.

To set the decimal to four places, the keystrokes are:

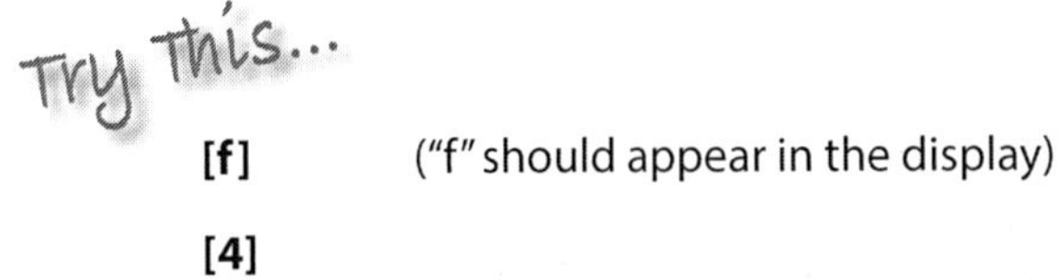

[f] ("f" should appear in the display)

[4]

Result: Four zeros should now be displayed to the right of the decimal point.

To set the decimal to six places, the keystrokes are:

[f]

[6]

Result: Six zeros should now be displayed to the right of the decimal point.

Changing the Decimal Setting Before, During, and After a Calculation

The decimal places can be changed at any time before, during, or after a calculation without fear of losing data or skewing the operation. Let's illustrate this point by inputting some lot dimensions to find the site in acres.

The residential building lot measures 105' x 263'. The keystrokes are:

Try this...

[f]

[2]

[CLX]

[105]

[ENTER] (105.00 should be displayed)

[f]

[4] (105.0000 should be displayed)

[263]

[x]

[43560]

[÷] (0.6340 should be displayed as the total site area in acres)

[f]

[6]

Result: **0.0633953** should be displayed as the total site area in acres.

Clearing the Prefix Keys

Occasionally, a prefix key might be pressed in error during the course of a calculation, such as pressing the gold [f] prefix instead of the blue [g] prefix key. A prefix key inadvertently pressed can be cleared without clearing everything else that has been keyed. Simply press the gold [f] prefix key and then the clear prefix key [ENTER]. Notice the word "PREFIX" is written in gold above the [ENTER] key, changing the function of this key to clear prefix when a prefix key is pressed prior to pressing [ENTER].

» *What You Have Learned...*

- *How to use the prefix keys to change the function of other keys.*
- *The method for changing the number of places displayed past the decimal point.*
- *How to clear the prefix keys without disturbing other entries.* «

Practice Problems

Before beginning the practice problems, set the decimal points on your calculator to 8, then key in 56.8278951.

1. Change the decimal points to 5. What is displayed?

2. Change the decimal points to 3. What is displayed?

Data Storage Registers

The HP 12c has 20 storage registers. The first ten data storage registers are named R_0 through R_9. The second set is named $R._0$ through $R._9$. The calculator's storage/recall function employs the use of the storage key [STO] and the recall key [RCL]. These keys are located in the bottom row, close to the [ENTER] key.

> ***For Example:*** To store numbers in the first set of registers, you need to press [STO] and [0], or whatever storage register you wish (0-9). To store a number in the second set of registers, you need to press [STO] [.] [0], or whatever storage register you wish (0-9).

The storage registers allow appraisers to store frequently used numbers (e.g., square feet in an acre, number of feet in a mile) so that the appraiser will not have to enter the numbers each time they are required in a calculation.

We will limit our discussion here to the first ten registers. The keystrokes for storing a number in a data storage register are:

1. Number to be stored

2. [STO]

3. Number on keyboard for the register in which to be stored

Let's use the example of the land area contained in a township section (640 acres). If we wanted to store this number in the first data storage register (R_0), the keystrokes are:

[640]

[STO]

[0]

Result: If the input has been entered correctly, **640.0000** (with more or less zeros after the decimal depending on the current setting) should be displayed.

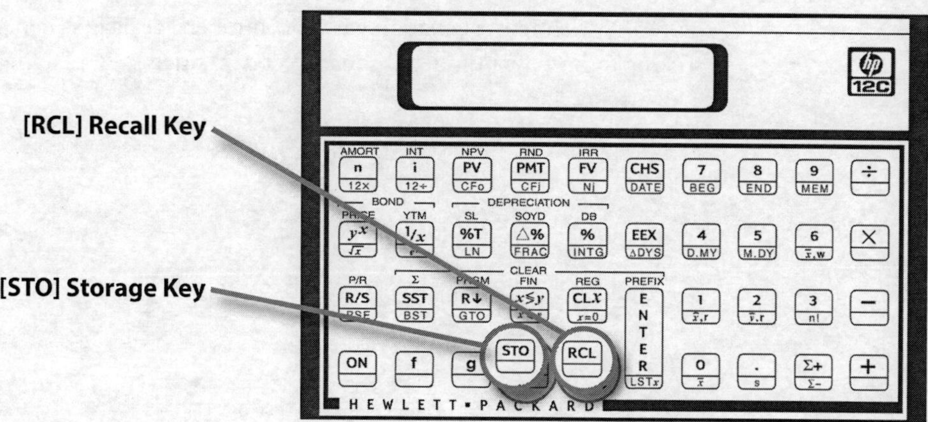

Base diagram of the HP 12c calculator: Courtesy, Hewlett-Packard Development Company, L.P.

Clearing Data Storage Registers

To recall a previously stored number, the keystrokes are:

Try this...

[CLX] (display should read all zeros (e.g., 0.00, again, this depends on your current setting)

[RCL]

[0] (recalls the stored number)

Result: You should see that the number **640** is stored for future use.

Let's store another frequently used number. To store the number of square feet in an acre, 43,560, in data storage register 1, the keystrokes are:

Try this...

[43560]

[STO]

[1]

Result: The number 43,560 should be stored.

Now let's try a simple calculation with the numbers we have stored. If an appraiser is seeking to find the number of square feet contained in ¼ of a township section, the keystrokes are:

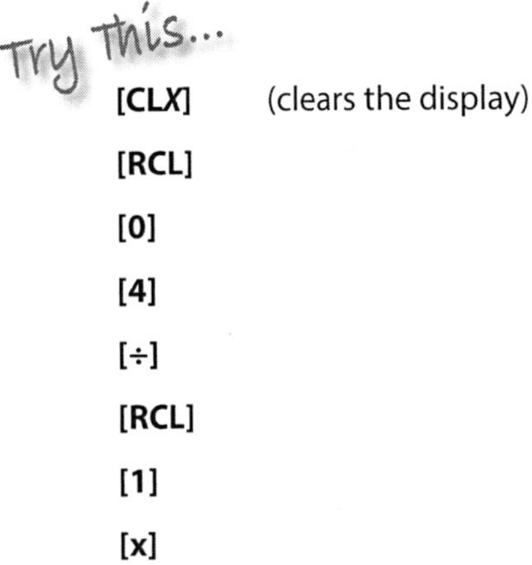

Try This...

[CLX] (clears the display)

[RCL]

[0]

[4]

[÷]

[RCL]

[1]

[x]

Result: If you have correctly followed this example**, 6,969,600.000** (depending on the set number of places past the decimal) should be displayed as the total site area in square feet.

To clear only one register, press the [RCL] key and then [0]. Next, press [STO] and then press the number of the register you desire to clear ("0" will now be stored in that register). If another number is to be stored in that register, enter a number other than "0". The keystrokes are:

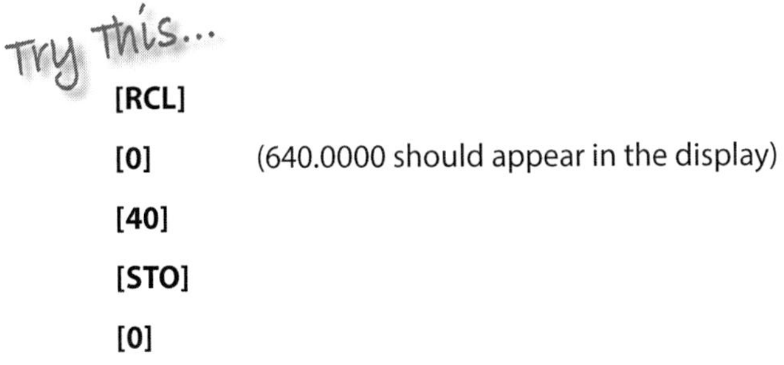

Try This...

[RCL]

[0] (640.0000 should appear in the display)

[40]

[STO]

[0]

Result: 40.0000 should now appear in the display.

To clear all of the registers, the keystrokes are:

Try This...

[f]

[CLX] (notice that the [CLX] key has "REG" above it in gold letters)

Result: All of the registers should be cleared.

To confirm the storage registers have been cleared, the keystrokes are:

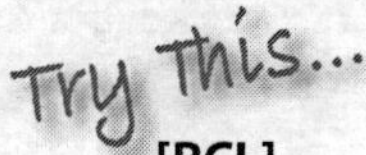

[RCL]

[0]

[RCL]

[1]

Result: All zeros and a decimal should appear in the display. All data storage registers are now cleared. The factory presets for the data registers are "0".

» *What You Have Learned...*

- *How to store and recall numbers in the data storage registers.*
- *How to clear the data storage registers.* «

Practice Problems

Before beginning the practice problems, set the data storage registers as follows:

$R_0 = 43560$

$R_1 = 27$

$R_2 = 640$

1. A land parcel contains 112,795 square feet. Rounded to six places, how many acres does the parcel contain?
2. Rounded to a whole number, how many cubic yards of concrete will be needed for a concrete slab 100' x 42' and 6 inches thick?
3. Rounded to the nearest ½ percent, what percent of a township section is 80 acres?
4. How many square feet are contained in ¼ of a township section?

Percentage Problems

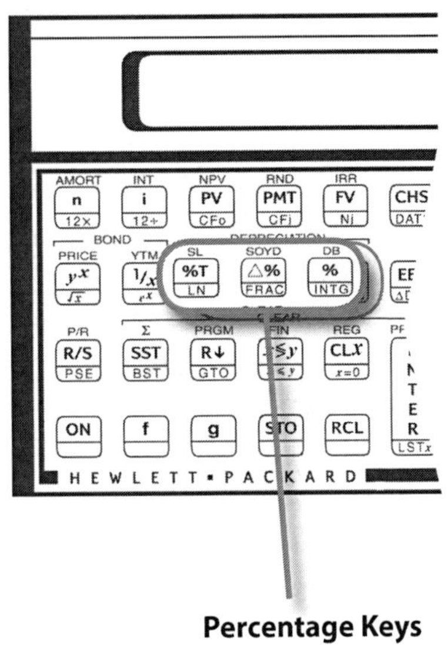

Percentage Keys
[%T], [Δ%], [%]

Base diagram of the HP 12c calculator: Courtesy, Hewlett-Packard Development Company, L.P.

Earlier in this chapter, we introduced the [%] key. As you look at your keyboard, you will see two additional percent keys (to the left of it). The [Δ%], or percent difference, key is used for determining the percent of difference between two numbers. The [%T], or percent of a total, key is used to determine the percent of total for one component in a problem.

When using the percent key to enter percents, the percent is entered as a whole number (e.g., 10), rather than a fractional derivative (e.g., 0.10).

So, to find 40% of 100, the keystrokes are:

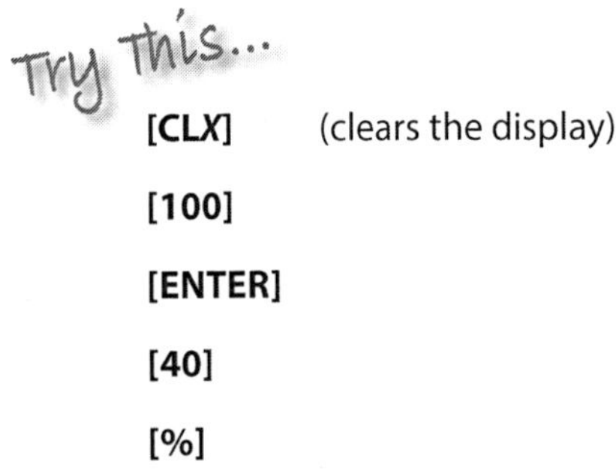
Try this...

[CLX] (clears the display)

[100]

[ENTER]

[40]

[%]

Result: If done correctly, **40.0000** should be displayed.

Net Amount

As one example of how to calculate the net amount, appraisers often need to determine the amount of a seller-paid financing concession for a residential transaction in terms of a percentage. The appraiser also needs to determine the adjusted sale price. The HP 12c makes such calculations simple.

Consider a transaction in which a house is selling for $150,000. The seller is paying 3.5% of the sale price toward the buyer's costs. The keystrokes are:

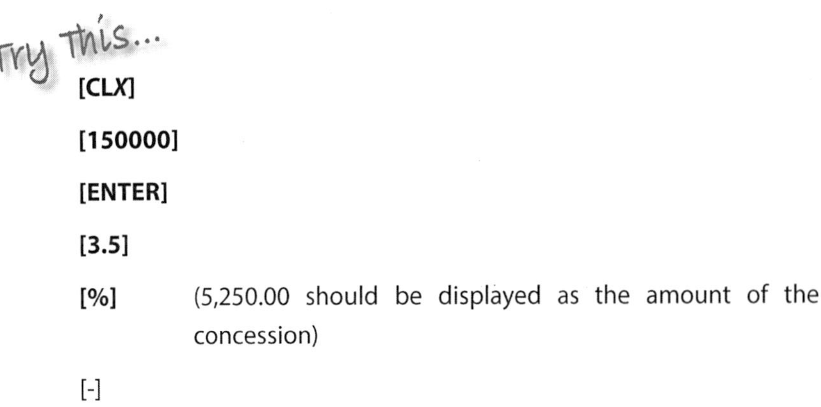
Try this...

[CLX]

[150000]

[ENTER]

[3.5]

[%] (5,250.00 should be displayed as the amount of the concession)

[-]

Result: If done correctly, **144,750.00** should be displayed. This is the net sale price.

Percent Difference

Appraisers often need to find the difference between two sale prices for determining adjustments for market conditions and other factors. The [Δ%] key makes this calculation simple on the HP 12c.

Let's use the example of a house that sold one year ago for $300,000 and sold again today for $360,000. What is the percent of increase in value? To find the solution, the keystrokes are:

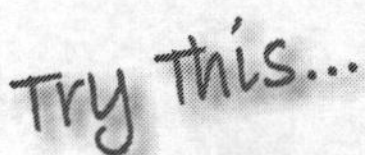

[CLX]

[300000]

[ENTER]

[360000]

[Δ%]

Result: If the data has been input correctly, **20.00** (again, depending on the decimal points set) should be displayed—indicating that the difference is 20%. The number appears as a positive so the percentage is also positive.

Using the same example, let's reverse the scenario using a declining market situation. In this case, the house sold one year ago for $360,000 and sold again today for $300,000. The keystrokes are:

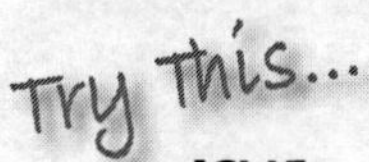

[CLX]

[360000]

[ENTER]

[300000]

[Δ%]

Result: This time, the calculator is figuring the downward trend as a percent of $360,000. So, correctly input, the downward percent should be **-16.6667**, or rounding to 2 places (press the [f], then [2]), -16.67%.

Percent of a Total

Calculating the percent of a total is a little more complex and uses the data storage registers discussed earlier. Once understood, the process is fairly straightforward. The process may seem a little involved for such a simple calculation; however, being familiar with the process will be advantageous in the appraiser's practice.

In order to demonstrate the process and math involved, we will go step-by-step through a simple example. Consider that a property sold for $145,000. The buyer obtained an $80,000 first mortgage from a bank and the seller held a

$20,000 second mortgage. The remainder of the sale price was paid by the buyer in cash. What percent of the sale price were the mortgages in the transaction (LTV)? The keystrokes are:

√ ***Note:*** For a computation such as this, changing the decimal place to at least six places is advisable.

Try This...

[f]

[CLX] (clears all data registers)

[145000]

[ENTER]

[80000]

[STO]

[0]

[%T] (55.172414 should be displayed as the percent of 145,000)

[CL**X**] (clears the 145,000, which is still in the stack register)

[20000]

[STO]

[+]

[0]

[%T] (13.793103 should be displayed as the percent of 145,000)

[RCL]

[0] (100,000.0000 should be displayed as the total mortgage contribution to the transaction)

[145000] (sale price)

[÷]

Result: If keyed correctly, **0.689655** should be displayed, or converted to 68.9655% as the LTV.

» *What You Have Learned...*

- *How to perform simple percentage calculations.*
- *How to determine a percent of difference.*
- *The method for determining the percent of the total.*
- *Additional uses of the [STO] and [RCL] keys.* «

Practice Problems

Before beginning the practice problems, the decimal should be set at six places.

1. A property that sold for $153,500 today sold for $172,000 eighteen months ago. What was the percent of downward change noted?

2. If a house sold for $400,000 six months ago and just resold for $420,000 today, what was the monthly appreciation in value?

3. Verification of a recent sale of a property for $205,000 has revealed that the seller carried a first mortgage of $155,000. What was the percent of the mortgage (LTV)?

4. The sale price of a property was $300,000. The purchaser obtained a 70% first mortgage though a bank and the seller carried a second mortgage of $10,000. What was LTV?

Time Value of Money Functions

Time value of money (TVM) is *the concept that a dollar today is usually worth more than receiving a dollar at some point in the future.* Time value of money functions reflect the six basic ways that money, time, and rates are tied together, known as the six functions of a dollar. Two functions involve the value of money in the future, two involve money today, and two functions deal with the size of a payment needed to either finance a reserve fund or savings account or pay off a loan.

The six functions of a dollar are:

1. Future value of $1
2. Future value of $1 per period (annuity)
3. Sinking fund factors
4. Present value of $1 (reversion)
5. Present value of $1 per period (annuity)
6. Payment to amortize $1.00 (amortization)

The six functions of a dollar are based on the theory of compound interest. **Compound interest** is *interest paid on previously earned interest based on the original principle amount. The more frequent the compounding period and the higher the effective interest rate, the greater the impact on the calculation.*

Before the creation of compound interest tables and the availability of financial calculators, long-hand math was the only option. This was extremely cumbersome and very time consuming. When tables were published, however, they were limited to specified interest rates, usually in 1/8 % increments, and specific compounding periods, such as monthly and yearly. The compound interest table books were often several hundreds of pages in order to cover as many rates as possible and the different compounding periods. The advantage to a financial calculator, such as the HP 12c, is that there are no limitations to the interest rate or number of compounding periods. Once a person learns the keystrokes, he can complete calculations quickly and simply.

Financial Registers

The financial register keys are located on the left side of the top row on the HP 12c calculator and are labeled "n", "i", "PV", "PMT", and "FV".

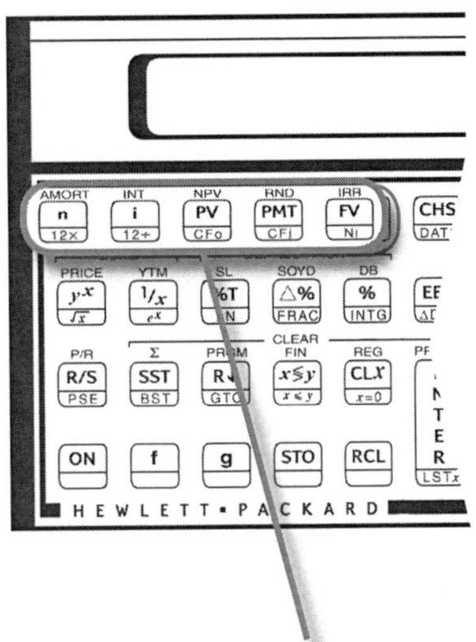

Financial Register Keys [n], [i], [PV], [PMT], [FV]

Base diagram of the HP 12c calculator: Courtesy, Hewlett-Packard Development Company, L.P.

Key	Function
[n]	Term or periods
[i]	Rate or interest rate
[PV]	Present value
[PMT]	Payment
[FV]	Future value

Notice on the lower face of the [n] key, in blue text, that "12x" appears. And, on the lower face of the [i] key, "12÷" appears in blue text. The blue prefix key [g] is pressed before pressing one of these keys whenever the term is in monthly periods and the amount of interest being earned will change with each deposit. It is very important that the frequency of compounding is consistent with the periodic interest rate. This will be illustrated later in this chapter.

Future Value of $1

The **future value** of $1 is an economic concept regarding the *amount of money that an investment (either a single payment or an annuity), at a fixed interest rate, for a specified period of time, will grow to in the future.* The concept also assumes that all monies earned (interest) is reinvested. Out of the six functions, this one is probably the easiest to understand because it works just like a savings account at the bank—a single amount of money placed in the bank now will grow due to accumulated interest over a period of time.

In order for a problem or calculation to fall into this category, one should determine that the deposit is made one time, and that the interest is not experiencing any changes during the deposit period.

Future value is often abbreviated FV. To calculate FV, the original amount of the investment must be known, along with the interest rate, represented by [i]. The length of the investment term, also referred to as the number of periods, needs to be known as well—this is represented by [n] in the data.

For Example: An investor puts $100 into a savings account. This represents the initial investment amount, or present value [PV]. The bank pays 6% interest, which is the interest rate [i]. By using simple math, after one year, the investment will have a future value of $106 ($100 x 1.06 = $106). How much will the investment have at the end of the second year?

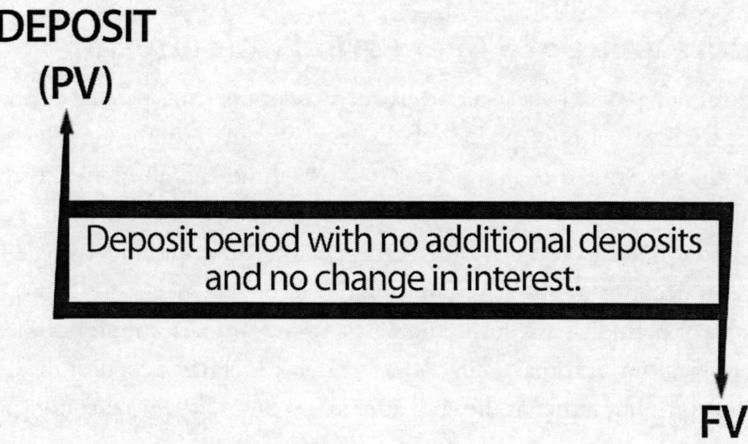

Before we demonstrate how to solve the previous example and the calculator input, we should cover a few important points:

- For all compounding problems, the display should be set at least six places past the decimal.
- There is no particular order that needs to be followed when inputting data.
- Most errors in these types of calculations stem from not having the calculator properly cleared. Make certain to clear the display and the storage registers before beginning a new problem.

In the previous example, **[n] = 2; [i] = 6; and the [PV] = $100**, the keystrokes are:

Try This...

[f]

[CLX] (clears the display and the storage registers)

[2]

[n]

[6]

[i]

[100]

[PV]

[FV]

Result: If the example has been followed correctly, **-112.360000** should be displayed, or $112.36.

√ ***Note:*** The HP-12c thinks in terms of cash flows. Hence, the $100 going into the bank is a positive cash flow for the bank. Therefore, at the end of the term when the principal and interest are returned, it is a negative.

Future Value of $1 Per Period (Annuity)

Future value of $1 per period is an economic concept that demonstrates what $1 invested on a periodic basis (e.g., weekly, monthly, yearly) will grow to if the investment is allowed to grow over time and all interest is reinvested (compounded). This is also known as an **annuity**. This function works very much like the future value of $1 except, rather than placing a single payment into an account at the beginning of the term, payments are deposited on a regular or periodic basis at the end of the term (ordinary annuity). In real estate, the reason for this is that an investment rarely generates income at the beginning of the term, but rather at the end, after all expenses have been paid.

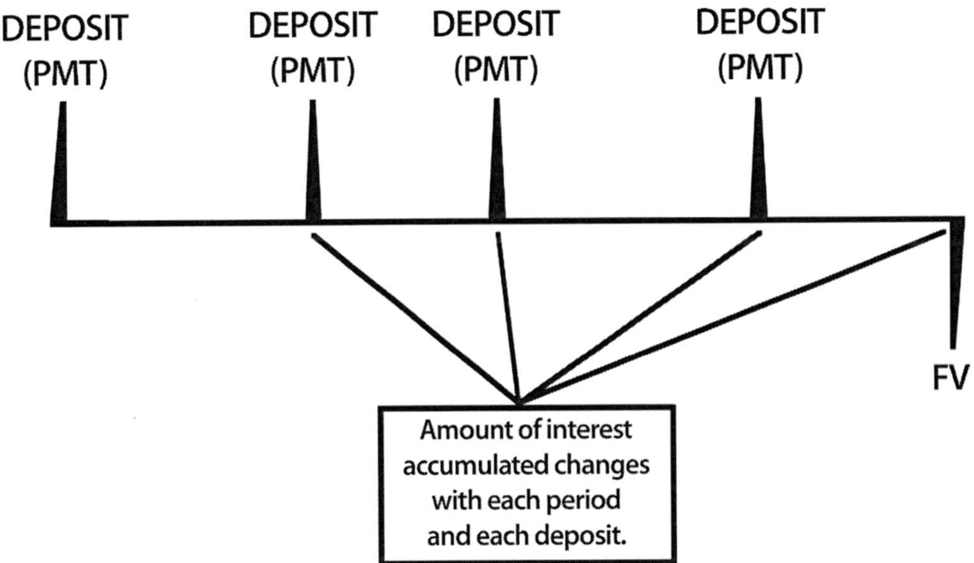

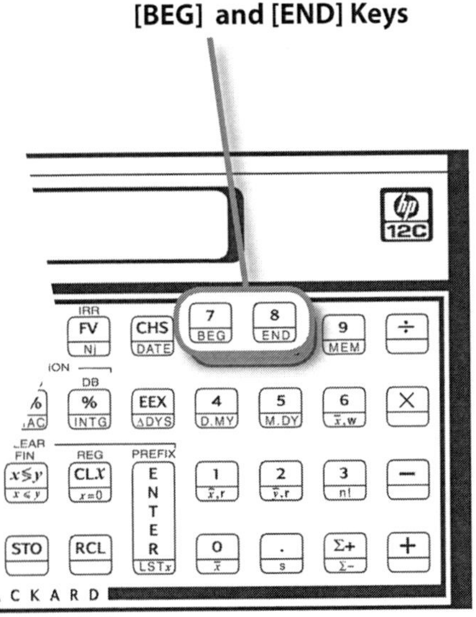

Base diagram of the HP 12c calculator: Courtesy, Hewlett-Packard Development Company, L.P.

A periodic payment placed in an account at the beginning of the period is called an *annuity in advance*. This is where the [BEG] and [END] keys are used. These keys are located on the lower face of the 7 and 8 number keys. Note that the text is in blue; therefore, the blue [g] prefix key must be pressed first before pressing one of these keys.

The HP-12c's default setting is for the end of the term. If the payment is at the beginning of the term, such as in an absolute net lease due at the first of each month, the calculator must be set for a "beginning term" calculation by pressing [g] [BEG].

Future value of $1 per period uses the same abbreviation as future value—[FV]. To calculate the future value of $1 per period, the payment to be invested each period, represented by [PMT] must be known, along with the interest rate, represented by [i], and the length of the investment term, also referred to as the number of periods and represented by [n] in the data.

For Example: After paying all expenses on a building, an investor will have $100 at the end of each year to deposit into a savings account. This represents the periodic payment [PMT]. The bank pays 6% interest, which is the interest rate [i]. Note that after the first year, the investment will have a future value of only $100, since the money was just placed in the account. At the end of year two, the total amount grows to $206. The first $100 deposit has now earned $6 interest and an additional $100 is added at the end of the second year. This amount will grow at 6% for the next year and equal $218.36 at the end of that time—at which time another $100 is deposited, bringing the total to $318.36 for three years [n].

In the previous example, **[n]** = **3, [i]** = **6,** and the **[PMT]** = **$100,** the keystrokes are:

Try This...

[f]

[CLX]

[3]

[n]

[6]

[i]

[100]

[PMT]

[FV]

Result: If the example has been followed correctly, **-318.360000** should be displayed, or $318.36.

The previous example demonstrates an annual deposit or payment. Let's look at an example where monthly deposits are being made and the interest is being figured on the balance at the end of each month.

For Example: After paying all expenses on a building, an investor will have $50 each month to deposit into a savings account. The interest rate is 6%. What will the balance be after three years of deposits?

Since the deposits are being made monthly and the amount of interest being earned will change with each deposit, both the term [n] and the rate [i] will need to be based on a monthly basis. Therefore, the term and the rate need to be converted to a monthly basis using the blue [g] prefix key prior to pressing the [n] or the [i] keys.

In the previous example, **[n] = 3; [i] = 6;** and the **[PMT] = $50,** the keystrokes are:

Try This...

[f]

[CLX]

[3]

[g]

[n]

[6]

[g]

[i]

[50]

[PMT]

[FV]

Result: If the example has been followed correctly, **-1,966.805248** should be displayed, or $1,966.81.

Sinking Fund Factor

The **sinking fund factor** is an economic concept regarding an *amount of money set aside on a periodic basis so that, when compounded at a given interest rate for a defined term, it will accumulate to a specified future sum.*

√ ***In Other Words:*** Sinking fund factors show the amount of regular payments that must be invested over a period of time at a specified interest rate, with reinvestment of all monies earned, so a desired or target amount is accumulated at the end of the investment term.

The concept is very similar to the present value annuity function except, with a sinking fund, the goal is a target amount at the end of the term. If no interest were involved, the problem would be easy to solve. If $1,000 is needed at the end of 10 years, $100 needs to be set aside per year to save $1,000. With compound interest, however, a smaller investment is required each period, since it will grow over time as interest payments are added to the principal. The sinking fund factor calculates this reduced payment based on the interest rate and the length of the compounding period.

To calculate sinking fund factors, the future value [FV] or target amount must be established; along with when the final amount is needed, or after how many intervals [n]; and how often contributions [PMT] will be made (e.g., monthly or annually). Finally, the interest rate [i] the investment will earn over time is needed.

For Example: An investor needs $1,000 at the end of 10 years. If the investment will earn 6% interest, how much must the investor deposit every year over the 10 years to end up with exactly $1,000?

In the previous example, **[n] = 10; [i] = 6;** and the **[FV] = $1,000,** the keystrokes are:

Try this...

[f]

[CLX]

[10]

[n]

[6]

[i]

[1000]

[FV]

[PMT]

Result: If the example has been followed correctly, **-75.867958** should be displayed, or $75.87 each year.

√ ***Note:*** The investor deposited $75.87 per year for 10 years ($758.70) to finish with $1,000; compound interest contributes the rest.

Let's now use the same sinking fund example, only in this case, monthly deposits are made. The keystrokes are:

Try this...

[f]

[CLX]

[10]

[g]

[n]

[6]

[g]

[i]

[1000]

FV]

[PMT]

Result: If the example has been followed correctly, **-6.102050** should be displayed, or $6.10 each month.

√ ***Note:*** Making deposits on a monthly basis rather than annual requires less total principle over the 10 year period ($732.25). This slight difference is due to monthly compounding rather than annual compounding.

Present Value of $1 (Reversion)

Present value is *an amount today that is equivalent to a future payment, or a series of payments (annuity), based on a specified interest rate, for a specific period of time.*

√ ***In Other Words:*** The present value of $1 is an economic concept that demonstrates how much must be invested today for the investment to grow to $1 at the end of a specified time period, with reinvestment of all monies earned.

Here, the amount in the future is known. So the question is: How much money (present value) invested today, with compound interest, is required to reach a specified amount in the future? The easiest way to understand this function is to think about present value as the opposite function of future value. In the future value example, $100 invested at 6% for two years is worth $112.36 after two years. Conversely, $112.36 received in two years at 6% is worth $100 today. Therefore, at 6%, $100 today and $112.36 received in two years are equal. Investors sometimes refer to converting monies due in the future to present value as discounting. **Discounting** is *the process that uses the principles of TVM to convert future income or cash flows into present value, at a specified interest rate.*

Present value is often abbreviated **PV**. To calculate [PV], the amount to be received in the future must first be established, along with the required interest rate [i] the investment will earn, and when in the future the amount is scheduled to be received (the term, [n]).

For Example: A promissory note for $1,000 is due in two years. A typical return on deposits is currently 8% annually with monthly compounding. How much is the note worth today?

In the previous example, **[n] = 2; [i] = 8;** and the **[FV] = $1,000,** the keystrokes are:

Try This...

[f]

[CLX]

[2]

[g]

[n]

[8]

[g]

[i]

[1000]

[FV]

[PV]

Result: If the example has been followed correctly, **-852.596376** should be displayed, or $852.60.

√ ***Note:*** The term and the rate have been converted to a monthly basis using the blue prefix [g] key, since the example specifies monthly compounding. If the question had specified annual compounding, the use of the prefix key before pressing [i] or [n] would be omitted. Even though no periodic payments are specified in the example, the compounding period and the periodic rate must always be consistent.

Present Value of $1 Per Period (Annuity)

Present value of $1 per period (annuity) is an economic concept that demonstrates how much money, in a single payment, must be invested today and compounded into the future to equal a series of periodic payments in the future. This is also a type of annuity calculation and works very much like the present value of a $1. An amount of money in the future is known, but, rather than it being a single amount, it is a series of equal payments received in the future on a periodic basis (e.g., weekly, monthly, yearly). This calculation can be useful when an investor wants to know, for example, how much ten years' worth of rent payments are worth today, or today's value of a series of land contracts being made in the future.

Present value of $1 per period uses the same abbreviation as present value—[PV]. To calculate the present value of $1 per period, the amount being received each period [PMT] must be known, along with the interest rate [i], and the length of the investment term, also referred to as the number of periods [n].

> ***For Example:*** A land contract will pay $1,000 per month for the next five years. If a potential purchaser of this land contract would like to make 8% interest on the investment, how much is the land contract worth in present value?

In the previous example, **[n] = 5; [i] = 8;** and the **[PMT] = $1,000,** the keystrokes are:

Try this...

[f]

[CLX]

[5]

[g]

[n]

[8]

[g]

[i]

[1000]

[PMT]

[PV]

Result: If the example has been followed correctly, **-49,318.43334** should be displayed, or a present value of $49,318.43.

Payment to Amortize $1

Amortization is *elimination of a debt with a series of equal payments (principle and interest) at a regular time intervals.* When a loan is fully amortized, the total payments retire the entire balance of principal and interest at the end of the loan term. The objective is to take a principal loan amount and determine the payment amount required to repay both the principal and all interest due over the life of the loan. For most people, this function is very familiar because it is the same concept as a fixed-rate, fixed-term home mortgage.

√ **Note:** This calculation will not work for variable-rate or variable-term loans.

To calculate the payment needed to amortize a loan, the amount borrowed [PV], the interest rate [i], and the length of the loan term [n] must be determined. Generally, loan payments are made monthly, but may be made weekly, quarterly, or annually.

For Example: A homeowner has a $100,000, 30-year mortgage at 6% interest. What are the monthly payments?

In the previous example, **[n] = 30; [i] = 6;** and the **[PV] = $100,000,** the keystrokes are:

Try this...

[f]

[CLX]

[30]

[g]

[n]

[6]

[g]

[i]

[100000]

[PV]

[PMT]

Result: If the example has been followed correctly, **-599.550525** should be displayed, or a monthly payment of $599.55.

» *What You Have Learned...*

- *Various examples of compound interest problems and the six functions of $1.*
- *How the financial register keys work and their functions.*
- *How deposits or payments made at the beginning or ending of a period are input.* «

Practice Problems

1. If $750 is deposited in a savings account earning 11.50% interest, how much will be in the account at the end of 3 years?

2. A heating system will need to be replaced in 10 years at a cost of $16,000. To have enough set aside when the replacement is necessary, what amount will need to be deposited monthly if the account will earn 2.5% interest?

3. The monthly debt service on a loan is $1,608.52. If the interest rate for the loan is 6.75% for a 30-year term, what was the original loan amount? (Round your answer to the nearest thousand.)

4. If $30 is deposited each month for a period of 6.5 years, what will the balance be in a savings account earning 3.25 percent?

Quiz

1. ***A residential dwelling measures 78' x 28', which includes a 2-car attached garage that has exterior dimensions of 24.5' x 28'. What is the gross living area of the dwelling?***
   a. 1,235
   b. 1,498
   c. 1,752
   d. 1,814

2. ***What is the current value of $25,000 discounted at 11%, due in one year (rounded to the nearest whole dollar)?***
   a. $22,250
   b. $22,523
   c. $22,755
   d. $23,122

3. ***What is the monthly debt service on a 30-year mortgage loan at 5.5% interest if the beginning principal balance is $92,000?***
   a. $497.22
   b. $502.22
   c. $522.37
   d. $532.22

4. ***The basement of a house has exterior foundation dimensions of 40' x 35'. The finished area is 1,100 square feet. What percent (rounded to a whole number) of the basement is finished?***
   a. 79%
   b. 81%
   c. 83%
   d. 85%

5. ***A comparable property sold for $112,000 and was financed with a 95% loan. If the sale price included 3.5 seller-paid points, what percent of the sale price were seller concessions?***
   a. 2.975%
   b. 3.125%
   c. 3.325%
   d. 3.500%

6. ***An investment property owner wants to assure that he has enough funds set away to replace these capital items in 15 years (furnace - $18,500, roof - $17,000). How much must be deposited each month in an account bearing 4% interest (rounded to the nearest whole cent)?***
   a. $114.37
   b. $121.52
   c. $138.49
   d. $144.26

7. ***What is the current value of $100,000 compounded monthly for 10 years at 8% interest (rounded to the nearest cent)?***
   a. $45,052.35
   b. $48,295.66
   c. $56,195.28
   d. $61,686.42

8. ***Rounded to four decimal places, what annual percent of increase is indicated as the market condition adjustment if a comparable property sold for $285,000 yesterday and the same property sold for $212,500 fourteen months ago?***
   a. 24.3972
   b. 29.2437
   c. 34.6643
   d. 37.5189

9. ***Over the next five years, a land contract disburses $400 payments at the end of each month. If an investor wanted to make a 10% return on investment, what is the value today of the land contract (rounded to a whole dollar)?***
   a. $18,153
   b. $18,826
   c. $18,983
   d. $24,000

10. ***Carpet in a 12.5 x 16' room and a 15.25' x 14.75 room needs to be replaced. Rounded to the nearest whole dollar, what will be the total cost of the carpet if it is priced at $26.50 per square yard, including installation?***
   a. $1,239
   b. $1,251
   c. $1,274
   d. $1,288

Introduction to *Income Fundamentals*

5

The income approach to real property appraisal requires the understanding of numerous principles, terms, and concepts related to its use. This chapter will provide illustration and discussion of the applicability of the income approach, leases, the fundamental elements of lease relationships, and important components used when applying various income methodologies.

The Income Approach—When and Why?

In reality, the income approach will not be developed as often for residential appraisal assignments as the sales comparison approach. In fact, depending on the particular market and neighborhood, the income approach may be thought of as somewhat of a "special" valuation tool for some appraisers. But, being prepared and equipped with knowledge of the income approach and how to use it when needed is essential to every appraiser.

Problem Identification and the Income Approach

In many, if not most, cases the appraiser will recognize when the income approach is needed for credible assignment results during problem identification (as we discussed in an earlier chapter). Common elements of problem identification that could cause this recognition might include:

- Intended use
- Relevant property characteristics
- Assignment conditions specified by the client or intended user

Obviously, if the intended use of the appraiser's conclusions is to determine what a property could rent for or what the value of that property is, based on its income producing potential, the income approach may be the appraiser's primary method for solving the problem. Or, possibly the intended use of the appraisal is to assist in the facilitation of mortgage financing with an investor/borrower.

Relevant property characteristics are very often the first and most obvious clue that the appraiser should consider the relevance of the income approach for a residential property. Some of the situations that often prompt this conclusion might include:

- Physical characteristics of the property
- Income history or existing leases for the property
- Location

KEY TERMS

Contract Rent What tenants are actually paying in rent, as stated in the terms of the lease.

Debt Service The amount of funds required to make periodic payments of principal and interest to the lender.

Deficit Rent The resulting difference when the market rent exceeds the contract rent.

Effective Gross Income (EGI) Potential gross income, less vacancy and collection losses.

Excess Rent The resulting difference when the contract rent exceeds the market rent.

Fee Simple The greatest estate (ownership) one can have in real property; it is freely transferable and inheritable, and of indefinite duration, with no conditions on the title. Often called **fee simple absolute** or **fee title.**

Fixed Expenses Ongoing operating expenses that do not vary based on occupancy levels of the property (e.g., taxes and insurance). *Compare:* **Variable Expenses.**

Gross Income Multiplier (GIM) A factor that takes into account income derived from all sources of a property (e.g., vending, storage units).

Gross Lease A property lease for which the landlord pays all expenses related to the operation of the property.

Gross Rent Multiplier (GRM) A factor derived from comparable rental data, which is then used to develop an opinion of value of the subject property.

Lease Conveyance of a leasehold estate from the fee owner to a tenant; a contract for which one party pays the other rent in exchange for possession of real estate.

Leased Fee Estate The landlord's ownership interest in property.

Leasehold Estate An estate that gives the holder (tenant) a temporary right to possession, without title. Also called **Less-than-Freehold Estate**.

Lessee A person who leases property; a tenant.

If the property consists of two or more living units, the appraiser undoubtedly will initially determine that the income approach has relevance in the assignment. When a property is currently rented or has an income history, the indication is probably the same. In the context of location, if the market area or neighborhood is, or is transitioning to, a significant number of tenant-occupied properties, this could also provide evidence to the appraiser that some type of income technique should be included in the scope of work. There are numerous scenarios based on these assignment elements (and possibly others) that could cause the appraiser to consider the income approach applicable and necessary for credible results. As a reminder, determination of the relevant property characteristics is solely the appraiser's responsibility.

In some assignments, the client may specify the income approach be developed and presented in the appraisal assignment. If the assignment is accepted with this client requirement, this would be an assignment condition with which the appraiser must comply. When the appraiser accepts an assignment with such a condition, the appraiser determines in the final analysis what the results of the income approach mean to the value opinion and the final results.

» The relevance of the income approach is often realized during problem identification, or possibly somewhere else in the development process «

Information or Conditions Discovered During Analysis

There will be occasions when the relevance of the income approach is not recognized during problem identification, but becomes evident sometime in the appraisal process.

> ***For Example:*** The income-producing characteristic or potential may reveal itself during the highest and best use analysis, or earlier, at the time of property inspection.

KEY TERMS

Lessor A person who leases property to another; a landlord.

Market Rent What the property could rent for in the open market if currently vacant and available.

Net Lease A property lease for which the tenant pays all utilities and certain expenses, in addition to rent payments.

Net Operating Income (NOI) Income after expenses.

Operating Expenses Day-to-day costs of running a building, like repairs and maintenance, but not including debt service or depreciation.

Overage Rent A percentage of business sales a tenant's business has generated paid in addition to rent payments.

Overall Capitalization Rate Used to interpret a property's single year net operating income to the property's value using direct capitalization. (Symbolized by R_0)

Overall Yield Rate Considers a series of annual figures over the entire investment period as well as reversion.

Potential Gross Income (PGI) The income that could be produced by a property in an ideal situation, with no vacancy or collection losses.

Reserves for Replacement An amount of money set aside for future replacement of major items, such as the roof or heating system. Also called **Reserves**.

Reversionary Benefit Typically a sum, often stated in a dollar amount, that a property owner will receive when or if he sells the property at the end of the investment term.

Variable Expenses Operating expenses necessary to the property, but usually dependent on the property's occupancy level.

As well, the appraiser might not recognize the transitioning of a market neighborhood to tenant occupancy until sometime in the market analysis. Following is a circumstance that occasionally might surface that illustrates these points:

Example

A real property appraiser, during the course of a single-family residential property inspection, found that the property features an apartment over the garage, which is permitted by public and private regulations. The appraiser was not aware of the additional living unit's existence when he accepted the assignment and decided on the initial scope of work. Although not predominate, there is a presence of tenant-occupied, single-family houses in the neighborhood, a fact revealed during the appraiser's market analysis. After analysis, the appraiser concludes the highest and best use of the property is as an income-producing property. Thus, the scope of work originally planned by the appraiser should be modified to include the development of the income approach.

Whether or not the appraiser in the previous example determines during reconciliation that the income approach yields meaningful direction for a credible indication of value could depend on many other things (e.g., the relevance of other valuation approaches that were developed and the quantity and quality of the income data used for analysis). The point to the previous example is that the appraiser learned of the income approach's applicability after the assignment commenced and the scope of work should be modified to include its development.

Likewise, there could be circumstances when the appraiser initially decides that the scope of work in the assignment will include the income approach, only to discover sometime into the assignment that the method is not applicable or would not produce credible results. Again, the scope of work should be modified to exclude the development of the income approach. Keep in mind, however, that Standards Rule 2-2 of USPAP requires that for all reporting options, the exclusion of the sales comparison approach, cost approach, or income approach must be explained in the appraisal report.

» *The appraiser decides what weight to give to the income approach during reconciliation* «

Lease Basics

A **lease** is *a conveyance of a leasehold estate from the fee owner to a tenant; a contract for which one party pays the other rent in exchange for possession of real estate.* In most residential lease scenarios, the arrangements between the *landlord* (**lessor**) and the *tenant* (**lessee**) are on a month-to-month or short-term basis.

In a month-to-month lease arrangement, there is no predetermined or firm date upon which the lease relationship will terminate. When the lessee pays the lessor a month rent and the lessor accepts the rent, the payment implies that the parties agree to provide or enjoy the benefits of the arrangement for that particular month.

√ ***In Other Words:*** The lease renews with each monthly rent payment.

In some cases, this same principle could apply when the period is one day or one week, which might possibly be the arrangement for a vacation rental.

Although there are no definitive number of years that universally describe a short-term lease, most consider a lease arrangement to be short-term if the period of the lease is for five years or less. Residential lease terms for a period greater than five years (which would be considered long-term) are rarer than short-term leases. As well, a short- or long-term lease might terminate but yet continue as month-to-month when the lessee continues to pay rent and the lessor accepts it.

It is important that appraisers be able to recognize the characteristics of the lease arrangements as well as the status of the property rights, and the partial interests that are present when a property is encumbered by lease. Ideally, this is part of the examination of the subject's lease. Appraisers should always commence the development of the income approach with an examination of the lease and its terms. The lease will spell out the term, the rent payment arrangements, which party is paying for certain expenses, and any personal property or other rights being assumed in the lease, to name a few.

Most leases are in writing in order to comply with many states' laws and regulations. However, states may allow certain leases *not* to be in writing, such as those which are month-to-month or for a term of less than one year. In some cases, a written lease may be required to be placed on public record (similar to the recording or filing of a deed), while in other states, placement on record might be an option.

Fee Simple, Leased Fee, & Leasehold Estates

When a property's owner enjoys all of the benefits of the bundle of rights, his ownership interests are said to be in **fee simple** (*the greatest ownership one can have in real property; it is freely transferable and inheritable, and of indefinite duration, with no conditions on the title*). The bundle of rights typically includes the right of quiet enjoyment, the right of disposal, and the right of use. However, when the property owner leases a property, he is temporarily (for the term of the lease) giving up, at the very least, all or part of the right of use, and probably some other elements in the bundle of rights as well. The party leasing the property from the owner temporarily is conveyed a possessory interest in the property, or defined portion of that property.

What results is the lessor (property owner) having the **leased fee estate** (*the landlord's ownership interest in the property*), and the lessee (tenant) having the **leasehold estate** (*an estate that gives the tenant a temporary right to possession without title*).

In the leased fee estate, the lessor owns the property and the other rights, but due to the lease, he cannot possess or occupy the property. The leased fee position is one in which the property owner, or lessor, does not have the right of possession. The lessee, on the other hand, does not own the property, but simply possesses the right to occupy it.

What is important for the appraiser to recognize in a particular appraisal assignment is the *interest being appraised* in that assignment. This discovery takes place during problem identification as part of determining relevant property characteristics. When the elements of an assignment direct the appraiser to value the fee simple interest, the property is valued as if unencumbered by the lease.

√ ***In Other Words:*** The property is valued as if the property were freely available to a new tenant at current market conditions.

This is often the case, especially in most residential assignments. Due to many (if not most) residential leases being of a short-term nature, the fee simple interest could usually be regained by the property owner, even if he did not have it at the time of the assignment, in a fairly short period of time.

√ ***Note:*** Just to be clear, this would certainly not dismiss the appraiser's duty to factually disclose and describe the terms of any lease arrangement that was currently related to the subject property.

When the subject of an assignment is the leased fee or the leasehold estate, that subject of that assignment is a **partial interest** (*any interest in real estate that one may have, other than the full bundle of rights*). We will talk more about partial interests and how they are valued in Chapter 7.

Types and Structures of Leases

Leases could be highly customized in nature with terms that address a specific property in specific (lessor/lessee) situations, and/or address the current condition and nature of a particular market. Leases can be broadly categorized as:

- Flat
- Variable
- Step-up
- Revaluation
- Annual increase
- Percentage

Not all of these categories are common to residential properties. Flat leases and, maybe occasionally, variable leases or annual increase leases will account for the majority of the leases seen in residential appraisal assignments. We will discuss all of these categories here.

Typically, leases are structured in either some type of a *gross lease* format or a *net lease* format. These lease types primarily refer to which party (lessee or lessor) is paying certain expenses in the arrangement. Let's look at each of these now, keeping in mind that there could be variations in different markets.

Gross Lease—A gross lease scenario is the most common for residential rentals. Most all apartment units would be classified as a gross lease, as well as many single-family rentals. In a **gross lease**, the *landlord pays for all expenses related to the ownership of the property*. These expenses typically include the real estate taxes, insurance on the property, and property maintenance and repairs. There could be markets and properties where the landlord pays the utilities, such as properties with shared metering. But with other markets and properties, tenants could pay their own utility expenses and still be termed a gross lease.

An alternative type of gross lease is a **modified gross lease**. In this scenario, which is also called semi-gross, the lessor and the lessee are sharing certain or all expenses.

Net Lease—In a **net lease** scenario, *the lessee is paying some or all of the expenses that are typically paid by the lessor* (such as in a gross lease). The term "net lease" is applied broadly, and to truly understand a particular lease's terms, a net lease is usually specified further into one of the following four categories (again, there could be variations):

1. **Single net**
   - Lessor pays for maintenance and building repairs, and real estate taxes *or* insurance
   - Lessee pays for *either* real estate taxes or insurance
2. **Double net** (sometimes referred to as **net/net**)
   - Lessor pays for maintenance *and* building repairs
   - Lessee pays for *both* real estate taxes and insurance
3. **Triple net** (sometimes referred to as **net/net/net**)
   - Lessor pays for building repairs
   - Lessee pays for real estate taxes, insurance, and maintenance
4. **Absolute net**
   - Lessee pays for real estate taxes, insurance, maintenance, and building repairs

Unless there are specific provisions or market customs otherwise, the lessee pays for utilities in all net lease scenarios. Net leases are not as common in most residential lease arrangements, but occasionally could be found. However, net lease scenarios are found frequently with many types of non-residential properties. Examination of lease documents provides clues as to the type of lease arrangement that is in place between the parties. The lease may or may not label the arrangement specifically as one of these classifications.

Flat Lease

A **flat lease** is *an arrangement where the rent payments to the lessor are consistent throughout the duration of the lease term*. This is the most common type of lease in short-term residential situations, especially gross lease scenarios, but could be found in net lease scenarios, as well. The flat lease may also be referred to as a **level lease** or a **level payment lease**.

> ***For Example:*** If the rent in a lease for a one-year period is specified as $750 per month, the rent would never change and would remain $750 per month for the entire year.

Variable Leases

A **variable lease** is *a lease with rental payments made at regular intervals, but payment amounts may change.* This is sometimes known as an **index lease**. The longer the lease term, the more likely it is to have some sort of adjustment mechanism written into it, especially net leases. Common mechanisms that trigger a change in lease rate or rent could be the Consumer Price Index, or simply variations in the owner's expenses in net lease scenarios.

> ***For Example:*** If the rent in a lease for a one-year period is specified as $750 per month, the rent could change at a specified frequency by some predetermined variable related to an index or other indicator and the rent may be adjusted higher or lower than $750 per month.

Step-up Leases

A **step-up** or **step-down lease** *provides for the rent amount change over time, usually a predetermined percentage at a predetermined interval.* Any interval can be specified, but annual increases are the most common (a step-down lease is far less common). This type of lease may also be referred to as **graduated rental lease**. On occasion, the appraiser might encounter a residential property that is the subject of such a lease scenario. However, these are usually leases of longer terms.

> ***For Example:*** The provisions of a lease specify that the rent for the first year will be $750 per month (or it could be an annual rent amount), with annual increases of 10%. Thus, the second year rent would be $825 per month, the third year $907.50 per month, and so on.

Revaluation Leases

A revaluation lease has *rental payments that change over time at a set interval, but the amount of the change is determined usually by a revaluation of the market rent, allowing the owner to maintain rents at market rates based on the current market.* This type of lease is very rarely, if ever, seen with residential properties. Most revaluation leases are found in long-term scenarios or short-term leases where there are renewal options.

> ***For Example:*** A lease stipulates that the rent for an office area might be $25 per square foot per year with a revaluation of the lease rate based on a revaluation of market rents bi-annually. The lessee will have the property rental rates revaluated and the current rental rate will be adjusted to reflect the current market.

Annual Increase Leases

The **annual increase lease** *operates very similarly to a step-up lease with one major exception—rather than a percentage increase, the periodic increase specified in the lease is a specific dollar amount.* This type of lease could be found with any type of property.

> ***For Example:*** The provisions of a lease specify that the rent for the first year will be $750 per month (or it could be an annual rent amount), with annual increases of $50. Thus, the second year rent would be $800 per month, the third year $850 per month, and so on.

Percentage Leases

The concept of a **percentage lease** typically does not lend itself to a residential property. This type of lease is most common to retail lessees and most frequently in high-profile retail environments, such as shopping complexes and malls. *There could be broad variations in percentage leases.* With some percentage leases, lessees could be paying a base or guaranteed minimum, which is often called a **breakpoint rent**, plus *a percentage of the sales their business has generated* (known as **overage rent**). In other cases, the rent is purely based on a percent of the sales volume. Even though this may seem somewhat precarious as far as the parties to the lease are concerned, percentage leases can be an advantage to the lessee, because the arrangement motivates the lessor to adequately promote and maintain the complex or facility.

» *Leases could be of many different types and structures. The appraiser must be able to recognize the characteristics of a lease in order to adequately analyze it* «

For Example: The Acme Department Store, located in the Valle Green Mall, is obligated, per its lease terms, to pay 3% of the annual sales as rent. Acme generated $10,000,000 in sales during the past year. Thus, the year's rent would be $300,000.

Income Concepts and Components

Appraisers must understand several concepts and components before they can effectively apply the income approach in an appraisal assignment. Some of these elements are fundamental to every assignment in which the income approach is applicable, while other elements may be part of a specific technique being applied.

Here we will discuss types of income and investment benefits, types of expenses, and the different factors and rates that may be employed in developing the income approach for a particular appraisal assignment.

Income vs. Rent

Depending on the particular income technique the appraiser chooses in the scope of work, distinguishing between the term "income" and "rent" may be critical (it is also very important for examination purposes). In some cases, the rent a particular property generates may be its income. In other circumstances, there may be other types of income aside from the rent the property generates for the living unit or units, such as income from parking spaces, garage spaces, storage spaces, vending machines, etc.

Recognizing the difference becomes important as you will learn later when we discuss the development of techniques such as the Gross Rent Multiplier (GRM) and the Gross Income Multiplier (GIM). The GRM technique considers only rent from the living units in its development, while the GIM technique (and others we will discuss) considers income from all sources.

Speaking strictly to rent, there are two defined concepts that we will discuss here—contract rent and market rent.

Contract Rent

Contract rent is *what the tenants are actually paying in rent, as stated in the terms of the lease.* It is the actual rent that the lessor and the lessee of a particular property have agreed upon. The contract rent, or what a particular property is actually generating, may or may not reflect what a typical lessor would expect, or what a typical lessee would pay.

Just as we discussed earlier about buyers and sellers in real estate sales transactions, one of the inefficiencies of the real estate market is that participants are not always well informed nor do they always act rationally. The same could often be true here, as well. There could be differences between the rent (and other income) a property should command and what it is actually generating.

Some landlords never adjust the rent for an income-producing property, or may opt to apply a rent adjustment only for a new tenant at the time of the initial lease or renewal. Other landlords may be quite knowledgeable of the rental market and maintain their leases with provisions for rent to reflect the current market. This is one of the important analyses that the appraiser must conduct when undertaking a *market value* assignment with an income property—determining if the rent being generated actually reflects that which would be typical in that particular marketplace. Therefore, the contract rent, while analyzed for its relevance to the market, is an important consideration in the income analysis but is not used as a basis for the analysis. The rent and income basis applied in any technique for which the assignment specifies *market value* would rely on what the typical market participant would do rather than what the parties in a particular agreement are doing.

There may be occasions when the contract rent is used in the income analysis; however, the type of value specified in those assignments would not be the common definition of market value, but rather some other type of value (such as a value in use or investment value).

Market Rent

Market rent (also referred to as **economic rent**) is *what the property could rent for in the open market if currently vacant and available.* It is the amount a property *should* command in an open and competitive market, and as we just mentioned, market rent could be more or less than contract rent. In some cases, the contract rent of a property may reflect, or be the same as, market rent.

When the market rent exceeds contract rent, the difference is called **deficit rent**. The lessee has the advantage and the lessor is at a disadvantage.

> ***For Example:*** A property is leasing for $750 per month. However, the appraiser's analysis indicates that property should be leasing for $900 per month. There is a $150 per month deficit.

When contract rent exceeds market rent, the difference is known as **excess rent**. In this case, the lessor has the advantage, leaving the lessee at a disadvantage. These terms become important as we discuss valuation of leasehold and leased fee positions in a later chapter.

> ***For Example:*** A property is leasing for $1,000 per month. The appraiser concludes that the market rent is $800 per month. There is a $200 per month excess rent.

Market rent is used in assignments when the fee simple interest (unencumbered by any lease and freely available) is the interest being appraised in an assignment at market value.

Measures of Income and Benefits

If one reflects on the fundamental principle of anticipation and an income-producing property, or a property for which there is income potential, there are several different benefits of owning the property that immediately come to mind. Obviously, the one thing that most owners of an income-producing property expect is an income flow. A return on the owner's investment is typically anticipated. And, most every investor expects the value of his investment will grow and a profit in an eventual sale of the property.

Appraisers have several mechanisms that are used as part of some or all income analysis to measure the efficiency of an investment, depending on the scope of work in the assignment. These concepts include:

- Potential gross income
- Effective gross income
- Net operating income
- Reversionary benefit

Potential Gross Income

Potential gross income (**PGI**) is *the income that could be produced by a property in an ideal situation, with no vacancy or collection losses (e.g., a tenant who failed to pay rent and it could not be collected*). The key here is that PGI is the income a property *could* generate if the property is fully rented and occupied during the particular period being analyzed. In most cases, PGI is based on an annual amount.

Effective Gross Income

Effective gross income (**EGI**) is *the potential gross income, less vacancy and collection losses.* EGI is the income that could be (or is) realized from an income property after deducting an amount for vacancy and collection losses, but before any operating expenses are considered. If PGI is what the property owner *could* have taken in, EGI can be thought of as what that property owner *did* take in. The formula for EGI is:

PGI - Vacancy and Collection Losses = EGI

Net Operating Income

Net operating income (**NOI**) is *the income after expenses.*

> ***In Other Words:*** Net operating income is the effective gross income minus operating expenses.

Operating expenses are discussed later in this chapter.

» *Anticipation, as applied to the income approach, could be the expected income, return on investment, and growth in property value* «

Do not confuse NOI with cash flow. Cash flow considers other obligations, such as payments toward loan debt and income tax obligations that are not considered in the NOI. The formula for NOI is:

PGI - Vacancy and Collection Losses =
EGI – Operating Expenses = NOI

As mentioned earlier, PGI and EGI are most commonly expressed in annual terms, as is NOI.

Reversionary Benefit

The **reversionary benefit** is *typically a sum, often stated in a dollar amount, that a property owner will receive when or if he sells the property at the end of the investment term*. There are several different methods of measuring the reversionary benefit, but to make it simple, it can be thought of as the net proceeds when and if the property is sold. In most cases, typical investors expect that the value of a property will grow over time for one reason or another.

√ ***Note:*** Analyses that consider reversionary benefits are not typically associated with most common residential income analyses and are beyond the scope of this course. However, appraisers should be familiar with these terms and concepts, which may be explored in greater detail in more advanced coursework.

Operating Expenses

Operating expenses are *day-to-day costs of running a building, like repairs and maintenance, but not including debt service or depreciation*. **Debt service** is *the amount of funds required to make periodic payments of principal and interest to the lender*. These are expenses that must be made by the property owner in order to adequately maintain a property at a level that it could continue to produce revenue. When income is analyzed at an annual level (as it usually is), the operating expenses are also considered on an annual basis.

As illustrated earlier in the discussion regarding contract rent vs. market rent, the discussion is applicable to operating expenses as well. For a market value opinion of the fee simple interest of a property using the income approach, market level expenses are used in the appraiser's analysis. As part of the diligence performed by the appraiser, he will compare the subject's actual expenses to similar properties in the market to determine if the subject's expenses are adequate and at a market level. The primary tool for this analysis is the reconstructed operating income statement. Here is a sample:

Sample Reconstructed Operating Income Statement

	Subject	Comp #1	Comp #2	Comp #3
	121 High St.	232 King Ave.	343 Main Rd.	454 Hill Blvd.
Net Rentable Area (sq. ft.)	35,000	42,500	37,500	40,000
Rent per square foot	$23.50	$21.75	$24.25	$22.50
Potential Gross Income	$822,500	$924,375	$909,375	$900,000
Vacancy and Collection =10%	$82,250	$92,438	$90,938	$90,000
Effective Gross Income	$740,250	$831,938	$818,438	$810,000
Expenses: Fixed				
Real Estate Taxes	$91,350	$107,100	$100,125	$99,200
Insurance	$2,450	$3,400	$2,625	$2,800
Expenses: Variable				
Utilities	$81,900	$108,800	$100,125	$92,800
Maintenance/Janitorial	$40,950	$56,525	$45,000	$46,400
Repairs	$14,000	$20,400	$15,375	$17,200
Management Fees	$8,400	$9,350	$9,000	$9,200
Other	$1,750	$2,550	$1,875	$2,400
Reserves (5% of EGI)				
Roof, HVAC	$37,100	$41,650	$40,875	$40,400
Total Expenses	$277,900	$349,775	$315,000	$310,400
Net Operating Income	$462,350	$482,163	$503,438	$499,600

You will note that operating expenses have been defined into three types:

1. Fixed expenses
2. Variable expenses
3. Reserves for replacement

When developing a reconstructed operating income statement, appraisers must identify certain expenses and assign them to the proper category. Therefore, it is important that the characteristics of each is clearly understood. Let's discuss each expense type a little further.

Fixed Expenses

When one considers **fixed expenses**, the primary thinking should reflect on *ongoing expenses that do not vary based on occupancy levels of the property.* Real estate taxes and insurance on the property are examples of items that are typically considered fixed expenses. Even though the cost of these items might vary from year to year, the change is usually not significant, and is not based upon occupancy.

Other examples of fixed expenses might be services that are contracted at a level rate for, perhaps, a year at a time. A good example might be refuse collection, where the lessor is paying for a certain number of collections per week or month, regardless of how much refuse there is. Another fixed expense might be the cost of a security light for a parking area or other common area where the expense is a reoccurring flat fee. Again, think of costs not associated with the occupancy.

√ **Note:** Keep in mind that debt service is not an expense that is required to maintain the property!

Variable Expenses

Variable expenses are *operating expenses necessary to the property, but dependent on the property's occupancy level.* Maintenance and repairs are typically considered a variable expense, as are any utilities to the living units furnished by the lessor. Another common variable expense is management fees (often expressed as a percent). Since it is not logical that property managers, or a management company, are rewarded for vacant units or property, the percentage is typically based upon EGI rather than PGI. Thus, management fees are considered a variable expense since the expense varies based on occupancy. Other examples of variable expenses *might* be legal and accounting fees that are charged on a non-consistent basis and other miscellaneous expenses.

Reserves for Replacement

There are certain components or items of any structure that will need to be replaced from time to time throughout the life of the building. For an income-producing property, the anticipated cost of replacing these components or items is addressed by *reserves for replacement.* **Reserves for replacement** (sometimes called just **reserves**) *refers to an amount of money set aside for future replacement of major items.* When used in an income analysis, the replacement reserve is most often applied as an annual dollar (or sometimes as a percentage) amount.

» *Operating expenses encompass all of the expenses that are necessary to adequately maintain a property and its income potential* «

Although there could certainly be others, common components or items for residential income properties for which a replacement reserve is typically considered include roof, heating and/or air conditioning systems, carpeting, and lessor furnished appliances.

Rent and Income Factors

Multipliers are **rent and income factors** frequently used in the valuation of many residential income properties. The use of rent and income factors as a technique in the income approach is an income capitalization method. As we will discuss in Chapter 6, in order for a meaningful and credible value opinion to result from applying multipliers, the data from which the multiplier is extracted must be very similar to the subject in many ways—physical features, lease terms, and income expense history.

A multiplier is not a percentage. A multiplier is identified as a factor derived by dividing the sale price (or sometimes value) of a comparable property by its *gross* income or, in some cases, rent. Multipliers are derived using this formula:

Sale Price (Value) ÷ Gross Income (or Rent) = Multiplier

There are two types of multipliers that can be applied. The type the appraiser will choose depends on the property characteristics and is decided in the scope of work of the assignment. These factors are known as *gross rent multipliers* and *gross income multipliers*.

Gross Rent Multipliers

A **gross rent multiplier,** or **GRM**, is *a factor derived from comparable rental data, which is then used to develop an opinion of value of the subject property.* A GRM is used when the property has income that is derived only from actual rent of the living units. Although the multiplier could be expressed as either a monthly or annual factor, it is most commonly derived on a *monthly* basis for residential properties. As we will see in Chapter 7, most residential appraisal forms report the development of the income approach by this technique in such a manner.

Some information sources discuss a **gross monthly rent multiplier**, or **GMRM**. While this may not be a widely used or applied term, when used, the term emphasizes that the factor is expressed as monthly. However, the term GRM is most prevalent and is applied most frequently on a monthly basis. The key is consistency. If extracted from comparable data as a monthly factor, the multiplier must be applied to monthly rent data as well.

Gross Income Multipliers

A **gross income multiplier**, or **GIM**, is *a factor that takes into account income derived from all sources of a property.* It is most often used when there are income-producing capabilities of a property other than rent derived from living units.

> ***For Example:*** A small residential income property with four units might have garage or parking spaces that rent to parties other than the occupants of the living units. Or, there might be a coin-operated laundry facility on the premises that derives income.

It is most common for GIMs to be derived from and applied to *annual* income. However, the process of derivation and application of the factor is much the same as the GRM.

The basis of income derived from, and applied to, the development of the GIM technique could be based on either potential gross income (PGI) or effective gross income (EGI). In such cases, the multiplier resulting would be either a **potential gross income multiplier**, or **PGIM,** or an **effective gross income multiplier**, or **EGIM**.

» *Rent and income factors, as well as rates of return can be extracted from market data and applied to the subject's rent or income to produce an indication of value* «

Application Example of PGIM vs. EGIM

If a comparable income property was significantly similar to the subject with the exception of its occupancy level, extracting an EGIM factor from the data would prove to be more meaningful than using the comparable property's PGIM. Of course, in such a case, the EGIM that was identified from the comparable property would be applied to the subject's EGI, rather than the PGI.

We will look at this application more closely in Chapter 6.

Rates of Return

There are various **rates of return** that can be used in different techniques for development of a value opinion using an income capitalization method. Two types of rates that will be discussed here are the overall capitalization rate (an income rate), and yield rate (reflects the anticipation of all future benefit returns).

Overall Capitalization Rate

As a component of one of the most common income capitalization methods, the **overall capitalization rate** is *used to interpret a property's single year net operating income to the property's value using direct capitalization.* There are two components that comprise the overall capitalization rate (signified by R_O—rate to overall). These components are the weighted average of the loan to value ratio (LTV) of the rate to mortgage ($M \times R_M$), and rate to the equity portion ($[1\text{-}M] \times R_E$); thus:

$$M \times R_M + (1\text{-}M) \times R_E = R_O$$

The formula in which the rate, stated as a percent, is extracted for application in direct capitalization—known as **IVR**, as follows:

(Net Operating) Income ÷ Value = Rate

Techniques for determining an overall capitalization rate as well as how the direct capitalization technique is developed will be fully illustrated in Chapter 6.

Overall Yield Rate

An **overall yield rate** differs from a direct capitalization rate as it *considers a series of annual figures over the entire investment period as well as reversion.* The use of yield capitalization in most residential appraising is not common. Thus, the term is being presented here only for the purpose of defining how the concept differs from that of the overall capitalization rate and direct capitalization.

Selected USPAP Illustrations and Guidance

The following USPAP Advisory Opinion (AO) and Frequently Asked Questions (FAQ) have been selected to illustrate the application of USPAP in specific circumstances discussed in this chapter.

FAQ 283—Reporting Work Not Done in an Assignment

FAQ 302—Developing "Unnecessary" Approach

Application Case Study

A real property appraiser has accepted an assignment for a single-family residential property located in an established residential neighborhood that is within his regular service area. The property has been owner-occupied by the same owner for over 40 years. The client, a local lender, has specified that they would need only the most abbreviated appraisal possible, developing and reporting only the sales comparison approach as an indication of the final value opinion. The appraiser has significant experience and familiarity with properties in the subject's neighborhood as well as the neighborhood characteristics. But, it has been about a year since he has performed an appraisal in the immediate subject area and therefore has not analyzed the market conditions and the neighborhood characteristics since his last appraisal assignment in that area. He, however, feels competency is not an issue (and for the purpose of this case study, it will be assumed that the appraiser possesses competency).

Based on the information received from the client, the appraiser concurs that developing only the sales comparison approach in the assignment should be sufficient in the scope of work to produce credible results.

During the course of analyzing the immediate subject market and neighborhood, the appraiser finds nine sales within the past year of single-family residential properties, similar to the subject. All of these sales are confirmed to be arm's-length transactions. In addition, the neighborhood market analysis conducted by the appraiser indicates the following trend in single-family residential dwelling occupancies of owner-occupied vs. tenant-occupied:

	12 Months Ago	Current
Owner-Occupied	60%	45%
Tenant-Occupied	40%	55%

Upon further discussion with parties to the nine sales transactions that the appraiser identified, the appraiser finds that six of the properties in those nine transactions sold to an investor and three to owner-occupants. Rental data was derived from the interviews regarding the tenant-occupied properties. It was also discovered that three of the tenant-occupied properties shared very similar physical characteristics with the subject (size, bedrooms, baths, etc.), and rented soon after the sale transactions for what appears to be market level rent.

How does this information change the appraiser's initial scope of work decision regarding the income approach?

How does the client's request to only develop the sales comparison approach in the assignment affect the appraiser's decision?

Is the sales comparison approach still applicable in the assignment?

Quiz

1. ***The best example of when the income approach should be considered applicable is when the subject property***
   a. has more than three bedrooms.
   b. has two or more living units.
   c. is in an undesirable location.
   d. is owner-occupied

2. ***If the client requests the income approach be developed and presented in the appraisal assignment and the appraiser accepts the assignment, the appraiser***
   a. can choose whether or not to do so.
   b. cannot accept requests for specific approaches in an assignment.
   c. must comply with the request.
   d. must develop the income approach but cannot consider it during reconciliation and final analysis.

3. ***The income-producing characteristic or potential may reveal itself***
   a. during the property inspection.
   b. in reconciliation.
   c. in the final analysis.
   d. while writing the report.

4. ***The scope of work***
   a. can be modified after the assignment commences.
   b. can be modified only if the client requests it.
   c. can be modified only with the client's permission.
   d. cannot be modified once the assignment commences.

5. ***The _______________ is the landlord's ownership interest in the property and the _______________ represents the temporary right of the tenant to possession, without title.***
   a. leased fee estate; leasehold estate
   b. leased fee estate; partial interest
   c. leasehold estate; leased fee estate
   d. leasehold estate; partial interest

6. ***What type of lease requires rental payments be made at regular intervals, but allows for the payment amount to change based on changes in market rent?***
   a. annual increase lease
   b. percentage lease
   c. revaluation lease
   d. variable lease

7. ***What type of lease is most likely to be seen with retail units inside a shopping mall?***
   a. net lease
   b. percentage lease
   c. revaluation lease
   d. variable lease

8. ***Ashley pays $900 a month for her 2-bedroom apartment. An appraiser concludes that the market rent is $1,200. There is a $300 per month _______ rent.***
   a. contract
   b. deficit
   c. excess
   d. overage

9. ***The potential gross income, less vacancy and collection losses is the***
   a. effective gross income (EGI).
   b. gross rent multiplier (GRM).
   c. net operating income (NOI).
   d. potential gross income (PGI).

10. ***Repairs, maintenance, and real estate taxes are alike in that they are all***
    a. fixed expenses.
    b. operating expenses.
    c. reserves for replacement.
    d. variable expenses.

Income Analysis

6

Income analysis, in a market value assignment, is an interpretation of what a *typical* investor's actions or reactions might be. In order to correctly make this interpretation, the appraiser must analyze data reflecting what typical investors have done in the past, and what they might do in the future and apply the conclusions of that analysis using accepted techniques. The income approach is closely related to the principle of anticipation, as the methodology analyzes the expectations of the typical investor for the benefit of a particular investment property.

Although there are numerous income techniques, in this chapter our discussion will be limited to two particular techniques of income analysis:

1. The use of multipliers, and
2. The use of direct capitalization using an overall capitalization rate.

Both of these techniques are methods of capitalization, and technically, both are categorized by some as being a form of direct capitalization. However, some sources in the industry make a distinction between them. Thus, we will treat these income capitalization techniques separately for ease of presentation and learning.

While in most small residential appraisal assignments the use of multipliers is appropriate, in others, the direct capitalization approach (using an overall capitalization rate) will be warranted in the scope of work. There is no standardized or uniform requirement for which approach is used in a particular assignment. However, generally accepted practices suggest that multipliers are typically used in small residential income properties consisting of one to four units and the direct capitalization approach is used for properties with more than four units. Clients and intended users may have guidelines or requirements specifying a particular approach (such as Fannie Mae).

When an income approach is necessary for credible results, the appraiser should be aware of competency requirements in developing the particular method or technique, which includes limitations of state regulatory agencies. Some jurisdictions may place limitations on development of a particular method or technique based on the appraiser's credentials. These limitations may also extend to the type of property being appraised, the complexity of the assignment, or a dollar value of the property being appraised. However, the techniques demonstrated in this chapter and their components are common topics for the national appraiser examinations. Therefore, students of appraisal should be knowledgeable of these techniques as well as their components and development.

USPAP provides guidance regarding the income approach in Standards Rule 1-4(c), which, among other things, requires the appraiser, when the income approach is appropriate, to (in part):

- Perform an analysis of the comparable rental data (as available), and analyze the earning potential of the subject to estimate the gross income potential of the property.
- Analyze comparable operating expense data (as available) to estimate a rate of capitalization.
- Establish projections of future rent or income potential and expenses on reasonably clear and appropriate evidence.

Multipliers

A **multiplier** is *a factor that is derived from market data and applied to the subject's market rent or income to produce a value indication in an income approach*. For the residential appraiser, the use of multipliers will be the most frequently employed income valuation technique in a market value assignment. The **gross rent multiplier (GRM)** and the **gross income multiplier (GIM)** are discussed here. While the use of these multipliers is fairly simple, the derivation and application of a multiplier must be carefully performed. Therefore, there are some very important things to keep in mind when using this technique:

- The GRM and the GIM consider only the *gross* rent or income of the property, and, therefore, do not consider expense items.
- The GRM, and the most common form of the GIM, do not consider any losses attributable to vacancy of the living unit(s) and/or inability to collect rent.
- The market rent used in the application of a GRM to the subject property (or in the case of a GIM, total income) must reflect market level.
- The comparable properties must be *very* similar physically, and in lease terms and conditions.

Gross Rent Multiplier—GRM

Developing a value opinion using the **GRM** technique of income capitalization consists of just two primary steps:

1. Determine the appropriate GRM from market data.

2. Apply the GRM to the subject's market rent to indicate a value conclusion.

While the actual steps in using a multiplier are relatively simple in application, the technique can yield misleading or false results if the data being used for the analysis is inconsistent, irrelevant, or not well analyzed. Let's take a closer look at how the GRM is derived and applied.

» *Inconsistent, irrelevant, or poorly analyzed information applied when utilizing the GRM or the GIM technique can lead to misleading or poor results* «

KEY TERMS

Band of Investment A technique for determining an overall capitalization rate by weighting and combining the various components of an investment.

Direct Capitalization An income method that takes a property's single-year net operating income or NOI into a value indication by applying an overall capitalization rate: NOI ÷ Overall Capitalization Rate = Value.

EGIM A factor derived and applied using EGI—the amount after estimated vacancy has been deducted from PGI.

Equity Capitalization Rate The capitalization rate applied to the expectation of return on equity (symbolized by R_E).

IVR A formula or technique that derives an overall capitalization rate: Income (NOI) ÷ Value (Sale Price) = Rate.

Mortgage Capitalization Rate A return on the money lent in an investment (symbolized by R_M).

Mortgage Constant The ratio between annual debt service and loan principal.

Multiplier A factor that is derived from market data and applied to the subject's market rent or income to produce a value indication in an income approach.

PGIM A fund factor derived from, and applied to, the total gross income generated by the property without vacancy being considered.

Rent Roll Briefly details the unit information, such as lease terms, contract rent, as well as the effective date of the leases that are in place for the property.

Rent Survey A compilation of the rents being generated (and often rent history) in a particular market for a particular property type.

VIM A formula used to derive the appropriate multiplier from the transaction data: V (sale price) ÷ I (gross monthly rent) = M (multiplier).

Determining the GRM from Market Data

To derive a GRM from market data, the value of the comparable property is divided by that property's gross market rent to conclude on a multiplier that can be used in later analysis.

When used in a market value appraisal assignment, this data will be extracted from arm's-length transactions of properties that were rented at the time of the sale transaction or rented soon after the sale at a verifiable market level rent. Ideally, this information comes from the appraiser's own files—data collected in the course of other appraisal assignments. However, the data could also come from other appraisers or parties to a transaction, or those who are familiar with a particular transaction (e.g., the real estate broker). The following is an example of data, that once verified, could lead to a significant error if used for analysis:

> ***For Example:*** John purchases his parents' home when his parents decide to move to an assisted care facility. John acquired the property to use as a rental. The transaction sale price was admittedly below market value and the sale did not reflect an arm's-length transaction.

In this case, this transaction should probably be discarded as it was not arm's-length.

In order for the analysis to be meaningful and produce true results, the market rent applied in the analysis should be consistent with the physical condition of the property.

> ***For Example:*** An investor purchases a rental property in below average condition. Immediately after the sale, the investor spends several thousand dollars on renovations prior to securing a tenant for the property at a market level rent based on the features and condition of the property after the renovations.

The appraiser must ensure that the sale price in a transaction is consistent with the rent being used in the analysis or misleading and false conclusions will result.

Determining Market Rent

Appraisers do consider the contract rent of the comparable data, as well as that of the subject, later when the GRM is applied. However, the purpose of this is to test the current (contract) rent against that of the market. In some cases, contract rent and market rent will be the same. But, to make this assumption only because two parties have agreed upon a certain level of rent is an unacceptable practice on the part of the appraiser. What the lessor and the lessee have agreed upon may represent something different than what typical parties would do in a similar transaction. This could be thought of as being similar to conditions of an arm's-length sales transaction, which were discussed in Chapter 3, where the parties might be related, unknowledgeable, under haste or duress, etc. Remember, real estate markets are imperfect and parties to a lease transaction may not behave in an informed, rational, and consistent manner, and conditions of a real estate market can change rapidly. Some other common examples of circumstances where market rent may be different from contract rent could be:

- The agreement was reached in a different market climate with different market conditions.

- The lessee is performing certain repairs or improvements to the property in exchange for reduced rent.
- The lessor is performing or providing specialized improvements, services, or items (that may not be recognized by other potential tenants) required by the specific lessee in exchange for a higher rent.
- The lease agreement could be for a temporary or an extended period of time, thus the contract rent could be higher or lower than that in a typical lease period.

When developing value opinions by any income method or technique, the appraiser must ensure that any rents being used in the assignment reflect a market level. Rent surveys provide a significant role in that determination. Here as well, consistency is important in producing a quality rent survey. The survey should include properties that share similar:

- Locational desirability.
- Physical characteristics.
- Lease terms and conditions.

For this process, the rental properties examined in the survey do not necessarily need to be properties that have recently transacted. In fact, many clients and intended users prefer the data come from properties other than those used to derive the GRM.

» In a market value assignment, the appraiser must ensure that any rents being used in the analysis reflect market level—rent surveys are typically performed to assist with the determination «

Let's look at some data that was gathered from single-family rental properties in a particular neighborhood. When looking at the following chart, assume the appraiser has already determined that the rental data reflects current market conditions and that the lease agreements are typical. The desirability of the properties being analyzed is also similar.

Rent Survey

	Rental #1	Rental #2	Rental #3	Rental #4	Rental #5	Rental #6
Bedrooms	3	2	3	3	3	3
Gross Living Area	1,100 +/-	1,100 +/-	1,100 +/-	1,250 +/-	1,250 +/-	1,000 +/-
Central Air-Conditioning	Yes	Yes	No	Yes	Yes	Yes
Garage	1-car	1-car	1-car	None	1-car	1-car
Monthly Rent	$600	$550	$575	$550	$600	$600

Broadly, what can be seen in the preceding chart is that a resulting rate of rent is between $550 and $600 per month, with $600 being the most frequently observed (mode). Obviously, rent surveys are necessary for different property types and markets. Once completed, they are treated as stored data by the appraiser. Just as we discussed in Chapter 3 (regarding comparable sale data becoming part of the appraiser's data bank), the information must be monitored and reanalyzed for relevance with each assignment.

Depending on the scope of work in the assignment, an unadjusted range ($550 - $600), or the mode ($600) may be sufficient to support the market rent of future data. However, some physical differences can be observed for which a dollar amount could be assigned for the possible adjustments, or to support that no adjustment is warranted for a particular characteristic or feature.

» *The reliability of the GRM or GIM technique requires that the comparable data be very similar to the subject physically, in lease terms, and in market conditions as of the effective date of the subject appraisal* «

The appraiser, in conducting the rent survey, chose certain characteristics or features as primary comparison points (e.g., number of bedrooms, gross living area, central air-conditioning, and garage provisions). These elements could vary depending on the particular property, the market, property type, size, price point, etc. Knowledge of the market and market participants will assist the appraiser in recognizing the most relevant analysis.

Adjusting Rent Data

The GRM itself is not usually adjusted, however, the market rent of a property can be adjusted from information extracted in the rent survey using paired data. Let's look at what the data in the rent survey revealed.

Bedrooms

When Rental #1 is paired with Rental #2, the difference in rent of a two-bedroom dwelling vs. a three-bedroom dwelling is revealed.

	Rental #1	Rental #2
Bedrooms	3	2
Gross Living Area	1,100 +/-	1,100 +/-
Central Air-Conditioning	Yes	Yes
Garage	1-car	1-car
Monthly Rent	$600	$550

The only difference between the properties is the additional bedroom of Rental #1, which can be associated with the $50 per month rent difference.

Gross Living Area

To examine the effect of the variation of gross living area, Rental #1, Rental #5, and Rental #6 are analyzed.

	Rental #1	Rental #5	Rental #6
Bedrooms	3	3	3
Gross Living Area	1,100 +/-	1,250 +/-	1,000 +/-
Central Air-Conditioning	Yes	Yes	Yes
Garage	1-car	1-car	1-car
Monthly Rent	$600	$600	$600

Interestingly enough, this analysis supports the appraiser's conclusion that, at least for this particular market segment, participants are not reacting to moderate differences in the size of the dwelling. Rather, they are associating the rent with the number of bedrooms. This certainly might not hold true in every market and with every property type. However, with some markets and properties, gross living area could have less to do with the typical renter's action than the utility of the property, which in this case is the number of bedrooms.

Central Air-Conditioning

Compare Rental #1 to Rental #3 to determine the effect of central air-conditioning.

	Rental #1	Rental #3
Bedrooms	3	3
Gross Living Area	1,100 +/-	1,100 +/-
Central Air-Conditioning	Yes	No
Garage	1-car	1-car
Monthly Rent	$600	$575

The analysis indicates that central air-conditioning contributes $25 to the monthly rent.

Garage

Compare Rental #4 to Rental #5 to determine the effect of a 1-car garage.

	Rental #4	Rental #5
Bedrooms	3	3
Gross Living Area	1,250 +/-	1,250 +/-
Central Air-Conditioning	Yes	Yes
Garage	None	1-car
Monthly Rent	$550	$600

The indicated contribution to the monthly rent of a 1-car garage is $50.

Of course, when identifying if adjustments are warranted, these comparisons can and should be made for any significant condition or characteristic of the property. And, like adjustments that are identified as typical for use in the sales comparison approach, adjustments extracted from rent data can be stored by the appraiser and applied in other assignments. However, great care must be taken to ensure that the adjustments reflect typical market response and are not applied simply as a predetermined or "canned" adjustment for which relevance has not been carefully considered.

» *In some appraisal assignments, it will be necessary for the appraiser to adjust the comparable rental data to more closely reflect the subject property* «

Here is an example of a circumstance when adjustments might be applied to rental data. For this example, the adjustments identified previously will be used:

Bedroom - $50 per month

Central Air-Conditioning - $25 per month

Garage - $50 per month

For Example: A residential real property appraiser is performing an appraisal of a single-family dwelling for a mortgage finance transaction. The lender-client has informed the appraiser that the borrower is purchasing the property for use as an investment and intends to rent the house. However, the property is currently vacant and does not have a recent rental history. The scope of work includes the appraiser determining a reasonable market rent for the subject property and developing a value opinion by the income approach.

The appraiser finds no rental properties in that particular market that share the exact same characteristics as the subject. However, rental properties with varying characteristics have been identified. If market conditions, conditions of the neighborhood, typical renter profile, etc., for the subject property are similar to the market in which the previous adjustments were identified, those adjustments could be applied to the rent data that is available for this particular market. Here are the subject's characteristics and the rent data obtained from the subject's neighborhood.

	Subject	**Rental #1**		**Rental #2**		**Rental #3**		**Rental #4**	
Contract Rent	—		$600		$510		$575		$500
Bedrooms	3	3		3		3		2	+ $50
Central A/C	Yes	Yes		No	+ $25	Yes		Yes	
Garage	None	1-car	- $50	None		1-car	- $50	None	
Adjusted Rent	—		$550		$535		$525		$550

From this information, the rent data, unadjusted, was far from conclusive and fairly broad ($500 - $600 per month). However, after adjusting the data, a reasonable market rent for the subject becomes more defined. As a conclusion, the appraiser chooses $550 per month as being a reasonable market rent to apply to the subject, as it appears most frequently (mode) among the adjusted rents, and thus is best supported. Also note that the appraiser's conclusion of $550 per month is bracketed within the current contract rents in the neighborhood ($500 - $600 per month).

Analysis of Transactional Data

Data derived from transactions of properties that were rented at the time of the sale, or shortly thereafter, reflect the expectation of the investor for the rent that is or could be collected. This is one of the more common expectations related to the principle of anticipation.

Once there is verification that the transaction is arm's-length, and that the rent produced reasonably represents market level, the process of indentifying a GRM from the transaction is fairly simple.

The appraiser begins the analysis by collecting information from arm's-length transactions of rental properties that are as similar to the subject as possible.

Again, as mentioned in Chapter 5, a GRM can be derived and applied as either a monthly or an annual factor, using either monthly or annual rent. The monthly method will be illustrated here as it most commonly reflects the application on most residential appraisal reporting forms.

The next step is to *derive the appropriate multiplier from the transaction data* by using a formula known as **VIM**, *value divided by income equals multiplier.*

V (sale price) ÷ I (gross monthly rent) = M (multiplier)

Let's continue on with the scenario in the previous example.

For Example: Once the appraiser determines a reasonable market rent for the subject property, he researches and analyzes transaction data from the market and identifies an indicated GRM by using VIM. The following is revealed:

	Sale Price	Monthly Rent	(Formula)	GRM
1	$66,200	$530	(66,200 ÷ 530)	124.91
2	$73,000	$590	(73,000 ÷ 590)	123.73
3	$75,000	$610	(75,000 ÷ 610)	122.95
4	$65,000	$525	(65,000 ÷ 525)	123.81
5	$65,500	$500	(65,500 ÷ 500)	131.00
6	$70,000	$575	(70,000 ÷ 575)	121.74
7	$72,800	$650	(72,800 ÷ 650)	112.00
8	$68,000	$520	(68,000 ÷ 520)	130.77

In the appraiser's final analysis of the developed range of GRMs, he notes that the most common result is around 123.00, with those results ranging from just slightly less than 123.00 to the upper 123.00 range.

	Sale Price	Monthly Rent	GRM
1	$66,200	$530	124.91
2	$73,000	$590	**123.73**
3	$75,000	$610	**122.95**
4	$65,000	$525	**123.81**
5	$65,500	$500	131.00
6	$70,000	$575	121.74
7	$72,800	$650	112.00
8	$68,000	$520	130.77

In reconciling a GRM conclusion, the appraiser could choose to use 123.00 as a GRM, or probably better, place most weight on #2 (123.73) and #4 (123.81), since the GRM from those transactions most closely brackets the subject's estimated market rent of $550. For this reason, the appraiser chooses a GRM of 123.75 to apply to the subject.

» *Multipliers are derived from comparable data by using a formula known as VIM: Value ÷ Income = Multiplier* «

Applying the GRM to the Subject

Developing a value indication for a subject property using a GRM is considered in the industry to be the simplest, if not one of the most time efficient, of the income capitalization techniques. However, as just illustrated, the simplicity and ease in this final step of the technique comes only after a very thorough analysis in determining an appropriate and relevant multiplier to apply, and a reasonable opinion of market rent to which the multiplier is applied.

To develop a value opinion using the GRM technique, the appraiser multiplies the monthly market rent of the subject by the selected multiplier.

M (multiplier) x I (monthly market rent) = V (value)

Let's illustrate this application by continuing with our previous example.

> ***For Example:*** The appraiser has chosen $550 per month as a reasonable opinion of market rent for the subject property and a GRM of 123.75 to apply to the rent. Thus, the results of the appraiser's conclusions are as follows:
>
> **123.75 x $550 = $68,062.50, or rounded, $68,000**

In summary, the GRM technique for use in the development of an indication of value by the income approach is the most common and frequently employed method in assignments of single-family and small residential income properties of 2-4 living units. As you'll see in Chapter 7, for residential assignments, for the most common intended use (mortgage finance transactions), many clients and intended users (e.g., Fannie Mae and others) specify that the GRM technique be developed and reported when an income approach is applicable.

In order for the GRM technique to produce meaningful and credible results, the subject property must be located in an area in which there is an established market for rental properties and data is available. When there is a scarcity or lack of relevant data, or where significant dissimilarities exist in available data, the method diminishes in reliability. *In many cases, these circumstances may cause the income approach to be inapplicable in an assignment.*

Gross Income Multipliers

Now that the fundamental concepts of the income approach using the GRM technique have been presented, the development and function of a **gross income multiplier**, or **GIM**, will be much easier to understand. Fundamental concepts of the GIM and the GRM are very similar in many respects, but some things are different.

The use of a GIM is appropriate when the subject property produces income in addition to rent from the living unit(s). With a GIM, both the rent and the other income are used for the analysis, while the GRM considers only rent.

There are some special things to know about using the GIM in a market value assignment. Each of these points will be discussed and illustrated:

- Other sources of income must be determined legally permissible and to reasonably have the potential to be ongoing.
- The rent and income derived from comparable data and applied to the subject property is considered on an annual basis.
- The income used in determining a GIM could be the potential gross income (PGI), or the effective gross income (EGI) and must be derived and applied consistently.
- The GIM is derived from properties with similar rent and (other) income flows.

The particular feature or additional use of the property for which other income is being considered must be legally permissible by private and public regulations. In addition, the appraiser must determine that the source of the income could be reasonably determined to be applicable and desirable to those who comprise the market for such property. Let's look at some examples.

> ***For Example:*** A single-family rental property has a garage located at the rear of the property. The garage is rented to an automotive mechanic. However, the subdivision restrictions, as well as zoning, prohibit such use of the garage. In this case, the use does not conform and the income should not be considered.

This example illustrates that the garage's use might be detracting from the rental dwelling, or not what the typical landlord's action might be. A better way to analyze the subject property might be to consider the garage as a feature of the rental dwelling. Following is a similar scenario where the garage would most likely be expected (or contribute more) as a common amenity of the rental dwelling from a market standpoint.

> ***For Example:*** Consider that a rental dwelling has been rented to the current lessee for an extended period of time. The lessee is somewhat unique in that he does not drive or own an automobile. Therefore, the garage is rented separately to the next-door neighbor for storage of her boat, while the rent of the dwelling is discounted due to the lessee not needing the garage.

In this example, the appraiser would need to consider if the typical tenant for such a property would expect a garage as a feature and have a use for it.

> √ ***In Other Words:*** Is the ongoing use, as it is currently, typical for landlords and tenants?

Very likely, a typical tenant would own an automobile and, thus, the typical landlord would rent the garage with the dwelling for use by the dwelling's occupant. In this case, the income from the rent of the garage to a third party should not be considered as other income, but rather analyzed with the rental dwelling, basing the market rent on similar houses with garages and using a GRM instead, ideally deriving the multiplier from properties that have garages included in the rent.

A good way to consider whether the feature or potential use generating the income should be considered in the analysis (therefore indicating the applicability of the GIM technique) is for the appraiser to think like a typical investor for such a property and to apply the principle of anticipation. Is this potential income source one that would be recognized and desired by most typical investors—one that does not detract from the rental unit(s) and would be considered an ongoing benefit to the investment?

The GIM technique could be applied to most non-residential properties, and may be relevant and ideal for some properties that are primarily residential in nature. In most residential cases, the GIM technique will be used more frequently for properties having two to four units or mixed-use properties, such as a non-residential use of a lower-floor unit, with a residential use of the upper floor. However, there may be circumstances in which the GIM could be applied to a single-family investment property.

The GIM, as mentioned earlier, could be developed using either PGI or EGI. The primary determinant of how the appraiser considers the multiplier depends on how the additional income flow is coming in. Very simply, is the source of the additional income based upon the occupancy level of the living units? This assists the appraiser in choosing to apply the GIM, defining the factor as either a **potential gross income multiplier (PGIM)**, or an **effective gross income multiplier (EGIM)**.

PGIM

The **PGIM** is *derived from, and applied to, the total gross income generated by the property without vacancy being considered.* This is probably the most common application of a GIM, and is appropriate when the source of the additional income is not influenced by the occupancy of the living unit(s).

> ***For Example:*** A rather large older residential dwelling in an established neighborhood features a four-stall garage, with each stall divided by an interior wall, and is situated at the rear of the property, along an alley. Two of the garage stalls are for the use of the renter of the dwelling and are included in its rent, while the other two have been rented for many years to other parties for storage. The two rented garage stalls generate $75 income per month each.

This example illustrates a circumstance when the PGIM would be perfectly logical, since the rental income of the garages is not influenced by the occupancy of the rental dwelling.

EGIM

EGIM is *derived using EGI—the amount after estimated vacancy has been deducted from PGI.* The EGIM is warranted when living unit occupancy is related to the potential for income from other sources.

> ***For Example:*** A four-unit apartment building has a small common laundry room with coin-operated washers, dryers, and vending services for the tenants' use. There are no provisions in the apartment units for washer/dryer hook-up by the lessee. At full occupancy, the laundry facility generates approximately $1,200 annually in additional income for the lessor.

» *A GIM can be based upon the potential gross income of a property (PGIM), or its effective gross income (EGIM)* «

In this example, the additional income is dependent on the occupancy level of the apartment building. The higher the vacancy, the less the laundry is used and, thus, income is diminished. Therefore, the income used in the GIM analysis might be best considered from the standpoint of EGI, using an EGIM.

Determining the GIM from Market Data

Deriving the GIM from market data is performed in much the same way as the GRM is derived using VIM:

Value ÷ (Annual) Income = Multiplier

Something to keep in mind when deriving the GIM: The factor must be derived consistently with how it will be applied to the subject data.

> ***For Example:*** If the subject property has an additional source of income that is not dependent on occupancy of the living unit(s), similar data (in this case using PGI) is analyzed. But, if the subject property has an additional income feature that is related to the occupancy of the living unit(s), the EGI of the comparable data is analyzed. The process of derivation and application must be consistent.

When analyzing market data for the purpose of deriving a GIM, the primary concern is that if the subject has constant income, the data analyzed also has constant income. Likewise, if the subject has an additional income source that fluctuates depending on occupancy, market data of other properties that have similar fluctuating income must be used in the analysis.

Ideally, if the subject has additional income from coin-operated vending, the data used to derive the GIM would similarly derive additional income through coin-operated vending. However, in reality, data with exact similarities is rarely available and the appraiser must seek to simply analyze data that has a similar benefit to the investor.

For Example: The subject of an appraisal, a leased residence generating $7,200 in market rent annually, has a small additional storage building that produces a consistent income of $1,200 per year, based on an annual lease to another party. No similar data featuring a storage building can be located by the appraiser.

The appraiser has located a similar rented residence generating $6,300 in market rent that has a billboard facing a highway at the rear of the property. The space on which the billboard is placed is leased, on an annual basis, to the advertising company for $1,200 per year. The property sold four months ago in similar market conditions for $179,000.

While the source of the income is not consistent, the income and the consistent basis from which it is derived are the same. Most likely this is what the typical investor would consider in forming his conclusions about the anticipatory benefit of the investment— consistent like dollars for consistent like dollars. Therefore, the GIM (in this case PGIM) could be derived from the property with the billboard and applied to the property with the storage building.

The PGIM is extracted from the sale data using VIM, producing the following conclusion:

$179,000 ÷ $7,500 ($6,300 + $1,200) = 23.87

The same process used in the previous example is used for identifying an EGIM (but with additional steps) when the flow of other income is dependent on the occupancy of the units. This is illustrated in the following example.

For Example: The subject property is a four-unit apartment building with a coin-operated laundry facility. PGI of the rental units totals $2,000 per month. At full occupancy, the laundry facility averages $100 per month.

A recently transacted comparable property has been found within the subject's market. It is a four-unit property with PGI of $1,800 per month, and four parking spaces that rent separately (and only) to the tenants for $25 per month each. The property indicated a vacancy rate of 4.8%, which was deemed to be consistent with the market. The transaction price of the property was $338,000.

While the sources of income are different in the example, both sources of income are controlled by the tenants and influenced by occupancy. Thus, it is appropriate to derive the GIM (in this case EGIM) from the recently transacted property.

(continued on next page)

For Example continued:

The steps for deriving an EGIM are as follows:

Step 1: Determine annual income from rent.

$1,800 monthly from rental units x 12 months = $21,600 annual income from rent

Step 2: Determine annual income from parking spaces.

4 parking spaces @ $25 per month =
$100 monthly x 12 months = $1,200 annual income

Step 3: Determine total PGI for the property.

$21,600 + $1,200 = $22,800

Step 4: Determine loss due to vacancy by applying the market vacancy rate to PGI.

$22,800 x 4.8% (0.048) = $1,094.40

Step 5: Determine EGI by subtracting vacancy loss from PGI

$22,800 - $1,094.40 = $21,705.60

Step 6: Use VIM to derive the EGIM.

$338,000 (Transaction Price) ÷ $21,705.60 (EGI) = 15.57 EGIM (rounded)

» *The GRM and the GIM are applied to the subject's market level rent or income by multiplying the rent or income by the multiplier* «

The preceding examples illustrate the basic steps taken to determine the GIM using PGI and EGI. There are certainly variations of doing so and specific situations could lead to modifications of these techniques that are discussed in more advanced coursework. The methodology of estimating vacancy rates will be discussed later in this chapter.

Applying the GIM to the Subject

The GIM is applied to the total market income of the subject property in a similar manner as was illustrated for applying a GRM to the subject property's market rent. As a reminder, the appraiser must be careful to apply the GIM consistently with how the multiplier was derived. If the multiplier was derived from PGI, then the multiplier (PGIM) must be applied to the subject's PGI. If the multiplier was derived from EGI, the multiplier (EGIM) must be applied to the EGI of the subject. We will use the subject's income and the derived PGIM or EGIM from the previous examples to illustrate.

Applying the PGIM

In a previous example, the subject property was a single-family dwelling generating $7,200 annually in market rent. A storage building on the property produced $1,200 per year in other income. The indicated PGIM derived from comparable market data was 23.87.

To develop an indication of the subject's value, the subject's determined PGI is multiplied by the PGIM:

$8,400 ($7,200 + $1,200) x 23.87 = $200,508

The appraiser would probably round the indication to $200,000, or maybe $201,000.

Applying the EGIM

In a previous example, the subject was a four-unit apartment building, generating $2,000 monthly market rent from the living units and $100 per month from the coin-operated laundry when the living units are at full occupancy. The market extracted vacancy rate given in the example was 4.8% and the indicated EGIM derived from comparable data was 15.57.

To develop an indication of value for the subject, PGI for the subject must first be calculated:

$24,000 ($2,000 rent x 12 months)
+ 1,200 ($100 laundry income x 12 months)
$25,200 PGI

Now the vacancy factor must be calculated and subtracted from PGI to result in EGI:

$25,200 x 4.8% (0.048) = $1,209.60 Vacancy
$25,200 - $1,209.60 = $23,990.40 EGI

As a final step, the subject's EGI is multiplied by the EGIM to indicate a value conclusion:

$23,990.40 x 15.57 = $373,530.53

Depending on the assignment, the appraiser would probably round the developed value indication to $374,000, or maybe even $375,000, in reconciling the conclusions of the income approach.

Direct Capitalization Using an Overall Rate

Direct capitalization (using an overall capitalization rate) is *an income method that converts a property's single-year net operating income (NOI) into a value indication by applying an overall capitalization rate:*

NOI ÷ Overall Capitalization Rate = Value

This direct capitalization technique is considered by most to interpret typical investor reactions and motivations of a particular property. Be careful, however, to not confuse direct capitalization with yield capitalization, which considers a series of cash flows rather than a single year's income.

The direct capitalization technique is most relevant when the property's occupancy and net operating income are stabilized or established. There must also be relevant comparable transaction data available that can be analyzed.

» *Direct capitalization using an overall capitalization rate uses the NOI of a single year to indicate an opinion of value* «

The development of the direct capitalization technique requires two major components that are used in the final analysis from which to form conclusions:

1. Net Operating Income
2. Overall Capitalization Rate

Determining Net Income of the Subject Property

The **net income** or **net operating income** (**NOI**) of the subject property is the estimated amount the property owner or investor should realize (or did realize) after accounting for certain losses and operating expenses (including replacement reserves) for the property.

The steps in estimating NOI require a systematic and careful analysis. These steps are:

1. Determine PGI

2. Estimate Rates of Vacancy and Collection Losses

3. Determine EGI

4. Estimate Operating Expenses

5. Determine NOI

While these five steps may seem outwardly simple, the appraiser may spend a significant amount of time in analyzing the various components leading to an estimated NOI. For direct capitalization, the method considers all of these components on an *annual* basis.

The mathematical formula for NOI is as follows:

PGI
- Vacancy and Collection Losses
= EGI
- Operating Expenses
= NOI

Estimating PGI

PGI is the amount of income that a property is capable of generating if all the units are occupied without vacancy for the full year and all rents and other anticipated income are received without collection losses. Of course, by the very nature of gross income, PGI is estimated before any operating expenses are deducted.

PGI, as we have discussed with any rent or income applied in the income approach, is based upon market rent. And, while the contract rent of the subject is analyzed, that analysis is for the purpose of determining if the subject's actual or contract rent reflects a market level. For this analysis, the appraiser reviews leases of the property, or in the case of more than one unit, possibly a **rent roll**.

A **rent roll** *briefly details the unit information, lease terms, contract rent, as well as the effective date of the leases that are in place for the property*. Some will have more or differing information than this but let's look at a simple rent roll.

For Example: The subject of an appraisal assignment is a four-unit apartment building. All apartment units are on the first floor and are identical, with each having a living room, kitchen, two bedrooms, and a full bath. Each of the building's units is currently rented by a flat gross lease. Here is the rent roll for the property provided by the owner:

Unit	Tenant	Original Lease Date	Lease Term	Rent	Term Remaining	Escalation Clause
1	Smith	24 months ago	3 years	$650	12 months	None
2	Jones	Last week	1 year	$700	12 months	None
3	Brown	3 months ago	1 year	$700	9 months	None
4	White	20 months ago	3 years	$600	4 months	None

At first glance, it can probably be concluded that rents being produced by Unit #1 and Unit #4 are probably not at market level. These leases have been in effect for a while and given that the more recent leases for Unit #2 and Unit #3 each are at $700 per month, it is likely that Unit #1 and Unit #4 can be supported at a higher rent for the purpose of estimating PGI. The appraiser, however, must confirm through analysis of similar market data, that $700 per month is a reasonable reflection of market level rent.

As part of the analysis, an appraiser may compile a **rent survey.** A **rent survey** is *a compilation of the rents being generated (and often a rent history) in a particular market for a particular property type.*

For Example: The appraiser has arrayed a current rent survey for other income-producing properties in the subject's market area having similar 2-bedroom apartment units on ground level revealing the following observations:

	Rent Comparable #1	Rent Comparable #2	Rent Comparable #3	Rent Comparable #4
Description	Three Two-bedroom Units	Four Two-bedroom Units	Four Two-bedroom Units	Five Two-bedroom Units
Rents	$700 $700 $675	$725 $675 $700 $715	$650 $675 $700 $700	$700 $710 $700 $685 $675

What can easily be seen from this rent survey is that the subject's most current level of rent ($700) is bracketed within the range of rents reflected in the survey. Also, of the 16 units represented in this survey, apartment units renting at $700 per month are observed most frequently. Therefore, the appraiser is well supported in concluding $700 per month rent as being a reasonable market level for the purpose of his estimation of PGI for the subject property.

» *Rent surveys should be conducted periodically for particular property types in particular markets and become part of the appraiser's stored data* «

The appraiser has estimated the PGI for the subject property as follows:

4 Units x $700 x 12 = $33,600

$33,600 - PGI

Estimating Vacancy and Collection Losses and EGI

In most cases, both losses due to vacancy and losses due to collection are based on a percentage of the PGI. The percentage applied in the development of NOI is derived from information obtained through the property owner, analysis of the leases or rent roll, and from market data of other similar properties. Let's continue with our previous example.

For Example: The subject's property owner indicates that, typically, each time a unit is vacated, the unit is vacant for a period of approximately 14 days for refurbishing and marketing. The subject's rental history indicates that, in most cases, two units are vacant for that period of time each year. So, using these numbers for the subject, 28 days divided by 1,460 days (365 x 4 units) equals a vacancy rate of 1.92%.

However, this number may be low or high depending on what market data reveals. The vacancy rate should represent an appropriate market level. The appraiser must now analyze market data to confirm if what is estimated does indeed align with the market.

To derive an indication of market level vacancy rate, the appraiser further analyzes the properties that he reviewed in the rent survey, which reveal the following:

	Rent Comparable #1	**Rent Comparable #2**	**Rent Comparable #3**	**Rent Comparable #4**
Description	Three Two-bedroom Units	Four Two-bedroom Units	Four Two-bedroom Units	Five Two-bedroom Units
Observed Vacancy (Annual)	1.72 %	2.51%	2.38%	3.60%

From this information, a trend can be seen that the more units there are, the greater the potential is for a higher rate of vacancy to occur. This analysis also confirms that using the subject property owner's estimation of vacancy would not be representative of market level. Since the subject property is a four-unit, most confidence would probably be given to the four-unit properties surveyed—somewhere between 2.38% and 2.51%. The appraiser has chosen to use 2.50% in his analysis as a reasonable rate of vacancy to apply to the subject's PGI in developing the estimated NOI.

Thus, when applying the market vacancy rate to the subject's PGI, the following vacancy loss is indicated:

$33,600 x 2.50% (0.025) = $840

The calculation for EGI results:

$33,600 (PGI)
- 840 (Vacancy Loss)
$32,760 (EGI)

» *Rates of vacancy are determined from market data most often discovered during the course of performing a rent survey in a market value assignment* «

An estimated amount for collection (or credit) loss is appropriate when the market supports that there is evidence in the market for its use. An allowance for collection losses is most often warranted when the property is large with numerous rental units, or when renters vacating without paying the rent owed is commonplace. This information can be derived from surveys similar to that which was performed to derive a market vacancy rate. In most residential assignments of smaller income properties, applying a number or percentage for collection loss may be less common. When a collection loss is warranted, it is applied to PGI in the same manner as the percentage for vacancy loss.

√ **Note:** If the property's income is comprised of rent income and income from other disconnected sources (e.g., parking spaces rented to parties other than the tenants of the rental units), the vacancy and/or collection loss may be a percent of rent from the units only. In this case, the other income is added after the vacancy and/or collection losses are deducted from PGI.

Estimating Operating Expenses and NOI

After EGI is estimated, the next step for the appraiser in determining an estimate of NOI is to sort out the various operating expenses for the subject property and categorize the expenses. Operating expenses are separated into three categories:

1. Fixed expenses
2. Variable expenses
3. Reserves for replacement

The initial gathering of specific property data for the subject should include collection of operating data for the property. Ideally, this data is provided by the property owner, or collected through an interview with the owner. In most cases, the property owner is able to provide the appraiser with an operating income statement which, in part, details the various expenses of the particular investment property. Quite often, the operating income statement may include expenses that are not directly related to the operation of the investment property, not categorized appropriately, or expenses that are not reasonable or at market level. Therefore, as part of the analysis after reviewing the data collected, the appraiser will typically develop a reconstructed operating income statement (as illustrated in Chapter 5), correctly categorizing the expenses at market level. Following is an illustration using the expenses reported by the property owner of the subject property from our previous examples.

» *NOI is determined by subtracting any vacancy and/or collection losses and operating expenses from PGI—in that order* «

Example:

The property owner has furnished the appraiser with a list of annual expenses incurred over each of the past three years. The expenses were not categorized.

Replace appliances (four units)	Miscellaneous supplies
Real estate taxes	Water
Trash dumpster	Landscape/snow removal
Lease payment for owner's wife's car	Insurance
Security light at rear	Depreciation
Building maintenance/repairs	Replace roof
Miscellaneous expenses	Extermination
Replace HVAC (four units)	Replace carpet (2,000 SF)
Entertainment expenses	Mortgage payments

The property owner also provided expenditures for these items, which the appraiser reviewed in the course of preparing the reconstructed operating income statement. In some cases the appraiser affirmed that the expense was market level, in other cases a market level expense was assigned to the item. The first determination made by the appraiser was that the following would not be considered operating expenses of the property:

- Lease payment on the owner's wife's car
- Entertainment expenses
- Depreciation
- Mortgage payments

While most of these items (except depreciation) were paid from the cash flow of the property, they were not necessary to the operation of the property. The annual payment for a mortgage (debt service) is voluntary and not every owner would have the same mortgage obligation, or possibly even a mortgage on the property at all. Thus, the amount of debt service has no influence on the value of the property. Depreciation is also not a building expense.

Fixed Expenses

In the reconstructed operating income statement, the appraiser has categorized the following as market level fixed expenses, based on the current year (with no significant change projected in the near future):

Fixed Expenses	
Real estate taxes	$2,778.59
Insurance	$1,855.60
Trash dumpster (annual level contract)	$600.00
Security light at rear (annual level contract)	$360.00
Total Annual Fixed Expenses	**$5,594.19**

Example continued:

Variable Expenses

The appraiser noted that the property owner did not report any expense for management. However, it is common in this market to either pay a property manager or compensate the owner for his management efforts. The following were categorized by the appraiser as variable expenses and assigned a market level expense amount, or confirmed that the owner's reported expense represented market level:

Variable Expenses	
Water	$1,200.00
Building maintenance/repairs	$1,500.00
Landscaping/snow removal	$1,800.00
Extermination (as needed)	$500.00
Miscellaneous supplies	$250.00
Miscellaneous expense	$500.00
Management fees (3% of EGI, $32,760)	$982.80
Total Annual Variable Expenses	**$6,732.80**

» Replacement reserves reflect the anticipated cost to replace an item at the end of its economic life, divided by the number of years until replacement is needed «

Replacement Reserves

There are four remaining items for which the appraiser determined it is appropriate to estimate an annual replacement reserve—roof, HVAC (four units), carpet, and appliances for the four living units. Even though all of these items have been replaced in the past three years, a replacement reserve should be considered. The appraiser has made the following estimates regarding these items:

√ ***Note:*** To derive the annual replacement reserve, the estimated cost of the component as of the point in time the component needs to be replaced is divided by the estimated number of years remaining until replacement is required.

Roof—The roof has approximately 25 years of economic life remaining and will need to be replaced at a cost of $25,000:

$25,000 ÷ 25 years = $1,000 annual replacement reserve

HVAC—The units serving each living unit (four) will need to be replaced in approximately 15 years at a cost of $7,500 each

4 x $7,500 = $30,000 ÷ 15 years = $2,000 annual replacement reserve

Carpet—All units (total of 2,000 square feet) have a remaining economic life of six years. Replacement is estimated to be $30.00 per square yard.

2,000 SF ÷ 9 = 222.22 (square yards)

222.22 x $30.00 = $6,666.67 ÷ 6 years = $1,111.10 annual replacement reserve

Appliances—Each unit has a refrigerator, range, and built-in dishwasher; there is an estimated 12 years remaining until they require replacement. Estimated replacement cost is $1,500 per unit.

4 x $1,500 = $6,000 ÷ 12 years = $500 annual replacement reserve

Example continued:

Replacement Reserves	
Roof	$1,000.00
HVAC	$2,000.00
Carpet	$1,110.10
Appliances	$500.00
Total Annual Replacement Reserves	**$4,610.10**

√ **Note:** In some cases, the replacement reserves may be determined using a sinking fund factor, which takes into consideration the reserves being deposited into an interest bearing account with compounding. This practice is not common for most small residential properties.

The appraiser's summary of expenses for the reconstructed operating income statement in this assignment looks like this:

Operating Expense Summary		
Fixed Expenses		
Real estate taxes	$2,778.59	
Insurance	$1,855.60	
Trash dumpster (annual level contract)	$600.00	
Security light at rear (annual level contract) Total *Fixed Expenses*	$360.00	*$5,594.19*
Variable Expenses		
Water	$1,200.00	
Building maintenance/repairs	$1,500.00	
Landscaping/snow removal	$1,800.00	
Extermination (as needed)	$500.00	
Miscellaneous supplies	$250.00	
Miscellaneous expenses	$500.00	
Management fees (3% of EGI, $32,760)	$982.80	
Total Variable Expenses		*$6,732.80*
Replacement Reserves		
Roof	$1,000.00	
HVAC	$2,000.00	
Carpet	$1,110.10	
Appliances	$500.00	
Total Replacement Reserves		*$4,610.10*
Total Operating Expenses		**$16,937.09**

» *Operating expenses are the sum of fixed expenses, variable expenses, and replacement reserves* «

Once the appraiser has estimated the operating expenses for the subject property, the next step is to develop NOI. Here is the appraiser's conclusion:

$33,600.00 (PGI)
\- 840.00 (Vacancy Loss)
$32,760.00 (EGI)
\- 16,937.09 (Operating Expense)
$15,822.91 (NOI)

Determining the Overall Capitalization Rate

After the NOI is estimated for the subject property, the next step in the process is to determine an applicable overall capitalization rate to apply to the subject's NOI. There are several techniques that can be used for deriving an overall capitalization rate for use in the income analysis. However, some of these techniques are not common, or often do not lend themselves well to residential appraisal assignments and, thus, are beyond the scope of this course.

The two most common techniques for deriving an overall capitalization rate involve:

1. Utilizing comparable sales of similar investment properties or market data, and
2. The analysis of mortgage and equity components, known as **band of investment**—*a technique for determining an overall capitalization rate by weighting and combining the various components of an investment.*

Using Market Data

Throughout this course it has been emphasized that identification of numerous components of an appraiser's analysis is best supported when the data is derived from the actions of the marketplace when sufficient market data is available. Derivation of the overall capitalization rate from market data of comparable sales is no exception and is the most common and preferred technique.

When employing the comparable sales technique for deriving an overall capitalization rate from income-producing properties that have been transacted, both the sales price and the NOI of the comparable data must be known. In real world appraising, this information ideally comes from previous appraisal assignments, or from other appraisers who have completed appraisal assignments for similar properties. However, the data can come from other sources as well, such as participants to a transaction, as long as those sources are credible. In order for market data to be reliable in the comparable sales technique for overall capitalization rate derivation, the appraiser must form certain conclusions about the data, such as:

- NOI calculations of the comparable must be consistent with how the net income of the subject was estimated.
- The lease terms of the comparable must be similar to those of the subject.
- The rents and income generated by the comparables should represent those typical for the market.
- Elements of comparison (e.g., terms of sale, conditions of sale, and market conditions) of the comparable data should be consistent with those found in an arm's-length transaction.

» Using the market technique to derive an overall capitalization rate, the appraiser identifies the rate from comparable data by using the formula of IVR: Income ÷ Value = Rate «

In some cases, adjustments could be made to the comparable data to align the data with the subject property in a market value assignment of the fee simple interest.

Once the comparable sales data has been gathered and analyzed for its reliability and relevance, the *process of deriving an overall capitalization rate* is fairly simple. Appraisers use a formula or technique known as **IVR**:

Income (NOI) ÷ Value (Sale Price) = Rate

For Example: In the course of analyzing an investment property that produces $38,000 NOI annually, the appraiser collected the following sales and income data:

	Sale Price	NOI	I ÷ V = R	Rate (%)
Sale #1	$425,000	$39,600	39,600 ÷ 425,000 = 0.0932	9.32%
Sale #2	$470,000	$42,300	42,300 ÷ 470,000 = 0.0900	9.00%
Sale #3	$395,000	$39,100	39,100 ÷ 395,000 = 0.0990	9.90%
Sale #4	$452,000	$40,900	40,900 ÷ 452,000 = 0.0905	9.05%
Sale #5	$405,000	$36,500	36,500 ÷ 405,000 = 0.0901	9.01%

In forming conclusions from this example, it can be noted that three of the five resulting indications are most closely related at 9.00% - 9.05%.

» *An overall capitalization rate, regardless of the technique being used to indicate it, is always derived from the market in a market value assignment* «

	Sale Price	NOI	I ÷ V = R	Rate (%)
Sale #1	$425,000	$39,600	39,600 ÷ 425,000 = .0932	9.32%
Sale #2	$470,000	$42,300	42,300 ÷ 470,000 = .0900	**9.00%**
Sale #3	$395,000	$39,100	39,100 ÷ 395,000 = .0990	9.90%
Sale #4	$452,000	**$40,900**	40,900 ÷ 452,000 = .0905	**9.05%**
Sale #5	$405,000	**$36,500**	36,500 ÷ 405,000 = .0901	**9.01%**

Thus, the appraiser has the best support for concluding somewhere within this range, and probably at the lower part, since two of those conclusions are suggesting 9.00% as being a reasonable indication for an overall capitalization rate. To further support the appraiser's evaluation of the data, it can be noted that the subject's NOI is bracketed between the 9.01% and the 9.05% conclusion.

Using the Band of Investment Technique

Once acquainted with the fundamentals of the band of investment technique, developing an indication of an overall capitalization rate is not particularly difficult. However, the basis for the technique and the components involved with the process are sometimes daunting when first introduced. There are different techniques that incorporate a band of investment formula using various components. But probably the most common version involves the analysis of mortgage (debt) and equity components separately to produce an indication of the overall capitalization rate, or $\mathbf{R_O}$.

This band of investment technique recognizes that most investors use a combination of debt and equity when acquiring an investment. As an explanation of debt, when an investor purchases an investment property, the lender is expecting *a return on the money lent in the investment.* This is called the **mortgage capitalization rate,** or $\mathbf{R_M}$. The investor, on the other hand, is usually making some type of initial investment in the purchase, very often in the form of a cash down payment. The investor expects a return on that investment. That expectation is related heavily to the risk involved with the investment, what other investments would have paid him, and what income he should realize in this investment. *The capitalization rate applied to the expectation of return on equity* is known as the **equity capitalization rate**, or $\mathbf{R_E}$. Thus, the overall capitalization rate, $\mathbf{R_O}$, is comprised of the weighted average of two components, R_M and R_E:

$$\mathbf{M \times R_M + (1\text{-}M) \times R_E = R_O}$$

Calculating the Mortgage Component

R_M should not be confused with the mortgage interest rate, although the interest rate being charged to the investor by the lender is a component remotely used in developing the R_M. The information needed to derive the mortgage component is:

- Loan-to-value ratio (LTV), also referred to as **M**
- **Mortgage constant** (*the ratio between annual debt service and loan principal*)

Assuming a purchase transaction of an investment property, M is the percent of the purchase price that is financed. The mortgage constant is the ratio of annual debt service to the dollar amount financed.

For Example: An investor is purchasing an investment property for $450,000. He has acquired a 30-year mortgage at 7.75% interest rate from a local bank for 70% of the purchase price. The monthly payment to the bank for principal and interest will be $2,256.70. The investor expects a 12% annual return on his equity portion of the investment.

The LTV, or M, is 70% of the purchase price, or $315,000 ($450,000 x 70%). The annual debt service is $27,080.38 ($2,256.70 x 12). Therefore:

M = 70%, or 0.70

Mortgage constant (R_M) = 0.0860 ($27,080.38 ÷ $315,000.00)

The mortgage component is calculated as the mortgage constant times the percent of the mortgage (LTV, or M):

(R_M) 0.0860 x (M) 0.70 = 0.0602

Solve this problem using your HP 12c calculator:

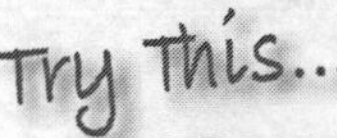

450000 [ENTER]	
70 [%]	(315,000 will appear in display)
[PV]	
7.75 [g] [i]	
30 [g] [n]	
[PMT]	(-2,256.6986 will appear in display)
12 [x]	(-27,080.38—annual debt service will appear in the display)
[CHS]	(changes the sign in the display from a negative—optional)
315000 [÷]	(0.0860 – mortgage constant R_M will appear in the display)
70 [%]	(0.0602 will appear in the display—mortgage component M x R_M)

Calculating the Equity Component

The equity component represents a ratio of annual equity dividend (expected return by the investor) to the amount of the equity investment (the percent of down payment or percent of initial equity investment), which is signified by the value or purchase price minus the mortgage, or 1-M. The calculation is fairly simple:

» *A mortgage constant is the ratio of the annual debt service to the mortgage amount* «

Equity investment (1-M) = 30%, or 0.30 (100% - 70% mortgage position)

Equity dividend (R_E) = 12%, or 0.12

The equity component is calculated as the equity dividend times the equity investment:

(R_E) 0.12 x (1-M) 0.30 = 0.0360

Calculating R_O

R_O is simply the weighted average of R_M plus the weighted average of R_E:

0.0602 ([M] 0.70 x R_M) + 0.0360 ([1-M] 0.30 x R_E) = 0.0962 (R_O)

The overall capitalization rate in our example is 9.62%.

The band of investment technique, similar to the market data technique, requires quality data from the market. However, in this case the appraiser must be particularly knowledgeable of current market interest rates and financing options from the lender's perspective, as well as what return on equity represents the typical investor's expectation.

Applying the Overall Capitalization Rate to the Subject

The final step in the direct capitalization technique is to apply the overall capitalization rate to NOI to produce a value indication. Here, the appraiser divides NOI by the overall capitalization rate. Thus, the formula in this step is commonly known as IRV:

(Net Operating) Income ÷ (Overall Capitalization) Rate = Value

For Example: A real property appraiser has estimated that a subject property has an NOI of $12,700. The overall capitalization rate indicated in this assignment is 10.25%.

$12,700 ÷ 10.25% = $123,902

Before leaving this topic, it is important to note that a capitalization rate can be very sensitive, especially in circumstances where larger NOI or property value is concerned. Because of this sensitivity, appraisers must be very cautious about rounding capitalization rates, both when deriving the rate and applying it. In some assignments, the appraiser might carry out the overall capitalization rate to four or six places past the decimal.

For Example: The calculations below show the effect of one-half of one percent when applying the overall capitalization rate to a property with NOI of $100,000.

$100,000 ÷ 10.00% = $1,000,000

$100,000 ÷ 10.50% = $952,381

Nearly a $50,000 variation is noted in the conclusion.

» *The process of applying an overall capitalization rate to NOI to indicate a value conclusion is known as IRV: Income ÷ Rate = Value* «

Reconciling the Income Approach

It may have been noted throughout the various analyses performed during income capitalization, whether using a multiplier or a direct capitalization rate, that reconciliation was an ongoing process. At nearly every step, the appraiser was weighing information and forming conclusions about the quality and appropriateness of the information and the resulting indications.

In the final reconciliation, the appraiser will consider the quantity and quality of the data used and the indications produced by the analysis in reaching his final conclusions regarding the relevance of the income approach in the appraisal assignment.

In some cases, the income approach may be the only valuation method developed. However, in most assignments of small residential income properties, the income approach will be developed in concert with at least the sales comparison approach. Even in the case of an income-producing property, some clients and intended users may require, as an assignment condition, that the income approach be used only as a basis of support for the final value opinion by the sales comparison approach.

Application Case Study #1
Valuation of a Single-Family Dwelling Using a GRM

A real property appraiser is appraising a property for use in assisting with a mortgage finance transaction. The purchase price of the single-family dwelling is $145,000. The parties to the transaction are the sellers (a retiring and relocating couple) and their son and daughter-in-law, who are purchasing the property to use as an investment property. The subject property has no income history; however, there is a presence of similar properties, which are rented, in the immediate market.

The appraiser has gathered data for his analysis and produced the following rent survey of similar properties that are rented in the immediate market:

Comparable Rental	#1	#2	#3	#4	#5	#6	#7	#8
Monthly Rent	$950	$925	$950	$975	$950	$910	$890	$950

In addition, the appraiser collected market level data from the subject market for sales transactions of other properties that were rented at the time of the transaction. The following sales were verified to reflect arm's-length transactions of similar single-family dwellings:

Comparable Sale	#1	#2	#3	#4	#5	#6
Sale Price	$177,500	$158,000	$159,000	$187,000	$175,000	$185,000
Monthly Rent	$925	$875	$890	$975	$910	$900

Based on the appraiser's best supported conclusion in the analysis, the appraiser's opinion of value, rounded to the nearest thousand should be $ ____________.

Selected USPAP Illustrations and Guidance

The following USPAP Frequently Asked Question (FAQ) has been selected to illustrate the application of USPAP in specific circumstances discussed in this chapter.

FAQ 223—Analyzing the Lease When Appraising Fee Simple Interest

Application Case Study #2
Valuing a Small Residential Four-unit Property Using a GIM

A four-unit apartment building is being appraised for mortgage refinancing purposes. The two apartments on the first floor each rent for $500 per month, while the two upstairs units each rent for $400 per month. All rents have been verified at market level.

A divided two-stall garage is at the rear of the property. The two stalls are rented to two of the tenants for $50 per month each.

A vacancy rate of 3.15% for the property has been observed from the market. Annual operating expenses for the property are $3,875 per year.

The appraiser analyzed data from two prior transactions to extract a GIM. His conclusions will be supported by the mean of the GIM indications.

	Sale Price	Monthly Income		
Comparable Sale #1	$497,000	$2,100		
Comparable Sale #2	$435,500	$1,800		

Rounded to the nearest five-hundred dollars, the appraiser's value opinion of the subject should be $_________.

Application Case Study #3
Appraising a Small Retail Property Using Direct Capitalization

A small retail property is being appraised. The market rent for the property is $1,625 per month. The property is leased to a long-term tenant with a net/net/net lease scenario, which is common for the market for this type of property. Insurance and real estate taxes total $2,945 per month. The monthly expenditure for maintenance varies, but averages approximately $150 per month. The roof on the building will need to be replaced in approximately 10 years at an estimated cost of $40,000. The HVAC system has an estimated remaining economic life of eight years, with estimated replacement cost of $35,000. The property owner does not use a sinking fund account for his replacement reserves. A market derived vacancy rate for the property is 1.65%.

Using the following market derived sales data, what is the indicated value of the subject property (rounded to the nearest dollar) if the overall capitalization rate is based on the median indicator of the data? $__________.

	Sale Price	NOI	
Comparable #1	$125,000	$11,375	
Comparable #2	$130,000	$11,895	
Comparable #3	$120,000	$10,890	

Quiz

1. ***Which is a TRUE statement regarding a GRM?***
   a. Annual rent is always used in the approach.
   b. Comparable properties must be very similar.
   c. Contract rent is always used as a basis.
   d. Expenses are subtracted after the multiplier is applied.

2. ***When developing conclusions using a GRM, which process is correct?***
   a. Rent of the subject is divided by the subject's value.
   b. Rent of the subject is multiplied by the GRM.
   c. Subject's value is divided by the rent.
   d. Subject's value is multiplied by the rent.

3. ***When either a GRM or a GIM is being derived from market data, which recognized formula is employed?***
   a. IRV
   b. IVR
   c. MIV
   d. VIM

4. ***Which is used as a component of the analysis when deriving or applying a GRM?***
   a. contract income
   b. effective gross income
   c. gross market rent
   d. net operating income

5. ***When considering data to be used for the purpose of deriving a GRM, which best represents transactional data that should be analyzed?***
   a. currently leased properties that are under option
   b. listed properties used for the purpose of investment
   c. properties that were rented at the time of the sale transaction
   d. sold properties that have not yet been rented

6. ***If a subject property has a market rent of $625 per month and a monthly GRM of 183.75 is deemed applicable, what is the appraiser's indicated value conclusion (rounded to the nearest one-thousand)?***
   a. $103,000
   b. $115,000
   c. $132,000
   d. $184,000

7. ***When an investor pays a particular price for a rental property with the expectation of income and other benefits associated with the investment, which fundamental principle explains the investor's actions?***
   a. anticipation
   b. effective demand
   c. increasing returns
   d. progression

8. ***When vacancy losses are subtracted from the amount a property could generate if it were rented for a full year with every unit rented, the result is***
   a. adjusted net income.
   b. effective gross income.
   c. market income.
   d. potential gross income.

9. ***Which would most clearly be categorized as a variable expense?***
   a. level payment services
   b. property insurance
   c. real estate taxes
   d. water for living units

10. ***A 13-year-old roof will need to be replaced in seven years at a cost of $10,000. Rounded to the nearest dollar, what amount will need to be considered as a replacement reserve for the roof?***
    a. $769
    b. $1,429
    c. $1,667
    d. $2,109

11. ***To derive a mortgage constant, the annual debt service is divided by the***
    a. equity capitalization rate.
    b. length of the mortgage.
    c. loan-to-value ratio.
    d. mortgage amount.

12. ***Using IRV, what would be the indicated value of a property, rounded to the nearest one hundred dollars, that has NOI of $8,000 if the overall capitalization rate is indicated at 9.25%?***
    a. $65,300
    b. $74,000
    c. $86,500
    d. $92,400

Using the *Sales Comparison and Income Approaches in Special Situations*

7

To this point, the content of this text has illustrated the fundamental principles and procedures of the sales comparison and income approaches. However, there are some special situations regarding the applications of these valuation methods that warrant discussion now that the fundamental concepts and techniques have been covered.

The application of the sales comparison approach and the income approach is not one-size-fits-all. Sometimes, the subject of a particular appraisal assignment may not be for the entire physical property or the full fee simple interest. In many assignments, there may be assignment conditions, such as Fannie Mae regulations and guidelines that have special requirements that affect some of the elements discussed throughout this text.

This chapter is certainly not intended to cover every special situation an appraiser could encounter. However, we will review and discuss the most common circumstances.

Appraising Partial Interests and Special Ownership

When the subject of an appraisal assignment involves a partial interest or a special ownership arrangement, the assignment is usually considered complex, especially for most residential appraisers. In both cases, the interest being appraised is something less than fee simple. There are many examples of a partial interest. In this portion of the chapter, we will review some of the more common situations relevant to residential appraisers.

Leasehold and Leased Fee Interests

There are various reasons why an appraisal of the leasehold or leased fee interest or the leasehold or leased fee estate may need to be appraised. In some cases the scope of the assignment may include only valuing this interest. One example might be when the lease is to be sold and assigned to another party. Another example might be when the new owner of a property, which is leased at below market level, desires to buy out the remaining term of the lease from the existing lessee.

There are several methods by which to value the leasehold and leased fee interests of a particular property. Most of these methods are income techniques. For residential properties, the simplest and most common method of developing a value opinion for the leasehold or leased fee interest is the GRM technique. The sales comparison approach is of little value unless comparable sales of similar leasehold or leased fee interests can be located.

The concept of leasehold and leased fee interests was introduced in Chapter 5. However, it is important to review and expand upon that discussion here. As noted earlier, the leased fee interest belongs to the lessor, and the leasehold interest belongs to the lessee. Let's look at an illustration and the important points that should be noted.

- *When contract rent is* ***less*** *than market rent, an advantage to the lessee occurs* and creates a **positive leasehold.**
- *When contract rent is* ***more*** *than market rent, an advantage to the lessor occurs* and creates a **negative leasehold.**
- The **leasehold interest** is *defined by the amount of rent that is less than market rent (amount of difference between contract and market rent).*
- The **leased fee interest** is *defined by the amount of contract rent over and above market rent.*

It should be obvious, from the illustration on the next page, that in order to develop an opinion of value of the leasehold or leased fee interest, the fee simple interest must be valued (as if the investment property were freely available to be leased at market level) as must the leased fee estate (based on what the property is generating per the terms of the lease).

Let's look first at an example of positive leasehold.

» Positive leasehold occurs when the lessee is paying less than market rent. Negative leasehold is when the lessee Is paying rent higher than market level «

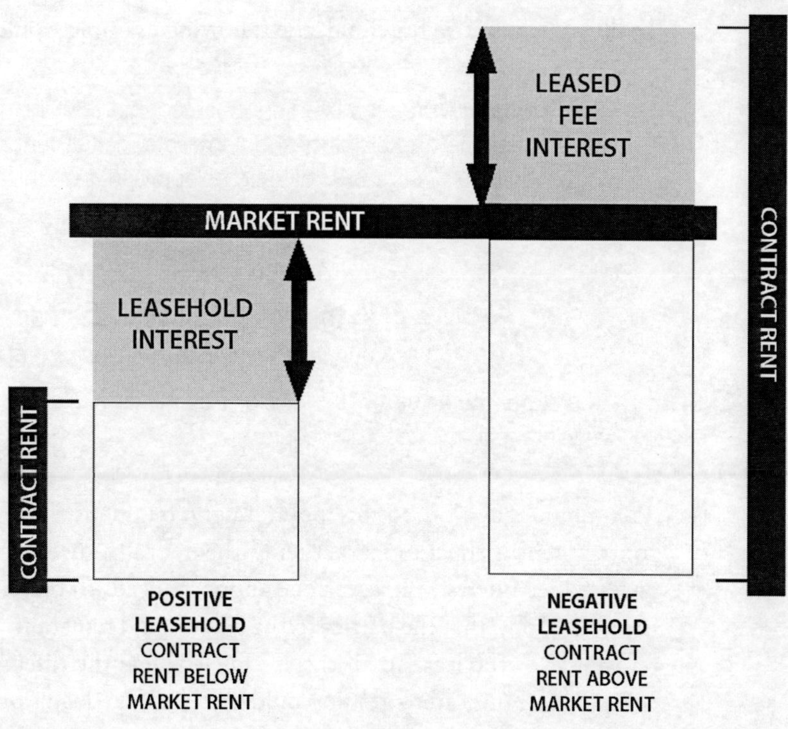

For Example: A property has a contract rent of $1,200 per month. The appraiser determines that the property should have a market rent of $1,350 per month. The appraiser selects a GRM of 110 to be appropriate in the assignment.

$1,350 x 110 = $148,500

$1,200 x 110 = $132,000

$148,500 – $132,000 = $16,500

Therefore, the value of the leasehold interest is $16,500, the amount of the advantage to the lessee, in dollars.

KEY TERMS

Appurtenant Rights Rights that go with ownership of real property. They are usually transferred with the property, but may be sold separately. This is a legal term referring to both physical and non-physical appurtenances.

Dominant Tenement A property that benefits from an easement.

Easement A right to use some part of another person's real property for a particular purpose. An easement is irrevocable and creates an interest in the property.

Easement Appurtenant An easement that burdens one piece of land for the benefit of another.

Easement in Gross An easement that benefits a person instead of a particular property; there is a dominant tenant, but no dominant tenement.

Leased Fee Interest Defined by the amount of contract rent over and above market rent.

Leasehold Interest Defined by the amount of rent that is less than market rent (amount of difference between contract and market rent).

Life Estate A freehold estate that lasts only as long as a specified person lives.

Life Tenant Someone who owns a life estate; the person entitled to possession of the property during the measuring life.

Negative Leasehold When contract rent is more than market rent (an advantage to the lessor).

Positive Leasehold When contract rent is less than market rent (an advantage to the lessee).

Remainderman The party in a life estate who is entitled to the remainder of the property interest after the life estate is terminated.

Servient Tenement A property that is burdened by an easement.

Timeshares Grant the right to use (or possess) a property for a specified period of time (the right may or may not be accompanied with an ownership interest in the property).

To illustrate negative leasehold, the following example would apply.

> ***For Example:*** A property has a contract rent of $1,500 per month. The appraiser determines that the property should have a market rent of $1,250 per month. The appraiser selects a GRM of 95 to be appropriate in the assignment.
>
> **$1,250 x 95 = $118,750**
>
> **$1,500 x 95 = $142,500**
>
> **$118,750 - $142,500 = -$23,750**
>
> (stated as a negative since a negative leasehold is created)
>
> Therefore, the value of the leased fee interest is $23,750, the amount of the advantage to the lessor, in dollars.

A common question at this point might be about what happens when the contract rent is equal to market rent. Theoretically, there would be no leasehold or leased fee interest. However, the appraiser needs to be very careful of making the assumption that the parties to the lease would remain in this position for the remainder of the lease in all cases. This is where the discussion becomes more complex and misleading results could occur if the conclusions of the analysis are not interpreted correctly. Assuming that rents are expected to rise during a lease period, if the lease is long term and there are no provisions for the rent to be adjusted upward, contract rent and market rent will *not* always remain the same as time goes on. In such case, a more complex analysis and/or technique must be used, which is beyond the scope of this course, but discussed in more advanced coursework.

Easements

An **easement** is *a right to use some part of another person's real property for a particular purpose. An easement is irrevocable and creates an interest in the property.*

> √ ***In Other Words:*** An easement constitutes a legal right that is granted for one party or entity to use another party's property (typically a defined area) for a particular purpose that benefits either a specific property or a specified party or entity.

There are two types of easements:

1. Easement appurtenant
2. Easement in gross

An **easement appurtenant** is *an easement that burdens one piece of land for the benefit of another.* The *burdened property* is the **servient tenement** and the *property benefiting from the easement* is the **dominant tenement.**

> ***For Example:*** Access easements (for ingress and egress purposes) are the most common example of an easement appurtenant.

An **easement in gross** *differs slightly from an easement appurtenant, in that the beneficiary is a person or entity rather than a property.*

> ***For Example:*** A common example of an easement in gross might be an easement for a cell tower. The beneficiary is the owner of the cell tower.

An easement in itself is theoretically not valued. The valuation of an easement is a measure in dollars of the effect of the burden on the servient tenement, or the amount of benefit in dollars that the easement contributes to the dominant tenement. And, the dollar amount of burden may not necessarily be equal to the dollar amount of benefit.

» The benefit or burden of an easement is most commonly valued using paired data of before and after scenarios «

Consider a five-acre property on which the servient tenement has an easement running along one of its side boundaries. The easement provides an access driveway to another property behind it, the dominant tenement. The driveway results in very little loss of utility or enjoyment to the servient property; however, the dominant property benefits greatly because without the easement, there would be no access.

The dollar amount attributable to the burden or benefit can best be derived by using a before and after scenario through market extraction using similar paired data. A common technique is for the dollar amount to be applied in the sales comparison approach as a percentage adjustment.

> ***For Example:*** A vacant subject site has a 30-foot access easement running along one side of it. The easement provides for future access to the site behind it. A nearly identical site next to the subject sold last week for $40,000, but was not subject to an easement.
>
> The appraiser located the sale of a vacant site in another area that has a similar easement, which sold for $30,000. In that same market with similar market conditions, a similar site without an easement sold for $32,000. What can be derived from this comparable data is that the easement burdened the comparable site by 6.25%.
>
> ($32,000 – 30,000 = $2,000. To find a downward percent adjustment, divide the indicated amount due to the negative influence by the amount the negative influence is from: $2,000 ÷ $32,000 = 6.25%.)
>
> Applying this percentage to the sale price of the site next to the subject ($40,000), a downward adjustment of $2,500 ($40,000 x 6.25%) is indicated as an adjustment due to the burden.

The benefit to the site behind the subject could be much more when analyzing before and after paired data. The method of deriving the adjustment is similar to how an adjustment for the burden of an easement is estimated.

> ***For Example:*** Consider an appraiser who found the sale of a land parcel that sold without access for $25,000. Soon after the sale, the owner arranged for an access easement to the property and the property resold for $35,000. The value of that property, assuming no change in market conditions, increased 40% ($10,000 ÷ $25,000). The same procedure could be applied if the appraiser is attempting to determine the downward adjustment when the subject has no access and a comparable sale does have access. Using the data from the previous comparable transaction, the downward adjustment would be 28.6% ($10,000 ÷ $35,000).

» Typically, only easements that are atypical and would result in a particular market reaction warrant an adjustment «

It should be clearly understood that not every easement warrants an adjustment. Only a thorough analysis by the appraiser will determine when an adjustment is appropriate. Common utility easements, etc., are seldom situations for which an adjustment is applied. In most cases, only easement scenarios that are atypical and would be perceived by the market as being such would warrant an adjustment. Easements and related methods of valuation are further discussed in more advanced coursework.

Other Appurtenant Rights

There could be innumerable **appurtenant rights** of real property ownership that may warrant analysis and possibly an adjustment when developing the sales comparison approach or the income approach. **Appurtenant rights** are *rights that go with ownership of real property. They are usually transferred with the property, but may be sold separately. This is a legal term referring to both physical and non-physical appurtenances.* These rights could include, among other things, the surface on, or the area below, the surface of a property; water adjacent or under the property surface; or the airspace above the property. Most, considered as part of property rights conveyed, will reveal themselves through analysis of differences between the subject property and the comparable data.

> ***For Example:*** A subject property lies in the path of an airport runway or approach zone. Airport zoning prohibits or limits certain building types and heights for the area. In this case, the air rights typically conveyed with real property are at issue. In certain jurisdictions and with some properties, the limitation may be specific, in the form of an airspace easement. The circumstance likely would require an adjustment if the limitations of use of the subject property's airspace are different from that found in the comparable data.

In addition to airspace, other examples of appurtenant rights might include, but are certainly not limited to:

- Mineral rights
- Riparian or littoral (water) rights
- Dock rights
- Timber rights
- Aggregate (gravel, sand, etc.) rights

When a property lacks, or has an appurtenant right that differs from, comparable data (something atypical), an adjustment is likely warranted if the difference would reflect in market actions. Depending on the market and the property, deriving the adjustment of the particular right may require extra effort and time. The adjustment can often be extracted from paired data and applied to the comparable data in the subject's appraisal, most often as a percentage. In some cases, the appraiser may be attempting to ascertain the value of only the appurtenant right. The procedure used to derive a value indication for the element is much the same. This procedure is very similar to that in the case of an easement.

For an income-producing property, if the particular right is affecting the potential income flow for the property, the adjustment could be applied in the income approach, similar to the procedure discussed in Chapter 6.

Timeshares

Timeshares *grant the right to use (or possess) a property for a specified period of time.* In some cases the right may be accompanied with an ownership interest in the property, while in other situations the timeshare represents a right of use without ownership.

In most cases, timeshares are valued using the sales comparison approach and utilizing comparable data representing the same property rights conveyed. Special courses are available that specifically address this topic.

Life Estates

Appraising a **life estate**, or a property interest subject to a life estate, is a complex procedure that requires scientific data, specialized skills, and competency. A **life estate** is *a freehold estate that lasts only as long as a specified person lives (that person is referred to as the* ***measuring life****).*

> ***For Example:*** When an elderly parent deeds her property to her son, while reserving for herself a life estate, or the right to live in the property, the parent is the **life tenant** (*someone who owns a life estate*) and the **measuring life**. The child owns the property, except for the right to live there. He cannot move into the property, or lease the property. He could sell the property; however, the possessory right would not transfer and a new owner would have to allow the parent to continue to live there (rent free).

√ ***In Other Words:*** The owner of the property subject to a life estate has a limited ownership of the property.

A life estate can be sold, as well. The parent could sell her right to possess the property to another party. However, the amount of time the other party could possess the property is based upon how long the parent (the measuring life) is expected to live. The measuring life *never* changes. Thus, the value of the life estate is based on the period of time that the third party could expect to enjoy possession before the measuring life passes on. When the life estate terminates, at the death of the measuring life, the right to possess the property (remainder of the rights) will pass to the child *who owns the property*, who is known as the **remainderman**.

Scientific data in the form of actuarial estimates are necessary to develop an opinion of value for the life estate, or a property subject to a life estate. The actuarial data estimates life expectancy. Such data is used similarly by life insurance companies to assess risk.

» *When the ownership of a property is subject to a life estate, the value of the property without the right of possession or the life estate itself can be valued* «

Following is a simplified example illustrating one technique with which a life estate could be valued.

For Example: John receives title to his mother's house. His mother, however, has reserved a life estate for herself, allowing for her to live in the house until she dies. The property's current value is estimated to be $175,000. John's mother is currently 67 years old and her life expectancy is estimated to be 18 more years (or until age 85). The appraiser has projected that the property value will appreciate consistently at 0.50% per year during that time. The safe rate of return (similar to what a savings account would earn) is 2.50%. John's mother will pay all expenses on the property during the term of the life estate.

The appraiser performs the following steps:

1. Find the future value of the property at the time of the estimated termination of the life estate.
2. Discount the future value by the safe rate to estimate the present value of the remainderman's interest.
3. Subtract the value of the discounted future value from the current property value to derive the value of the life estate.

Find the future value of the property . Solve this problem using your HP 12c calculator:

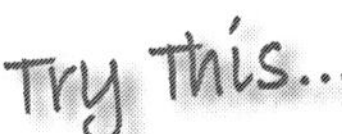

175000 [PV]

0.5 [i]

18 [n]

[FV]

$191,437.56 should be displayed as the future value of the property at the time the life estate terminates, given that the property increases in value 0.50% per year for 18 years.

Estimate the present value of the remainderman's interest. Solve this problem using your HP 12c calculator:

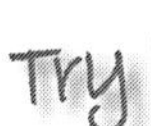

191437.56 [FV] (or press [enter] if still in the display)

2.5 **[i]**

18 [n]

[PV]

$122,743.24 should be displayed as the present value of the remainderman's interest, given a 2.5% safe rate over the projected 18-year period.

Find the value of the life estate

$175,000.00 - $122,743.24 = $52,256.76

The indicated value of the life estate is $52,256.76.

Great care and caution must be exercised by the appraiser when valuing a property subject to a life estate (property without the right of possession), or a life estate (possessory right). The technique used in the previous example might not be sufficient for most assignments where a life estate is a relevant property characteristic.

For Example: The resulting value indication of the life estate ($52,256.76) might reflect only what the remainderman would pay the life tenant for the right of possession. The open market would probably pay less than this. Other more complex issues might include the possibility of the life tenant living beyond the projected number of years.

Very often, the analysis of a life estate is based on a complex analysis of a series of scenarios, not just a single scenario, as in the example. These techniques are beyond the scope of this course.

Using Combined Approaches

On occasion, appraisers can use the sales comparison and income methods in combination to form value conclusions. Most often, these circumstances arise from the subject property being unique or complex.

For Example: An adjustment based on income can sometimes be made in the sales comparison approach, and income techniques can be used in a cost approach. Advanced coursework will expand on these techniques.

Employing combined approaches requires market competence inasmuch as any combined technique must truly represent an anticipated market reaction. There could be many combinations. When contemplating the use of combined approaches, the appraiser must ensure that doing so will be consistent with any assignment conditions and the intended use of the appraisal. Here, using an income technique as the basis for an adjustment in the sales comparison approach and as the basis of depreciation will be examined.

» *When using combined valuation approaches, the appraiser must be careful that any indications produced by the analysis reflect typical market actions* «

Using the Income Approach as a Basis for an Adjustment

For some properties in some assignments, adjustments for application in the sales comparison approach can be derived using an income technique when the particular adjustment cannot be derived from paired data. Similar transaction data may not be found, or existing data could prove inconclusive due to significant differences.

For Example: The subject property consists of an owner-occupied, single-family residential property that has a studio apartment over the garage and has a long history of being consistently rented. There are no public or private restrictions conflicting with the current improvements. The appraiser has been unable to locate comparable data with similar improvements. However, the appraiser derived a market rent for the unit of $250 per month and a reasonable GRM of 85.

$250 x 85 = $21,250 (contributory value)

In the previous example, since the typical owner's anticipated benefit of the studio apartment is for the unit's potential to produce income, the appraiser could estimate the contributory value of the studio apartment by an income technique and apply the results as an adjustment in the sales comparison approach. Again, the appraiser must be careful that the adjustment reflects market reaction.

Using the Income Approach as the Basis for Depreciation

In some cases, depreciation due to physical deterioration, functional obsolescence, or external obsolescence can be estimated for use in the cost approach by an income technique. Often, this may actually be the best reflection of the loss in value when the particular deficiency is somehow affecting a property's income-producing ability. Let's look at an example in which functional obsolescence can be addressed using an income technique.

> ***For Example:*** A four-unit apartment building in a warm climate area has no central air-conditioning. Several industry professionals agree that due to the age and design of the property, installing central air-conditioning would be physically prohibitive. However, estimates reveal that if the central air-conditioning was added along with the construction of the building, the cost if installed new would be $16,000. Market data supports that each unit rents for $50 per month less than comparable units that have central air-conditioning. The appraiser determined that a GRM for the property is 125.
>
> **4 x $50 = $200 x 125 = $25,000**
>
> (loss in rental income) - $16,000 (cost if installed when new) = $9,000 (functional depreciation due to lack of central air-conditioning)

Of course, the use of combined approaches should be accompanied by thorough commentary in the appraisal report of the appraiser's rationale for using the combined technique.

Special Requirements for Appraisals Used in Residential Lending

While the discussion of special requirements often found in residential lending has been placed in this chapter regarding the use of the sales comparison and income approaches, most residential appraisers will find the content of this section relevant in the majority of their assignments.

Many, if not most, residential appraisal assignments will be for the lender to use in facilitating a mortgage transaction—to construct, purchase, or refinance a property. And very often these assignments will have assignment conditions in the form of regulations, guidelines, and/or client requirements that are expected to be observed by the appraiser. As stated in earlier chapters, USPAP requires the appraiser to recognize and comply with assignment conditions present in an appraisal assignment.

» When the intended use of the appraisal is to assist with a mortgage finance transaction, the appraiser must be especially aware of any assignment conditions that may affect the analysis and development in the assignment «

Lending regulations and guidelines, as well as particular client requirements, may be directed to the development or reporting of an appraisal. The purpose of this section is to provide an *overview* of some of these requirements; it is not intended to be all-inclusive. In some cases, special courses have been designed to specifically address most of these topics, such as specific reporting forms, FHA and VA appraisal, appraising for Fannie Mae, etc.

As this chapter focuses specifically on appraisal development using the sales comparison and income approaches for specific residential lending situations, the discussion of special assignment conditions will be concentrated on that function of the appraisal process. However, reporting forms that are most often used in residential appraisals for lending transactions will be illustrated as appropriate. A full range of applicable Fannie Mae residential appraisal forms can be found in the Appendix of this text.

Observing Fannie Mae Requirements and Guidelines

Fannie Mae provides specific regulations and guidelines for appraisal development and reporting in Fannie Mae's *Selling Guide*. Many of these regulations and guidelines are related directly to the sales comparison approach and the income approach. Other secondary market participants, such as Freddie Mac and FHA, often mirror Fannie Mae in most of their requirements. In some cases, other lenders, such as a primary market or portfolio lenders, impose assignment conditions that require appraisers to observe guidelines, such as Fannie Mae's, for mortgage lending appraisals. If a lender adopts Fannie Mae requirements and guidelines into their standards, the appraisal will be done in a manner that will allow the lender the option of selling the loan to Fannie Mae at a later date.

» *Fannie Mae regulations and guidelines are often used as a benchmark by other lending entities* «

The **Ethics Rule** requires that, when any of these assignment conditions are an element of an assignment, the appraiser must observe them. The **Competency Rule** requires the appraiser to recognize the special requirements, know what they are, and how to apply them in an assignment.

For our discussion here, Fannie Mae general requirements and guidelines specific to the sales comparison approach and the income approach as addressed in the Fannie Mae *Selling Guide* will be discussed separately.

Sales Comparison Approach

Fannie Mae considers the sales comparison approach to be the most reliable valuation method of the three approaches to value. The following is intended as an *overview* of some of the most important requirements and guidelines from the Fannie Mae *Selling Guide* in developing the sales comparison approach. We will discuss special handling of the requirements and guidelines and how these particular elements differ from traditional appraisal practices. *Excerpts and paraphrased content from the* Selling Guide *are noted in italics.*

In general, the appraiser must, at a minimum:

1. Perform a complete visual inspection of the interior and exterior areas of the subject property (except for exterior-only appraisals).
2. Inspect the neighborhood.
3. Inspect the comparable sales from, at least, the street.
4. Research, verify, and analyze data from reliable public and/or private sources.
5. Report the analysis, opinions, and conclusions in the appraisal report.

USPAP does not specifically address property inspection, other than being one of the options the appraiser may use to properly identify the property. In most assignments, the appraiser includes an inspection within the scope of work.

One major difference, specific to Fannie Mae, from what the appraiser might typically do, is the requirement to inspect from the exterior (or to drive by) the comparable properties used in the sales comparison analysis (or data that is used as transaction or rental data for the income approach). Following are some excerpts regarding this requirement from the *Selling Guide:*

- *Although it is preferable for the appraiser to provide comparables from the subject's neighborhood, Fannie Mae allows for the use of comparable sales that are located in competing neighborhoods, as these may simply be the best comparables available and the most appropriate for the appraiser's analysis. If this situation arises, the appraiser must not expand the neighborhood boundaries just to encompass the comparables selected. The appraiser must indicate the comparables are from a competing neighborhood and address any differences that exist.*
- *The* Selling Guide *states that when a property is located in an area in which there is a shortage of truly comparable sales—either because of the nature of the property improvements or the relatively low number of sales transactions in the neighborhood—the appraiser may need to use, as comparable sales, properties that are not truly comparable to the subject property or properties that are located in competing neighborhoods.*
- *If the appraiser utilizes comparable sales outside of the subject's neighborhood when closer comparable sales appear to be available, Fannie Mae has added a requirement that the appraiser provide an explanation as to why he or she used the specific comparable sales in the appraisal report. This will add transparency to the appraiser's selection of comparable sales and may assist the lender in underwriting the appraisal.*

USPAP requires that the appraiser analyze only such comparable data as is available. The Fannie Mae requirement offers guidance on how the data is classified and any limitations, necessary commentary, or disclosures required when the data is from outside the subject's defined neighborhood:

- *When the appraiser is provided with comparable sales data by a party that has a financial interest in either the sale or financing of the subject property, Fannie Mae requires the appraiser to verify the data with a party that does not have a financial interest in the subject transaction.*

Again, the requirement is more specific than the appraiser's obligations according to USPAP:

- *If in the analysis and completion of the sales comparison approach, the appraiser determines that time adjustments are required, the adjustments may be either positive or negative. The adjustments, however, must reflect the difference in market conditions between the date of sale of the comparable and the effective date of appraisal for the subject property.*

Although the application of a market condition (time) adjustment (either quantitatively or qualitatively) is an element of necessary practice when applicable in any appraisal, Fannie Mae is quite specific that adjustments are expected and how they should be considered. Notice that, according to Fannie Mae, the appraiser deems when and if a market condition adjustment is warranted:

- *In compliance with Fannie Mae, a minimum of **three** closed comparable sales must be analyzed and reported. Additional comparable sales, land contract purchase data, pending sales, and active listings may be used beyond the first three comparables as support for the value opinion.*

- *Fannie Mae allows the prior sale of the subject property to be used as a comparable sale for additional support, but not as one of the first three closed sale transactions.*
- *Comparable sales should be closed within the last **12 months.** Older sales can be used if the appraiser believes they are appropriate for the situation and the best indicator of value.*
- *The appraiser must explain the reasons for using any comparable sale more than **six months** old.*

It is generally accepted, as good practice, that the more data the appraiser analyzes, and the more recent the data is, the more credible the results will be. However, USPAP does not reference the number of comparable sales the appraiser must analyze in the sales comparison approach or limit how old comparable data can be. As can be seen, Fannie Mae has requirements that extend beyond the minimum requirements established by USPAP regarding those issues:

» *Fannie Mae requires that at least three comparable sales, preferably closed within the past twelve months, be used in the sales comparison analysis* «

- *Fannie Mae requires using quantitative adjustments for any differences between the subject property and the comparable sales. The adjustments must be based on supported market reaction to the difference, and not personal opinion. Qualitative analysis is not permitted.*

Quantitative and qualitative adjustments have been discussed in previous chapters. USPAP does not specifically address how a difference between the comparable property and the subject property is handled in terms of an adjustment. Fannie Mae requires that when a difference is present, it must be addressed with a dollar adjustment (or a percent stated as a dollar adjustment) that reflects market reaction to that particular element of difference. Be careful not to interpret this to mean that every difference must be addressed with an adjustment. Every difference for which the market evidence supports requiring an adjustment must be adjusted, or alternatively, be addressed by commentary in the report, discussing why an adjustment was not applied. USPAP does not specifically address the quantity (number of adjustments) or amount (in dollars) of adjustments in the sales comparison approach.

» *Significant differences between the comparables and the subject must be addressed with a quantitative adjustment that reflects market reaction to the difference* «

- *Fannie Mae has no specific guideline for what constitutes an acceptable range of value resulting from the sales comparison approach. However, if there is a large discrepancy among the indicated values, comments should be added to the appraisal report to explain the difference.*

Appraisers, as well as underwriters, may have some individual measures regarding the final adjusted range resulting in the sales comparison approach, such as a 10% overall range, but Fannie Mae has no specific guideline for this issue.

To better illustrate, appraisers and underwriters alike often prefer to have a narrow range result from the adjusted comparable data.

> ***For Example:*** If three comparable sales were adjusted to result in a range of value of $150,000 to $160,000, that range would be considered, by most interpretations, fairly narrow. However, if the resulting adjusted value range were $150,000 to $180,000, that would represent a significantly large spread in the indicated value range and the appraiser should discuss why the results are so broad.

SALES COMPARISON APPROACH

There are comparable properties currently offered for sale in the subject neighborhood ranging in price from $ to $.
There are comparable sales in the subject neighborhood within the past twelve months ranging in sale price from $ to $.

FEATURE	SUBJECT	COMPARABLE SALE # 1		COMPARABLE SALE # 2		COMPARABLE SALE # 3	
Address							
Proximity to Subject							
Sale Price	$		$		$		$
Sale Price/Gross Liv. Area	$ sq. ft.	$ sq. ft.		$ sq. ft.		$ sq. ft.	
Data Source(s)							
Verification Source(s)							
VALUE ADJUSTMENTS	DESCRIPTION	DESCRIPTION	+(-) $ Adjustment	DESCRIPTION	+(-) $ Adjustment	DESCRIPTION	+(-) $ Adjustment
Sale or Financing Concessions							
Date of Sale/Time							
Location							
Leasehold/Fee Simple							
Site							
View							
Design (Style)							
Quality of Construction							
Actual Age							
Condition							
Above Grade Room Count	Total Bdrms. Baths	Total Bdrms. Baths		Total Bdrms. Baths		Total Bdrms. Baths	
Gross Living Area	sq. ft.	sq. ft.		sq. ft.		sq. ft.	
Basement & Finished Rooms Below Grade							
Functional Utility							
Heating/Cooling							
Energy Efficient Items							
Garage/Carport							
Porch/Patio/Deck							
Net Adjustment (Total)		☐ + ☐ -	$	☐ + ☐ -	$	☐ + ☐ -	$
Adjusted Sale Price of Comparables		Net Adj. % Gross Adj. %	$	Net Adj. % Gross Adj. %	$	Net Adj. % Gross Adj. %	$

I ☐ did ☐ did not research the sale or transfer history of the subject property and comparable sales. If not, explain

My research ☐ did ☐ did not reveal any prior sales or transfers of the subject property for the three years prior to the effective date of this appraisal.
Data source(s)
My research ☐ did ☐ did not reveal any prior sales or transfers of the comparable sales for the year prior to the date of sale of the comparable sale.
Data source(s)
Report the results of the research and analysis of the prior sale or transfer history of the subject property and comparable sales (report additional prior sales on page 3).

ITEM	SUBJECT	COMPARABLE SALE # 1	COMPARABLE SALE # 2	COMPARABLE SALE # 3
Date of Prior Sale/Transfer				
Price of Prior Sale/Transfer				
Data Source(s)				
Effective Date of Data Source(s)				

Analysis of prior sale or transfer history of the subject property and comparable sales

Summary of Sales Comparison Approach

Indicated Value by Sales Comparison Approach $

Sales comparison approach section from Fannie Mae Uniform Residential Appraisal Report (URAR) form 1004. The URAR is one of the Fannie Mae forms in which the sales comparison approach is reported.

In addition to the requirement to analyze the sales history of the subject property for the three-year period prior to the effective date of the appraisal, as required by USPAP, Fannie Mae has requirements for comparable sales as well:

- *Prior sales for each comparable sale must be reported for the 12 months prior to the date of sale of each comparable.*

USPAP does not address analysis of the sales history of the comparable sale data used in the sales comparison approach.

» *Net adjustments should not exceed 15% and gross adjustments should not exceed 25% in the sales comparison approach for appraisals complying with Fannie Mae guidelines without convincing commentary explaining why the excessive adjustments were warranted* «

Income Approach

For single-family residential appraisal assignments, the income approach is generally appropriate in neighborhoods with a significant presence of tenant-occupied, single-family properties, or when the subject is a two- to four-family property.

Many of the Fannie Mae requirements for employing the income approach in a residential assignment are similar to those that have been discussed in this text as being good practice. There are some requirements that go beyond, or are more specific than, those practices that have been previously illustrated. Again, excerpts and paraphrased content from Fannie Mae's *Selling Guide* are noted in *italics.*

- *The GRM technique is employed using data extracted from other comparable rentals in the neighborhood. The sale prices of comparable properties are divided by their monthly market rent to develop the multiplier. The estimated gross monthly market rent of the subject is then multiplied by the multiplier to indicate a value.*

Fannie Mae specifies the use of the GRM technique, as illustrated in Chapter 6, as being the acceptable income valuation method in assignments used by Fannie Mae.

- *For two- to four-family investment properties, at least* ***three*** *comparable rental properties must be analyzed to support the market rent of the subject property. The rental comparables used in the analysis do not need to be the same comparables used in the sales comparison approach.*
- *The rental rates of two- to four-family investment properties should reflect unfurnished rent with the same type of utilities as used in the subject property, and the sales used to derive the GRM.*

Again, Fannie Mae has requirements for the quantity and type of data used in the preliminary income analysis of a two- to four-family investment property using the GRM technique.

INCOME	INCOME APPROACH TO VALUE (not required by Fannie Mae)			
	Estimated Monthly Market Rent $	X Gross Rent Multiplier	= $	Indicated Value by Income Approach
	Summary of Income Approach (including support for market rent and GRM)			

Income approach section from Fannie Mae Uniform Residential Appraisal Report (URAR) form 1004.

For single-family or two- to four-family residential properties that will serve as a rental property, the appraiser must also determine the property's cash flow and operating income:

- *The* ***Form 1007 Single-Family Comparable Rent Schedule*** *should be completed by the appraiser for single-family investment properties.* (shown on page 199.)
- ***Form 216 Operating Income Statement*** *should be completed for two- to four-family investment properties.*

» *Specific data must be gathered and analyzed in order to complete reporting Forms 1007 and 216, which are used for residential investment properties* «

The Fannie Mae Form 216 Operating Income Statement consists of three primary sections for which the appraiser must develop the information required (if part of the scope of work):

1. Replacement Reserve Schedule (shown on page 200.)
2. Annual Income and Expense Projection for the Next 12 Months (shown on page 200.)
3. Operating Income Reconciliation (shown on page 201.)

The form is presented in its entirety in the Appendix.

Operating Income Reconciliation

$ ________	–	$ ________	=	$ ________	÷ 12 =	$ ________
Effective Gross Income		Total Operating Expenses		Operating Income		Monthly Operating Income
$ ________	–	$ ________	=	$ ________		
Monthly Operating Income		Monthly Housing Expense		Net Cash Flow		

(Note: Monthly Housing Expense includes principal and interest on the mortgage, hazard insurance premiums, real estate taxes, mortgage insurance premiums, HOA dues, leasehold payments, and subordinate financing payments.)

The Operating Income Reconciliation converts the annual operating income to a monthly level and then deducts monthly housing expenses to arrive at net cash flow. It should be noted that for the purpose of completing this form, the appraiser must develop the monthly housing expense to include mortgage principal and interest (debt service), insurance, real estate taxes, mortgage insurance premiums and other miscellaneous elements.

- *The* ***lender*** *must make certain that the appraiser has been provided operating statements, expense statements relating to mortgage insurance premiums, and if applicable, owner's association dues, or other pertinent information related to the property.*

» *When compiling the information to complete the Annual Income and Expense section of Form 216 Operating Income Statement, income and expenses for owner-occupied units are not included* «

Completion of Form 1007 and Form 216 will be more fully discussed in appropriate coursework dedicated to the topic of residential report writing and/or the appraisal of investment properties.

Fannie Mae 1004MC Market Conditions Addendum

In several sections of this course there have been discussions regarding the appraiser's obligation to analyze the conditions of supply and demand, as well as other relevant market conditions in a market value appraisal assignment.

SINGLE FAMILY COMPARABLE RENT SCHEDULE

This form is intended to provide the appraiser with a familiar format to estimate the market rent of the subject property. Adjustments should be made only for items of significant difference between the comparables and the subject property.

ITEM	SUBJECT	COMPARABLE NO. 1		COMPARABLE NO. 2		COMPARABLE NO. 3	
Address							
Proximity to Subject							
Date Lease Begins Date Lease Expires							
Monthly Rental	If Currently Rented: $	$		$		$	
Less: Utilities Furniture	$	$		$		$	
Adjusted Monthly Rent	$	$		$		$	
Data Source							
RENT ADJUSTMENTS	DESCRIPTION	DESCRIPTION	+(–) $ Adjustment	DESCRIPTION	+(–) $ Adjustment	DESCRIPTION	+(–) $ Adjustment
Rent Concessions							
Location/View							
Design and Appeal							
Age/Condition							
Above Grade Room Count	Total / Bdrms / Baths	Total / Bdrms / Baths		Total / Bdrms / Baths		Total / Bdrms / Baths	
Gross Living Area	Sq. Ft.	Sq. Ft.		Sq. Ft.		Sq. Ft.	
Other (e.g., basement, etc.)							
Other:							
Net Adj. (total)		☐ + ☐ –	$	☐ + ☐ –	$	☐ + ☐ –	$
Indicated Monthly Market Rent			$		$		$

Comments on market data, including the range of rents for single family properties, an estimate of vacancy for single family rental properties, the general trend of rents and vacancy, and support for the above adjustments. (Rent concessions should be adjusted to the market, not to the subject property.)

Final Reconciliation of Market Rent:

I (WE) ESTIMATE THE MONTHLY MARKET RENT OF THE SUBJECT AS OF ______________________ 19____ TO BE $__________

Appraiser(s) SIGNATURE ______________________ Review Appraiser (If applicable) SIGNATURE ______________________

NAME ______________________ NAME ______________________

This form must be reproduced by the Seller.

Freddie Mac Form 1000 (8/88) Fannie Mae Form 1007 (8/88)

The Fannie Mae Form 1007 Single-Family Comparable Rent Schedule is similar to the discussion in Chapter 6 of elements that might be found in a rent schedule. Note that comparable rentals are adjusted first for any utilities or furniture included in the monthly rental and then adjustments are applied for rent concessions, or significant locational or physical differences between the subject and the comparable property.

Replacement Reserve Schedule

Adequate replacement reserves must be calculated regardless of whether actual reserves are provided for on the owner's operating statements or are customary in the local market. This represents the total average yearly reserves. Generally, all equipment and components that have a remaining life of more than one year—such as refrigerators, stoves, clothes washers/dryers, trash compactors, furnaces, roofs, and carpeting, etc.—should be expensed on a replacement cost basis.

Equipment	Replacement Cost		Remaining Life			By Applicant/ Appraiser	Lender Adjustments
Stoves/Ranges	@ $ ______	ea. ÷	____ Yrs. x	______	Units =	$ ______	$ ______
Refrigerators	@ $ ______	ea. ÷	____ Yrs. x	______	Units =	$ ______	$ ______
Dishwashers	@ $ ______	ea. ÷	____ Yrs. x	______	Units =	$ ______	$ ______
A/C Units	@ $ ______	ea. ÷	____ Yrs. x	______	Units =	$ ______	$ ______
C. Washer/Dryers	@ $ ______	ea. ÷	____ Yrs. x	______	Units =	$ ______	$ ______
HW Heaters	@ $ ______	ea. ÷	____ Yrs. x	______	Units =	$ ______	$ ______
Furnace(s)	@ $ ______	ea. ÷	____ Yrs. x	______	Units =	$ ______	$ ______
(Other)	@ $ ______	ea. ÷	____ Yrs. x	______	Units =	$ ______	$ ______
Roof	@ $ ______	÷	____ Yrs. x One Bldg. =			$ ______	$ ______

Carpeting (Wall to Wall) — Remaining Life

				By Applicant/ Appraiser	Lender Adjustments
(Units)	____ Total Sq. Yds. @ $____	Per Sq. Yd. ÷	____Yrs. =	$ ______	$ ______
(Public Areas)	____ Total Sq. Yds. @ $____	Per Sq. Yd. ÷	____Yrs. =	$ ______	$ ______

Total Replacement Reserves. (Enter on Pg. 1) $ ______ $ ______

The information for the Replacement Reserve Schedule is developed as illustrated in Chapter 6, with one major difference; the replacement costs and remaining life of the component are first defined per unit and then multiplied by the number of units.

Annual Income and Expense Projection for Next 12 months

Income *(Do not include income for owner-occupied units)*	By Applicant/Appraiser	Adjustments by Lender's Underwriter
Gross Annual Rental *(from unit(s) to be rented)*	$ ______	$ ______
Other Income *(include sources)*	+ ______	+ ______
Total	$ ______	$ ______
Less Vacancy/Rent Loss	− ______ (%)	− ______ (%)
Effective Gross Income	$ ______	$ ______
Expenses *(Do not include expenses for owner-occupied units)*		
Electricity	______	______
Gas	______	______
Fuel Oil	______	______
Fuel ....(Type - ______)	______	______
Water/Sewer	______	______
Trash Removal	______	______
Pest Control	______	______
Other Taxes or Licenses	______	______
Casual Labor .... This includes the costs for public area cleaning, snow removal, etc., even though the applicant may not elect to contract for such services.	______	______
Interior Paint/Decorating .... This includes the costs of contract labor and materials that are required to maintain the interiors of the living units.	______	______
General Repairs/Maintenance .... This includes the costs of contract labor and materials that are required to maintain the public corridors, stairways, roofs, mechanical systems, grounds, etc.	______	______
Management Expenses .... These are the customary expenses that a professional management company would charge to manage the property.	______	______
Supplies .... This includes the costs of items like light bulbs, janitorial supplies, etc.	______	______
Total Replacement Reserves - See Schedule on Pg. 2........	______	______
Miscellaneous	______	______
....	______	______
Total Operating Expenses	$ ______	$ ______

The information for the Annual Income and Expense Projection for the Next 12 Months is very similar to that which was developed for the Income and Expense Summary in Chapter 6. Key differences are that income and expenses for owner-occupied units are not included and the expenses are not specifically defined as being either fixed or variable. Real estate taxes and insurance are also not considered in this step, but will be considered during reconciliation. It should also be noted that management expenses are to be estimated based on what a professional management company would charge to manage the property.

Being aware of economic and supply and demand factors of the subject market is part of the appraiser's market competency.

Due to increased risk during particularly volatile economic climates, Fannie Mae now requires the development and completion of the 1004MC Market Conditions Addendum as part of appraisals performed for use by Fannie Mae. A reproduction of the form can be found in the Appendix of this text. While the reporting format may exceed the level common in many residential appraisal assignments, the analysis required to develop the appraiser's opinions should not be entirely new. Correctly analyzing most of these factors is embedded in the appraiser's obligation in compliance with Standards Rule 1-3 of USPAP.

The following has been reproduced from Fannie Mae Announcement 08-30 in its entirety. Illustrations of each form section are also provided.

Implementation of the Market Conditions Addendum

Fannie Mae purchases or securitizes mortgages in all markets and under all market conditions. The current appraisal report forms require the appraiser to report on the primary indicators of market condition for properties in the subject neighborhood by noting the trend of property values (increasing, stable, or declining), the supply of properties in the subject neighborhood (shortage, in-balance, or over-supply), and the marketing time for properties (under three months, three to six months, or over six months) as of the effective date of the appraisal. Fannie Mae also expects the appraiser to provide their conclusions for the reasons a market is experiencing declining market values, an over-supply of properties, or marketing times over six months.

To further enhance the transparency of the conclusions made by the appraiser related to market trends and conditions, the Form 1004MC will be required for all mortgage loans delivered to Fannie Mae with appraisals of one- to four-unit properties with an effective date on or after April 1, 2009.

Guidelines for Using Form 1004MC

The Form 1004MC is intended to provide the lender with a clear and accurate understanding of the market trends and conditions prevalent in the subject neighborhood. The form provides the appraiser with a structured format to report the data and to more easily identify current market trends and conditions. The appraiser's conclusions are to be reported in the "Neighborhood" section of the appraisal report.

Fannie Mae recognizes that all of the requested data elements for analysis are not equally available in all markets. In some markets it may not be possible to retrieve the total number of comparable active listings from earlier periods. If this is the case, the appraiser must explain the attempt to obtain such information. Also, there may be markets in which the data is available in terms of an "average" as opposed to a "median." In this case, the appraiser needs to note that his or her analysis has been based on an "average" representation of the data. Regardless of whether all requested information is available, the appraiser must provide support for his or her conclusions regarding market trends and conditions.

» *The information needed to complete the 1004MC Market Conditions Addendum can be gathered from a variety of public and private information sources and should be considered part of the appraiser's market analysis in the appraisal process* «

Inventory Analysis Section

The "Inventory Analysis" section assists the appraiser in analyzing important supply and demand factors in order to reach a conclusion regarding housing trends and market conditions. When completing this section, the appraiser must include the comparable data that reflects the total pool of comparable properties from which a buyer may select a property in order to analyze the sales activity and the local housing supply. One of the tools used to monitor these trends is the absorption rate. The absorption rate is the rate at which properties for sale have been or can be sold (marketed) within a given area. To determine the absorption rate, the appraiser divides the total number of settled sales by the time frame being analyzed. The months of housing supply is based on the total listings for the applicable period divided by the absorption rate.

Inventory Analysis	Prior 7–12 Months	Prior 4–6 Months	Current – 3 Months	Overall Trend		
Total # of Comparable Sales (Settled)				☐ Increasing	☐ Stable	☐ Declining
Absorption Rate (Total Sales/Months)				☐ Increasing	☐ Stable	☐ Declining
Total # of Comparable Active Listings				☐ Declining	☐ Stable	☐ Increasing
Months of Housing Supply (Total Listings/Ab.Rate)				☐ Declining	☐ Stable	☐ Increasing

For Example:

Step 1: Calculate the absorption rate. If there were 60 sales during a six-month period (e.g., "Prior 7 – 12 Months" column), the absorption rate is 10 sales per month (60 ÷ 6).

Step 2: Calculate the months of housing supply. If there are 240 active listings, there is a 24-month supply of homes on the market (240 active sales ÷ 10 sales per month). This may support the appraiser's conclusion that there is an over-supply of homes on the market. Anomalies in the data, such as seasonal markets, new construction, or other factors, must be addressed in the form.

Median Sale & List Price, DOM, List/Sale Ratio Section

The appraiser must analyze additional trends, including the changes in median prices and days on the market (DOM) for both sales and listings, as well as a change in list-to-sales price ratios.

Median Sale & List Price, DOM, Sale/List %	Prior 7–12 Months	Prior 4–6 Months	Current – 3 Months	Overall Trend		
Median Comparable Sale Price				☐ Increasing	☐ Stable	☐ Declining
Median Comparable Sales Days on Market				☐ Declining	☐ Stable	☐ Increasing
Median Comparable List Price				☐ Increasing	☐ Stable	☐ Declining
Median Comparable Listings Days on Market				☐ Declining	☐ Stable	☐ Increasing
Median Sale Price as % of List Price				☐ Increasing	☐ Stable	☐ Declining
Seller-(developer, builder, etc.) paid financial assistance prevalent? ☐ Yes ☐ No				☐ Declining	☐ Stable	☐ Increasing

For Example: If the median comparable sale prices are $300,000, $295,000, and $305,000 for their respective time periods, the overall trend for the prior 12 months is relatively "stable."

Overall Trend Section

The "Overall Trend" section is designed to reflect potential positive trends, neutral trends, or negative trends in inventory, median sale and list price, days on market, list-to- sale price ratio, and seller concessions.

For Example: An increase in the absorption rate is generally viewed as a positive trend, whereas a decrease in the absorption rate may be viewed as a negative trend. Furthermore, a decrease in the number of days on the market, either sales or listings, more than likely represents an overall positive trend.

Seller Concessions

Form 1004MC also provides a section for comments on the prevalence of seller concessions and the trend in seller concessions for the past 12 months. The change in seller concessions within the market provides the lender with additional insight into current market conditions. The appraiser should consider and report on seller-paid (or third-party) costs.

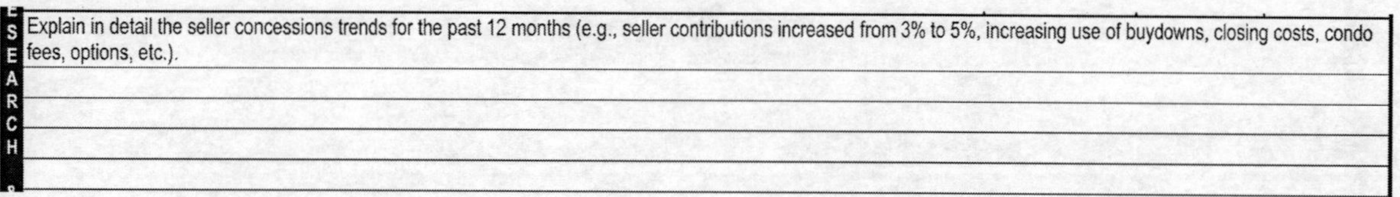

Explain in detail the seller concessions trends for the past 12 months (e.g., seller contributions increased from 3% to 5%, increasing use of buydowns, closing costs, condo fees, options, etc.).

For Example: These items include, but are not limited to, mortgage payments, points and fees, and in condominium or cooperative projects, items such as homeowners' association fees and guaranteed rental programs.

Seller concessions must be carefully analyzed by the appraiser, since excessive concessions often lead to inflated property values.

There are a number of markets across the country where, due to current conditions, there has been an increase in the prevalence of seller concessions. The following excerpt from the Selling Guide, Part XI, Section 406.5 (C) provides guidance for these circumstances:

> *"The need to make negative dollar adjustments for sales and financing concessions and the amount of the adjustments to the comparable sales are not based on how typical the concessions might be for a segment of the market area—large sales concessions can be relatively typical in a particular segment of the market and still result in sale prices that reflect more than the value of the real estate. Adjustments based on dollar-for-dollar deductions that are equal to the cost of the concessions to the seller (as a strict cash equivalency approach would dictate) are not appropriate. We recognize that the effect of the sales concessions on sale prices can vary with the amount of the concessions and differences in various markets. The adjustments must reflect the difference between what the comparables actually sold for with the sales concessions and what they would have sold for without the concessions, so that the dollar amount of the adjustments will approximate the reaction of the market to the concessions."*

Foreclosure Sales and Summary/Analysis of Data

The presence and extent of foreclosure/REO sales are worthy of comment when analyzing market data and must be reported on the form. The form also allows for the appraiser to summarize the data and provide other data analysis or additional information, such as analysis of pending sales, which over time can show a market trend.

& ANALYSIS

Are foreclosure sales (REO sales) a factor in the market? ☐ Yes ☐ No If yes, explain (including the trends in listings and sales of foreclosed properties).

Cite data sources for above information.

Summarize the above information as support for your conclusions in the Neighborhood section of the appraisal report form. If you used any additional information, such as an analysis of pending sales and/or expired and withdrawn listings, to formulate your conclusions, provide both an explanation and support for your conclusions.

Selected USPAP Illustrations and Guidance

The following USPAP Frequently Asked Questions (FAQ) have been selected to illustrate the application of USPAP in specific circumstances discussed in this chapter.

FAQ 185—Physical Segments (5-Acre Portion)

FAQ 199—Adjustments in Sales Comparison Approach

FAQ 228—Pending Sales as Comparables

FAQ 229—Subject Property as a Comparable Sale

FAQ 233—Analysis of Sales History for Comparable Sales

FAQ 235—Obligation to Analyze Prior Listings of Subject Property

Application Case Study

A residential investment property is generating $1,250 per month. Using the mean of the data provided rounded to the nearest one-hundred dollars and a GRM of 127, determine if the scenario represents a positive leasehold or a negative leasehold and the value of the leased fee or leasehold interest.

Rent Comparable	Monthly Rent
1	$1,475
2	$1,275
3	$1,150
4	$1,175
5	$1,200
6	$1,250
7	$1,400
8	$1,425
9	$1,375
10	$1,300

Quiz

1. ***The contract rent of a property is $1,000 per month. However, the market rent is indicated at $1,250. Which does this scenario represent?***
   a. negative leasehold/leased fee interest
   b. negative leasehold/leasehold interest
   c. positive leasehold/leased fee interest
   d. positive leasehold/leasehold interest

2. ***Which best describes a servient tenement?***
   a. individual conveyed the right to use an easement
   b. party benefiting from an access easement
   c. property burdened by an easement
   d. public entity in a gross easement

3. ***The party in a life estate situation to whom the right of possession will pass upon the death of the life tenant is the***
   a. dominant tenement.
   b. measuring life.
   c. remainderman.
   d. reversionary tenant.

4. ***A 3-unit income property does not feature a popular amenity, and the condition is incurable. The cost new to add the amenity at time of the construction if the building were being built today would be $8,500. The appraiser concludes that the property is renting for $40 per month less than properties which feature the amenity. Using an income technique, what would be the indicated functional depreciation due to lack of the amenity if the monthly GRM was 90?***
   a. $1,290
   b. $2,300
   c. $3,580
   d. $4,700

5. ***In the sales comparison approach, observing Fannie Mae guidelines, which is a TRUE statement if the subject property sold two months ago?***
   a. Subject can be used, but not as one of the first three comparable sales.
   b. Subject can be used with a qualitative adjustment applied for market conditions.
   c. Subject must be one of the three comparables used.
   d. Subject property cannot be used as a comparable in the approach.

6. ***The income technique required by Fannie Mae is the***
   a. gross income multiplier.
   b. gross rent multiplier.
   c. overall capitalization rate method.
   d. yield capitalization method.

7. ***For the Income/Expense Projection of the Fannie Mae Operating Income Statement,***
   a. expenses for an owner-occupied unit are included.
   b. management fees must be estimated.
   c. real estate taxes and insurance are considered fixed expenses.
   d. replacement reserves are not included.

8. ***For which is there NO requirement of USPAP, but is commonly an assignment condition of Fannie Mae and other major lending entities?***
   a. Reporting of prior sales of the subject property for the previous 3 years.
   b. Reporting the reasoning for not developing one or more approaches to value.
   c. Reporting sales history of the comparable sales for the prior 12 months.
   d. Reporting the scope of work performed.

Appendix

APPENDIX 1: SAMPLE FORMS

Uniform Residential Appraisal Report—1004

Market Conditions Addendum to the Appraisal Report—1004MC

Small Residential Income Property Appraisal Report—1025

Exterior-Only Inspection Residential Appraisal Report—2055

Operating Income Statement—216

APPENDIX 2: COMMON FORMULA & CONCEPTS

Uniform Residential Appraisal Report

File #

The purpose of this summary appraisal report is to provide the lender/client with an accurate, and adequately supported, opinion of the market value of the subject property.

SUBJECT

Property Address | City | State | Zip Code

Borrower | Owner of Public Record | County

Legal Description

Assessor's Parcel # | Tax Year | R.E. Taxes $

Neighborhood Name | Map Reference | Census Tract

Occupant ☐ Owner ☐ Tenant ☐ Vacant | Special Assessments $ | ☐ PUD | HOA $ | ☐ per year ☐ per month

Property Rights Appraised ☐ Fee Simple ☐ Leasehold ☐ Other (describe)

Assignment Type ☐ Purchase Transaction ☐ Refinance Transaction ☐ Other (describe)

Lender/Client | Address

Is the subject property currently offered for sale or has it been offered for sale in the twelve months prior to the effective date of this appraisal? ☐ Yes ☐ No

Report data source(s) used, offering price(s), and date(s).

CONTRACT

I ☐ did ☐ did not analyze the contract for sale for the subject purchase transaction. Explain the results of the analysis of the contract for sale or why the analysis was not performed.

Contract Price $ | Date of Contract | Is the property seller the owner of public record? ☐ Yes ☐ No | Data Source(s)

Is there any financial assistance (loan charges, sale concessions, gift or downpayment assistance, etc.) to be paid by any party on behalf of the borrower? ☐ Yes ☐ No

If Yes, report the total dollar amount and describe the items to be paid.

NEIGHBORHOOD

Note: Race and the racial composition of the neighborhood are not appraisal factors.

Neighborhood Characteristics				One-Unit Housing Trends				One-Unit Housing		Present Land Use %	
Location	☐ Urban	☐ Suburban	☐ Rural	Property Values	☐ Increasing	☐ Stable	☐ Declining	PRICE	AGE	One-Unit	%
Built-Up	☐ Over 75%	☐ 25–75%	☐ Under 25%	Demand/Supply	☐ Shortage	☐ In Balance	☐ Over Supply	$ (000)	(yrs)	2-4 Unit	%
Growth	☐ Rapid	☐ Stable	☐ Slow	Marketing Time	☐ Under 3 mths	☐ 3–6 mths	☐ Over 6 mths	Low		Multi-Family	%
Neighborhood Boundaries								High		Commercial	%
								Pred.		Other	%

Neighborhood Description

Market Conditions (including support for the above conclusions)

SITE

Dimensions | Area | Shape | View

Specific Zoning Classification | Zoning Description

Zoning Compliance ☐ Legal ☐ Legal Nonconforming (Grandfathered Use) ☐ No Zoning ☐ Illegal (describe)

Is the highest and best use of the subject property as improved (or as proposed per plans and specifications) the present use? ☐ Yes ☐ No If No, describe

Utilities	Public	Other (describe)		Public	Other (describe)	Off-site Improvements—Type	Public	Private
Electricity	☐	☐	Water	☐	☐	Street	☐	☐
Gas	☐	☐	Sanitary Sewer	☐	☐	Alley	☐	☐

FEMA Special Flood Hazard Area ☐ Yes ☐ No | FEMA Flood Zone | FEMA Map # | FEMA Map Date

Are the utilities and off-site improvements typical for the market area? ☐ Yes ☐ No If No, describe

Are there any adverse site conditions or external factors (easements, encroachments, environmental conditions, land uses, etc.)? ☐ Yes ☐ No If Yes, describe

IMPROVEMENTS

General Description		Foundation		Exterior Description	materials/condition	Interior	materials/condition
Units ☐ One ☐ One with Accessory Unit		☐ Concrete Slab ☐ Crawl Space		Foundation Walls		Floors	
# of Stories		☐ Full Basement ☐ Partial Basement		Exterior Walls		Walls	
Type ☐ Det. ☐ Att. ☐ S-Det./End Unit		Basement Area	sq. ft.	Roof Surface		Trim/Finish	
☐ Existing ☐ Proposed ☐ Under Const.		Basement Finish	%	Gutters & Downspouts		Bath Floor	
Design (Style)		☐ Outside Entry/Exit ☐ Sump Pump		Window Type		Bath Wainscot	
Year Built		Evidence of ☐ Infestation		Storm Sash/Insulated		Car Storage ☐ None	
Effective Age (Yrs)		☐ Dampness ☐ Settlement		Screens		☐ Driveway # of Cars	
Attic	☐ None	Heating ☐ FWA ☐ HWBB ☐ Radiant		Amenities	☐ Woodstove(s) #	Driveway Surface	
☐ Drop Stair	☐ Stairs	☐ Other	Fuel	☐ Fireplace(s) #	☐ Fence	☐ Garage # of Cars	
☐ Floor	☐ Scuttle	Cooling ☐ Central Air Conditioning		☐ Patio/Deck	☐ Porch	☐ Carport # of Cars	
☐ Finished	☐ Heated	☐ Individual	☐ Other	☐ Pool	☐ Other	☐ Att. ☐ Det. ☐ Built-in	

Appliances ☐ Refrigerator ☐ Range/Oven ☐ Dishwasher ☐ Disposal ☐ Microwave ☐ Washer/Dryer ☐ Other (describe)

Finished area **above** grade contains: | Rooms | Bedrooms | Bath(s) | Square Feet of Gross Living Area Above Grade

Additional features (special energy efficient items, etc.)

Describe the condition of the property (including needed repairs, deterioration, renovations, remodeling, etc.).

Are there any physical deficiencies or adverse conditions that affect the livability, soundness, or structural integrity of the property? ☐ Yes ☐ No If Yes, describe

Does the property generally conform to the neighborhood (functional utility, style, condition, use, construction, etc.)? ☐ Yes ☐ No If No, describe

Freddie Mac Form 70 March 2005 | Page 1 of 6 | Fannie Mae Form 1004 March 2005

Uniform Residential Appraisal Report

File #

SALES COMPARISON APPROACH

There are comparable properties currently offered for sale in the subject neighborhood ranging in price from $ to $.

There are comparable sales in the subject neighborhood within the past twelve months ranging in sale price from $ to $.

FEATURE	SUBJECT	COMPARABLE SALE # 1		COMPARABLE SALE # 2		COMPARABLE SALE # 3	
Address							
Proximity to Subject							
Sale Price	$		$		$		$
Sale Price/Gross Liv. Area	$ sq. ft.	$ sq. ft.		$ sq. ft.		$ sq. ft.	
Data Source(s)							
Verification Source(s)							
VALUE ADJUSTMENTS	DESCRIPTION	DESCRIPTION	+(-) $ Adjustment	DESCRIPTION	+(-) $ Adjustment	DESCRIPTION	+(-) $ Adjustment
Sale or Financing Concessions							
Date of Sale/Time							
Location							
Leasehold/Fee Simple							
Site							
View							
Design (Style)							
Quality of Construction							
Actual Age							
Condition							
Above Grade Room Count	Total / Bdrms. / Baths	Total / Bdrms. / Baths		Total / Bdrms. / Baths		Total / Bdrms. / Baths	
Gross Living Area	sq. ft.	sq. ft.		sq. ft.		sq. ft.	
Basement & Finished Rooms Below Grade							
Functional Utility							
Heating/Cooling							
Energy Efficient Items							
Garage/Carport							
Porch/Patio/Deck							
Net Adjustment (Total)		☐ + ☐ -	$	☐ + ☐ -	$	☐ + ☐ -	$
Adjusted Sale Price of Comparables		Net Adj. % Gross Adj. %	$	Net Adj. % Gross Adj. %	$	Net Adj. % Gross Adj. %	$

I ☐ did ☐ did not research the sale or transfer history of the subject property and comparable sales. If not, explain

My research ☐ did ☐ did not reveal any prior sales or transfers of the subject property for the three years prior to the effective date of this appraisal.

Data source(s)

My research ☐ did ☐ did not reveal any prior sales or transfers of the comparable sales for the year prior to the date of sale of the comparable sale.

Data source(s)

Report the results of the research and analysis of the prior sale or transfer history of the subject property and comparable sales (report additional prior sales on page 3).

ITEM	SUBJECT	COMPARABLE SALE # 1	COMPARABLE SALE # 2	COMPARABLE SALE # 3
Date of Prior Sale/Transfer				
Price of Prior Sale/Transfer				
Data Source(s)				
Effective Date of Data Source(s)				

Analysis of prior sale or transfer history of the subject property and comparable sales

Summary of Sales Comparison Approach

Indicated Value by Sales Comparison Approach $

RECONCILIATION

Indicated Value by: Sales Comparison Approach $ Cost Approach (if developed) $ Income Approach (if developed) $

This appraisal is made ☐ "as is", ☐ subject to completion per plans and specifications on the basis of a hypothetical condition that the improvements have been completed, ☐ subject to the following repairs or alterations on the basis of a hypothetical condition that the repairs or alterations have been completed, or ☐ subject to the following required inspection based on the extraordinary assumption that the condition or deficiency does not require alteration or repair:

Based on a complete visual inspection of the interior and exterior areas of the subject property, defined scope of work, statement of assumptions and limiting conditions, and appraiser's certification, my (our) opinion of the market value, as defined, of the real property that is the subject of this report is $, as of , which is the date of inspection and the effective date of this appraisal.

Uniform Residential Appraisal Report—1004

Uniform Residential Appraisal Report

File #

ADDITIONAL COMMENTS

COST APPROACH

COST APPROACH TO VALUE (not required by Fannie Mae)

Provide adequate information for the lender/client to replicate the below cost figures and calculations.

Support for the opinion of site value (summary of comparable land sales or other methods for estimating site value)

ESTIMATED ☐ REPRODUCTION OR ☐ REPLACEMENT COST NEW	OPINION OF SITE VALUE .... = $
Source of cost data	Dwelling Sq. Ft. @ $ .... =$
Quality rating from cost service Effective date of cost data	Sq. Ft. @ $ .... =$
Comments on Cost Approach (gross living area calculations, depreciation, etc.)	
	Garage/Carport Sq. Ft. @ $ .... =$
	Total Estimate of Cost-New .... = $
	Less Physical | Functional | External
	Depreciation =$( )
	Depreciated Cost of Improvements............ =$
	"As-is" Value of Site Improvements............ =$
Estimated Remaining Economic Life (HUD and VA only) Years	Indicated Value By Cost Approach .... =$

INCOME

INCOME APPROACH TO VALUE (not required by Fannie Mae)

Estimated Monthly Market Rent $ X Gross Rent Multiplier = $ Indicated Value by Income Approach

Summary of Income Approach (including support for market rent and GRM)

PUD INFORMATION

PROJECT INFORMATION FOR PUDs (if applicable)

Is the developer/builder in control of the Homeowners' Association (HOA)? ☐ Yes ☐ No Unit type(s) ☐ Detached ☐ Attached

Provide the following information for PUDs ONLY if the developer/builder is in control of the HOA and the subject property is an attached dwelling unit.

Legal name of project

Total number of phases Total number of units Total number of units sold

Total number of units rented Total number of units for sale Data source(s)

Was the project created by the conversion of an existing building(s) into a PUD? ☐ Yes ☐ No If Yes, date of conversion

Does the project contain any multi-dwelling units? ☐ Yes ☐ No Data source(s)

Are the units, common elements, and recreation facilities complete? ☐ Yes ☐ No If No, describe the status of completion.

Are the common elements leased to or by the Homeowners' Association? ☐ Yes ☐ No If Yes, describe the rental terms and options.

Describe common elements and recreational facilities

Freddie Mac Form 70 March 2005 Page 3 of 6 Fannie Mae Form 1004 March 2005

Uniform Residential Appraisal Report

File #

This report form is designed to report an appraisal of a one-unit property or a one-unit property with an accessory unit; including a unit in a planned unit development (PUD). This report form is not designed to report an appraisal of a manufactured home or a unit in a condominium or cooperative project.

This appraisal report is subject to the following scope of work, intended use, intended user, definition of market value, statement of assumptions and limiting conditions, and certifications. Modifications, additions, or deletions to the intended use, intended user, definition of market value, or assumptions and limiting conditions are not permitted. The appraiser may expand the scope of work to include any additional research or analysis necessary based on the complexity of this appraisal assignment. Modifications or deletions to the certifications are also not permitted. However, additional certifications that do not constitute material alterations to this appraisal report, such as those required by law or those related to the appraiser's continuing education or membership in an appraisal organization, are permitted.

SCOPE OF WORK: The scope of work for this appraisal is defined by the complexity of this appraisal assignment and the reporting requirements of this appraisal report form, including the following definition of market value, statement of assumptions and limiting conditions, and certifications. The appraiser must, at a minimum: (1) perform a complete visual inspection of the interior and exterior areas of the subject property, (2) inspect the neighborhood, (3) inspect each of the comparable sales from at least the street, (4) research, verify, and analyze data from reliable public and/or private sources, and (5) report his or her analysis, opinions, and conclusions in this appraisal report.

INTENDED USE: The intended use of this appraisal report is for the lender/client to evaluate the property that is the subject of this appraisal for a mortgage finance transaction.

INTENDED USER: The intended user of this appraisal report is the lender/client.

DEFINITION OF MARKET VALUE: The most probable price which a property should bring in a competitive and open market under all conditions requisite to a fair sale, the buyer and seller, each acting prudently, knowledgeably and assuming the price is not affected by undue stimulus. Implicit in this definition is the consummation of a sale as of a specified date and the passing of title from seller to buyer under conditions whereby: (1) buyer and seller are typically motivated; (2) both parties are well informed or well advised, and each acting in what he or she considers his or her own best interest; (3) a reasonable time is allowed for exposure in the open market; (4) payment is made in terms of cash in U. S. dollars or in terms of financial arrangements comparable thereto; and (5) the price represents the normal consideration for the property sold unaffected by special or creative financing or sales concessions* granted by anyone associated with the sale.

*Adjustments to the comparables must be made for special or creative financing or sales concessions. No adjustments are necessary for those costs which are normally paid by sellers as a result of tradition or law in a market area; these costs are readily identifiable since the seller pays these costs in virtually all sales transactions. Special or creative financing adjustments can be made to the comparable property by comparisons to financing terms offered by a third party institutional lender that is not already involved in the property or transaction. Any adjustment should not be calculated on a mechanical dollar for dollar cost of the financing or concession but the dollar amount of any adjustment should approximate the market's reaction to the financing or concessions based on the appraiser's judgment.

STATEMENT OF ASSUMPTIONS AND LIMITING CONDITIONS: The appraiser's certification in this report is subject to the following assumptions and limiting conditions:

1. The appraiser will not be responsible for matters of a legal nature that affect either the property being appraised or the title to it, except for information that he or she became aware of during the research involved in performing this appraisal. The appraiser assumes that the title is good and marketable and will not render any opinions about the title.

2. The appraiser has provided a sketch in this appraisal report to show the approximate dimensions of the improvements. The sketch is included only to assist the reader in visualizing the property and understanding the appraiser's determination of its size.

3. The appraiser has examined the available flood maps that are provided by the Federal Emergency Management Agency (or other data sources) and has noted in this appraisal report whether any portion of the subject site is located in an identified Special Flood Hazard Area. Because the appraiser is not a surveyor, he or she makes no guarantees, express or implied, regarding this determination.

4. The appraiser will not give testimony or appear in court because he or she made an appraisal of the property in question, unless specific arrangements to do so have been made beforehand, or as otherwise required by law.

5. The appraiser has noted in this appraisal report any adverse conditions (such as needed repairs, deterioration, the presence of hazardous wastes, toxic substances, etc.) observed during the inspection of the subject property or that he or she became aware of during the research involved in performing this appraisal. Unless otherwise stated in this appraisal report, the appraiser has no knowledge of any hidden or unapparent physical deficiencies or adverse conditions of the property (such as, but not limited to, needed repairs, deterioration, the presence of hazardous wastes, toxic substances, adverse environmental conditions, etc.) that would make the property less valuable, and has assumed that there are no such conditions and makes no guarantees or warranties, express or implied. The appraiser will not be responsible for any such conditions that do exist or for any engineering or testing that might be required to discover whether such conditions exist. Because the appraiser is not an expert in the field of environmental hazards, this appraisal report must not be considered as an environmental assessment of the property.

6. The appraiser has based his or her appraisal report and valuation conclusion for an appraisal that is subject to satisfactory completion, repairs, or alterations on the assumption that the completion, repairs, or alterations of the subject property will be performed in a professional manner.

Uniform Residential Appraisal Report

File #

APPRAISER'S CERTIFICATION: The Appraiser certifies and agrees that:

1. I have, at a minimum, developed and reported this appraisal in accordance with the scope of work requirements stated in this appraisal report.

2. I performed a complete visual inspection of the interior and exterior areas of the subject property. I reported the condition of the improvements in factual, specific terms. I identified and reported the physical deficiencies that could affect the livability, soundness, or structural integrity of the property.

3. I performed this appraisal in accordance with the requirements of the Uniform Standards of Professional Appraisal Practice that were adopted and promulgated by the Appraisal Standards Board of The Appraisal Foundation and that were in place at the time this appraisal report was prepared.

4. I developed my opinion of the market value of the real property that is the subject of this report based on the sales comparison approach to value. I have adequate comparable market data to develop a reliable sales comparison approach for this appraisal assignment. I further certify that I considered the cost and income approaches to value but did not develop them, unless otherwise indicated in this report.

5. I researched, verified, analyzed, and reported on any current agreement for sale for the subject property, any offering for sale of the subject property in the twelve months prior to the effective date of this appraisal, and the prior sales of the subject property for a minimum of three years prior to the effective date of this appraisal, unless otherwise indicated in this report.

6. I researched, verified, analyzed, and reported on the prior sales of the comparable sales for a minimum of one year prior to the date of sale of the comparable sale, unless otherwise indicated in this report.

7. I selected and used comparable sales that are locationally, physically, and functionally the most similar to the subject property.

8. I have not used comparable sales that were the result of combining a land sale with the contract purchase price of a home that has been built or will be built on the land.

9. I have reported adjustments to the comparable sales that reflect the market's reaction to the differences between the subject property and the comparable sales.

10. I verified, from a disinterested source, all information in this report that was provided by parties who have a financial interest in the sale or financing of the subject property.

11. I have knowledge and experience in appraising this type of property in this market area.

12. I am aware of, and have access to, the necessary and appropriate public and private data sources, such as multiple listing services, tax assessment records, public land records and other such data sources for the area in which the property is located.

13. I obtained the information, estimates, and opinions furnished by other parties and expressed in this appraisal report from reliable sources that I believe to be true and correct.

14. I have taken into consideration the factors that have an impact on value with respect to the subject neighborhood, subject property, and the proximity of the subject property to adverse influences in the development of my opinion of market value. I have noted in this appraisal report any adverse conditions (such as, but not limited to, needed repairs, deterioration, the presence of hazardous wastes, toxic substances, adverse environmental conditions, etc.) observed during the inspection of the subject property or that I became aware of during the research involved in performing this appraisal. I have considered these adverse conditions in my analysis of the property value, and have reported on the effect of the conditions on the value and marketability of the subject property.

15. I have not knowingly withheld any significant information from this appraisal report and, to the best of my knowledge, all statements and information in this appraisal report are true and correct.

16. I stated in this appraisal report my own personal, unbiased, and professional analysis, opinions, and conclusions, which are subject only to the assumptions and limiting conditions in this appraisal report.

17. I have no present or prospective interest in the property that is the subject of this report, and I have no present or prospective personal interest or bias with respect to the participants in the transaction. I did not base, either partially or completely, my analysis and/or opinion of market value in this appraisal report on the race, color, religion, sex, age, marital status, handicap, familial status, or national origin of either the prospective owners or occupants of the subject property or of the present owners or occupants of the properties in the vicinity of the subject property or on any other basis prohibited by law.

18. My employment and/or compensation for performing this appraisal or any future or anticipated appraisals was not conditioned on any agreement or understanding, written or otherwise, that I would report (or present analysis supporting) a predetermined specific value, a predetermined minimum value, a range or direction in value, a value that favors the cause of any party, or the attainment of a specific result or occurrence of a specific subsequent event (such as approval of a pending mortgage loan application).

19. I personally prepared all conclusions and opinions about the real estate that were set forth in this appraisal report. If I relied on significant real property appraisal assistance from any individual or individuals in the performance of this appraisal or the preparation of this appraisal report, I have named such individual(s) and disclosed the specific tasks performed in this appraisal report. I certify that any individual so named is qualified to perform the tasks. I have not authorized anyone to make a change to any item in this appraisal report; therefore, any change made to this appraisal is unauthorized and I will take no responsibility for it.

20. I identified the lender/client in this appraisal report who is the individual, organization, or agent for the organization that ordered and will receive this appraisal report.

Uniform Residential Appraisal Report

File #

21. The lender/client may disclose or distribute this appraisal report to: the borrower; another lender at the request of the borrower; the mortgagee or its successors and assigns; mortgage insurers; government sponsored enterprises; other secondary market participants; data collection or reporting services; professional appraisal organizations; any department, agency, or instrumentality of the United States; and any state, the District of Columbia, or other jurisdictions; without having to obtain the appraiser's or supervisory appraiser's (if applicable) consent. Such consent must be obtained before this appraisal report may be disclosed or distributed to any other party (including, but not limited to, the public through advertising, public relations, news, sales, or other media).

22. I am aware that any disclosure or distribution of this appraisal report by me or the lender/client may be subject to certain laws and regulations. Further, I am also subject to the provisions of the Uniform Standards of Professional Appraisal Practice that pertain to disclosure or distribution by me.

23. The borrower, another lender at the request of the borrower, the mortgagee or its successors and assigns, mortgage insurers, government sponsored enterprises, and other secondary market participants may rely on this appraisal report as part of any mortgage finance transaction that involves any one or more of these parties.

24. If this appraisal report was transmitted as an "electronic record" containing my "electronic signature," as those terms are defined in applicable federal and/or state laws (excluding audio and video recordings), or a facsimile transmission of this appraisal report containing a copy or representation of my signature, the appraisal report shall be as effective, enforceable and valid as if a paper version of this appraisal report were delivered containing my original hand written signature.

25. Any intentional or negligent misrepresentation(s) contained in this appraisal report may result in civil liability and/or criminal penalties including, but not limited to, fine or imprisonment or both under the provisions of Title 18, United States Code, Section 1001, et seq., or similar state laws.

SUPERVISORY APPRAISER'S CERTIFICATION: The Supervisory Appraiser certifies and agrees that:

1. I directly supervised the appraiser for this appraisal assignment, have read the appraisal report, and agree with the appraiser's analysis, opinions, statements, conclusions, and the appraiser's certification.

2. I accept full responsibility for the contents of this appraisal report including, but not limited to, the appraiser's analysis, opinions, statements, conclusions, and the appraiser's certification.

3. The appraiser identified in this appraisal report is either a sub-contractor or an employee of the supervisory appraiser (or the appraisal firm), is qualified to perform this appraisal, and is acceptable to perform this appraisal under the applicable state law.

4. This appraisal report complies with the Uniform Standards of Professional Appraisal Practice that were adopted and promulgated by the Appraisal Standards Board of The Appraisal Foundation and that were in place at the time this appraisal report was prepared.

5. If this appraisal report was transmitted as an "electronic record" containing my "electronic signature," as those terms are defined in applicable federal and/or state laws (excluding audio and video recordings), or a facsimile transmission of this appraisal report containing a copy or representation of my signature, the appraisal report shall be as effective, enforceable and valid as if a paper version of this appraisal report were delivered containing my original hand written signature.

APPRAISER

Signature ______________________
Name ______________________
Company Name ______________________
Company Address ______________________
____
Telephone Number ______________________
Email Address ______________________
Date of Signature and Report ______________________
Effective Date of Appraisal ______________________
State Certification # ______________________
or State License # ______________________
or Other (describe) ______________ State # ______________
State ______________________
Expiration Date of Certification or License ______________________

ADDRESS OF PROPERTY APPRAISED

____
____

APPRAISED VALUE OF SUBJECT PROPERTY $ ______________

LENDER/CLIENT

Name ______________________
Company Name ______________________
Company Address ______________________
____
Email Address ______________________

SUPERVISORY APPRAISER (ONLY IF REQUIRED)

Signature ______________________
Name ______________________
Company Name ______________________
Company Address ______________________
____
Telephone Number ______________________
Email Address ______________________
Date of Signature ______________________
State Certification # ______________________
or State License # ______________________
State ______________________
Expiration Date of Certification or License ______________________

SUBJECT PROPERTY

☐ Did not inspect subject property
☐ Did inspect exterior of subject property from street
Date of Inspection ______________________
☐ Did inspect interior and exterior of subject property
Date of Inspection ______________________

COMPARABLE SALES

☐ Did not inspect exterior of comparable sales from street
☐ Did inspect exterior of comparable sales from street
Date of Inspection ______________________

Market Conditions Addendum to the Appraisal Report—1004MC

Market Conditions Addendum to the Appraisal Report

File No.

The purpose of this addendum is to provide the lender/client with a clear and accurate understanding of the market trends and conditions prevalent in the subject neighborhood. This is a required addendum for all appraisal reports with an effective date on or after April 1, 2009.

Property Address | City | State | ZIP Code

Borrower

Instructions: The appraiser must use the information required on this form as the basis for his/her conclusions, and must provide support for those conclusions, regarding housing trends and overall market conditions as reported in the Neighborhood section of the appraisal report form. The appraiser must fill in all the information to the extent it is available and reliable and must provide analysis as indicated below. If any required data is unavailable or is considered unreliable, the appraiser must provide an explanation. It is recognized that not all data sources will be able to provide data for the shaded areas below; if it is available, however, the appraiser must include the data in the analysis. If data sources provide the required information as an average instead of the median, the appraiser should report the available figure and identify it as an average. Sales and listings must be properties that compete with the subject property, determined by applying the criteria that would be used by a prospective buyer of the subject property. The appraiser must explain any anomalies in the data, such as seasonal markets, new construction, foreclosures, etc.

MARKET RESEARCH & ANALYSIS

Inventory Analysis	Prior 7–12 Months	Prior 4–6 Months	Current – 3 Months	Overall Trend		
Total # of Comparable Sales (Settled)				☐ Increasing	☐ Stable	☐ Declining
Absorption Rate (Total Sales/Months)				☐ Increasing	☐ Stable	☐ Declining
Total # of Comparable Active Listings				☐ Declining	☐ Stable	☐ Increasing
Months of Housing Supply (Total Listings/Ab.Rate)				☐ Declining	☐ Stable	☐ Increasing
Median Sale & List Price, DOM, Sale/List %	Prior 7–12 Months	Prior 4–6 Months	Current – 3 Months	Overall Trend		
Median Comparable Sale Price				☐ Increasing	☐ Stable	☐ Declining
Median Comparable Sales Days on Market				☐ Declining	☐ Stable	☐ Increasing
Median Comparable List Price				☐ Increasing	☐ Stable	☐ Declining
Median Comparable Listings Days on Market				☐ Declining	☐ Stable	☐ Increasing
Median Sale Price as % of List Price				☐ Increasing	☐ Stable	☐ Declining
Seller-(developer, builder, etc.) paid financial assistance prevalent? ☐ Yes ☐ No				☐ Declining	☐ Stable	☐ Increasing

Explain in detail the seller concessions trends for the past 12 months (e.g., seller contributions increased from 3% to 5%, increasing use of buydowns, closing costs, condo fees, options, etc.).

Are foreclosure sales (REO sales) a factor in the market? ☐ Yes ☐ No If yes, explain (including the trends in listings and sales of foreclosed properties).

Cite data sources for above information.

Summarize the above information as support for your conclusions in the Neighborhood section of the appraisal report form. If you used any additional information, such as an analysis of pending sales and/or expired and withdrawn listings, to formulate your conclusions, provide both an explanation and support for your conclusions.

CONDO/CO-OP PROJECTS

If the subject is a unit in a condominium or cooperative project , complete the following: **Project Name:**

Subject Project Data	Prior 7-12 Months	Prior 4-6 Months	Current – 3 Months	Overall Trend		
Total # of Comparable Sales (Settled)				☐ Increasing	☐ Stable	☐ Declining
Absorption Rate (Total Sales/Months)				☐ Increasing	☐ Stable	☐ Declining
Total # of Active Comparable Listings				☐ Declining	☐ Stable	☐ Increasing
Months of Unit Supply (Total Listings/Ab. Rate)				☐ Declining	☐ Stable	☐ Increasing

Are foreclosure sales (REO sales) a factor in the project? ☐ Yes ☐ No If yes, indicate the number of REO listings and explain the trends in listings and sales of foreclosed properties.

Summarize the above trends and address the impact on the subject unit and project.

APPRAISER

Signature	Signature
Appraiser Name	Supervisory Appraiser Name
Company Name	Company Name
Company Address	Company Address
State License/Certification # State	State License/Certification # State
Email Address	Email Address

Freddie Mac Form 71 March 2009 Page 1 of 1 Fannie Mae Form 1004MC March 2009

Small Residential Income Property Appraisal Report

File #

The purpose of this summary appraisal report is to provide the lender/client with an accurate, and adequately supported, opinion of the market value of the subject property.

SUBJECT

Property Address | City | State | Zip Code
Borrower | Owner of Public Record | County
Legal Description
Assessor's Parcel # | Tax Year | R.E. Taxes $
Neighborhood Name | Map Reference | Census Tract
Occupant ☐ Owner ☐ Tenant ☐ Vacant | Special Assessments $ | ☐ PUD | HOA $ | ☐ per year ☐ per month
Property Rights Appraised ☐ Fee Simple ☐ Leasehold ☐ Other (describe)
Assignment Type ☐ Purchase Transaction ☐ Refinance Transaction ☐ Other (describe)
Lender/Client | Address
Is the subject property currently offered for sale or has it been offered for sale in the twelve months prior to the effective date of this appraisal? ☐ Yes ☐ No
Report data source(s) used, offering price(s), and date(s).

CONTRACT

I ☐ did ☐ did not analyze the contract for sale for the subject purchase transaction. Explain the results of the analysis of the contract for sale or why the analysis was not performed.

Contract Price $ | Date of Contract | Is the property seller the owner of public record? ☐ Yes ☐ No | Data Source(s)
Is there any financial assistance (loan charges, sale concessions, gift or downpayment assistance, etc.) to be paid by any party on behalf of the borrower? ☐ Yes ☐ No
If Yes, report the total dollar amount and describe the items to be paid.

NEIGHBORHOOD

Note: Race and the racial composition of the neighborhood are not appraisal factors.

Neighborhood Characteristics				2-4 Unit Housing Trends				2-4 Unit Housing		Present Land Use %	
Location	☐ Urban	☐ Suburban	☐ Rural	Property Values	☐ Increasing	☐ Stable	☐ Declining	PRICE	AGE	One-Unit	%
Built-Up	☐ Over 75%	☐ 25–75%	☐ Under 25%	Demand/Supply	☐ Shortage	☐ In Balance	☐ Over Supply	$ (000)	(yrs)	2-4 Unit	%
Growth	☐ Rapid	☐ Stable	☐ Slow	Marketing Time	☐ Under 3 mths	☐ 3–6 mths	☐ Over 6 mths	Low		Multi-Family	%
Neighborhood Boundaries								High		Commercial	%
								Pred.		Other	%

Neighborhood Description

Market Conditions (including support for the above conclusions)

SITE

Dimensions | Area | Shape | View
Specific Zoning Classification | Zoning Description
Zoning Compliance ☐ Legal ☐ Legal Nonconforming (Grandfathered Use) ☐ No Zoning ☐ Illegal (describe)
Is the highest and best use of the subject property as improved (or as proposed per plans and specifications) the present use? ☐ Yes ☐ No If No, describe

Utilities	Public	Other (describe)		Public	Other (describe)	Off-site Improvements—Type	Public	Private
Electricity	☐	☐	Water	☐	☐	Street	☐	☐
Gas	☐	☐	Sanitary Sewer	☐	☐	Alley	☐	☐

FEMA Special Flood Hazard Area ☐ Yes ☐ No | FEMA Flood Zone | FEMA Map # | FEMA Map Date
Are the utilities and off-site improvements typical for the market area? ☐ Yes ☐ No If No, describe
Are there any adverse site conditions or external factors (easements, encroachments, environmental conditions, land uses, etc.)? ☐ Yes ☐ No If Yes, describe

IMPROVEMENTS

General Description		Foundation		Exterior Description	materials/condition	Interior	materials/condition
Units ☐ Two ☐ Three ☐ Four		☐ Concrete Slab	☐ Crawl Space	Foundation Walls		Floors	
☐ Accessory Unit (describe below)		☐ Full Basement	☐ Partial Basement	Exterior Walls		Walls	
# of Stories	# of bldgs.	Basement Area	sq. ft.	Roof Surface		Trim/Finish	
Type ☐ Det. ☐ Att. ☐ S-Det./End Unit		Basement Finish	%	Gutters & Downspouts		Bath Floor	
☐ Existing ☐ Proposed ☐ Under Const.		☐ Outside Entry/Exit	☐ Sump Pump	Window Type		Bath Wainscot	
Design (Style)		Evidence of	☐ Infestation	Storm Sash/Insulated		**Car Storage**	
Year Built		☐ Dampness	☐ Settlement	Screens		☐ None	
Effective Age (Yrs)		**Heating/Cooling**		**Amenities**		☐ Driveway	# of Cars
Attic	☐ None	☐ FWA ☐ HWBB	☐ Radiant	☐ Fireplace(s) #	☐ Woodstove(s) #	Driveway Surface	
☐ Drop Stair	☐ Stairs	☐ Other	Fuel	☐ Patio/Deck	☐ Fence	☐ Garage	# of Cars
☐ Floor	☐ Scuttle	☐ Central Air Conditioning		☐ Pool	☐ Porch	☐ Carport	# of Cars
☐ Finished	☐ Heated	☐ Individual	☐ Other	☐ Other		☐ Att. ☐ Det.	☐ Built-in

# of Appliances	Refrigerator	Range/Oven	Dishwasher	Disposal	Microwave	Washer/Dryer	Other (describe)

Unit # 1 contains:	Rooms	Bedroom(s)	Bath(s)	Square feet of Gross Living Area
Unit # 2 contains:	Rooms	Bedroom(s)	Bath(s)	Square feet of Gross Living Area
Unit # 3 contains:	Rooms	Bedroom(s)	Bath(s)	Square feet of Gross Living Area
Unit # 4 contains:	Rooms	Bedroom(s)	Bath(s)	Square feet of Gross Living Area

Additional features (special energy efficient items, etc.)

Describe the condition of the property (including needed repairs, deterioration, renovations, remodeling, etc.).

Small Residential Income Property Appraisal Report

File #

IMPROVEMENTS

Are there any physical deficiencies or adverse conditions that affect the livability, soundness, or structural integrity of the property? ☐ Yes ☐ No If Yes, describe

Does the property generally conform to the neighborhood (functional utility, style, condition, use, construction, etc.)? ☐ Yes ☐ No If No, describe

Is the property subject to rent control? ☐ Yes ☐ No If Yes, describe

COMPARABLE RENTAL DATA

The following properties represent the most current, similar, and proximate comparable rental properties to the subject property. This analysis is intended to support the opinion of the market rent for the subject property.

FEATURE	SUBJECT	COMPARABLE RENTAL # 1	COMPARABLE RENTAL # 2	COMPARABLE RENTAL # 3
Address				
Proximity to Subject				
Current Monthly Rent	$	$	$	$
Rent/Gross Bldg. Area	$ sq. ft.	$ sq. ft.	$ sq. ft.	$ sq. ft.
Rent Control	☐ Yes ☐ No	☐ Yes ☐ No	☐ Yes ☐ No	☐ Yes ☐ No
Data Source(s)				
Date of Lease(s)				
Location				
Actual Age				
Condition				
Gross Building Area				

Unit Breakdown	Rm Count			Size Sq. Ft.	Rm Count			Size Sq. Ft.	Monthly Rent	Rm Count			Size Sq. Ft.	Monthly Rent	Rm Count			Size Sq. Ft.	Monthly Rent
	Tot	Br	Ba		Tot	Br	Ba			Tot	Br	Ba			Tot	Br	Ba		
Unit # 1									$					$					$
Unit # 2									$					$					$
Unit # 3									$					$					$
Unit # 4									$					$					$
Utilities Included																			

Analysis of rental data and support for estimated market rents for the individual subject units reported below (including the adequacy of the comparables, rental concessions, etc.)

SUBJECT RENT SCHEDULE

Rent Schedule: The appraiser must reconcile the applicable indicated monthly market rents to provide an opinion of the market rent for each unit in the subject property.

Leases			**Actual Rent**			**Opinion Of Market Rent**		
	Lease Date		Per Unit		Total	Per Unit		Total
Unit #	Begin Date	End Date	Unfurnished	Furnished	Rent	Unfurnished	Furnished	Rent
1			$	$	$	$	$	$
2								
3								
4								
Comment on lease data			Total Actual Monthly Rent		$	Total Gross Monthly Rent		$
			Other Monthly Income (itemize)		$	Other Monthly Income (itemize)		$
			Total Actual Monthly Income		$	Total Estimated Monthly Income		$

Utilities included in estimated rents ☐ Electric ☐ Water ☐ Sewer ☐ Gas ☐ Oil ☐ Cable ☐ Trash collection ☐ Other (describe)

Comments on actual or estimated rents and other monthly income (including personal property)

PRIOR SALE HISTORY

I ☐ did ☐ did not research the sale or transfer history of the subject property and comparable sales. If not, explain

My research ☐ did ☐ did not reveal any prior sales or transfers of the subject property for the three years prior to the effective date of this appraisal.

Data source(s)

My research ☐ did ☐ did not reveal any prior sales or transfers of the comparable sales for the year prior to the date of sale of the comparable sale.

Data source(s)

Report the results of the research and analysis of the prior sale history of the subject property and comparable sales (report additional prior sales on page 4).

ITEM	SUBJECT	COMPARABLE SALE # 1	COMPARABLE SALE # 2	COMPARABLE SALE # 3
Date of Prior Sale/Transfer				
Price of Prior Sale/Transfer				
Data Source(s)				
Effective Date of Data Source(s)				

Analysis of prior sale history for the subject property and comparable sales

Freddie Mac Form 72 March 2005 Page 2 of 7 Fannie Mae Form 1025 March 2005

Small Residential Income Property Appraisal Report

File #

There are comparable properties currently offered for sale in the subject neighborhood ranging in price from $ to $.

There are comparable sales in the subject neighborhood within the past twelve months ranging in sale price from $ to $.

SALES COMPARISON APPROACH

FEATURE	SUBJECT	COMPARABLE SALE # 1		COMPARABLE SALE # 2		COMPARABLE SALE # 3	
Address							
Proximity to Subject							
Sale Price	$		$		$		$
Sale Price/Gross Bldg. Area	$ sq. ft.	$ sq. ft.		$ sq. ft.		$ sq. ft.	
Gross Monthly Rent	$	$		$		$	
Gross Rent Multiplier							
Price Per Unit	$	$		$		$	
Price Per Room	$	$		$		$	
Price Per Bedroom	$	$		$		$	
Rent Control	☐ Yes ☐ No	☐ Yes ☐ No		☐ Yes ☐ No		☐ Yes ☐ No	
Data Source(s)							
Verification Source(s)							
VALUE ADJUSTMENTS	DESCRIPTION	DESCRIPTION	+ (-) Adjustment	DESCRIPTION	+ (-) Adjustment	DESCRIPTION	+ (-) Adjustment
Sale or Financing Concessions							
Date of Sale/Time							
Location							
Leasehold/Fee Simple							
Site							
View							
Design (Style)							
Quality of Construction							
Actual Age							
Condition							
Gross Building Area							
Unit Breakdown	Total / Bedrooms / Baths	Total / Bdrms / Baths		Total / Bdrms / Baths		Total / Bdrms / Baths	
Unit # 1							
Unit # 2							
Unit # 3							
Unit # 4							
Basement Description							
Basement Finished Rooms							
Functional Utility							
Heating/Cooling							
Energy Efficient Items							
Parking On/Off Site							
Porch/Patio/Deck							
Net Adjustment (Total)		☐ + ☐ -	$	☐ + ☐ -	$	☐ + ☐ -	$
Adjusted Sale Price of Comparables		Net Adj. % Gross Adj. %	$	Net Adj. % Gross Adj. %	$	Net Adj. % Gross Adj. %	$
Adj. Price Per Unit (Adj. SP Comp / # of Comp Units)		$		$		$	
Adj. Price Per Room (Adj. SP Comp / # of Comp Rooms)		$		$		$	
Adj. Price Per Bedrm (Adj. SP Comp / # of Comp Bedrooms)		$		$		$	

Value Per Unit $ ________ X ________ Units = $ ________ Value Per GBA $ ________ X ________ GBA = $ ________

Value Per Rm. $ ________ X ________ Rooms = $ ________ Value Per Bdrms. $ ________ X ________ Bdrms. = $ ________

Summary of Sales Comparison Approach including reconciliation of the above indicators of value.

Indicated Value by Sales Comparison Approach $

INCOME

Total gross monthly rent $ X gross rent multiplier (GRM) = $ Indicated value by the Income Approach

Comments on income approach including reconciliation of the GRM

RECONCILIATION

Indicated Value by: Sales Comparison Approach $ Income Approach $ Cost Approach (if developed) $

This appraisal is made ☐ "as is", ☐ subject to completion per plans and specifications on the basis of a hypothetical condition that the improvements have been completed, ☐ subject to the following repairs or alterations on the basis of a hypothetical condition that the repairs or alterations have been completed, or ☐ subject to the following required inspection based on the extraordinary assumption that the condition or deficiency does not require alteration or repair:

Based on a complete visual inspection of the interior and exterior areas of the subject property, defined scope of work, statement of assumptions and limiting conditions, and appraiser's certification, my (our) opinion of the market value, as defined, of the real property that is the subject of this report is $, as of , which is the date of inspection and the effective date of this appraisal.

Small Residential Income Property Appraisal Report File

ADDITIONAL COMMENTS

COST APPROACH TO VALUE (not required by Fannie Mae)

Provide adequate information for the lender/client to replicate the below cost figures and calculations.

Support for the opinion of site value (summary of comparable land sales or other methods for estimating site value)

ESTIMATED ☐ REPRODUCTION OR ☐ REPLACEMENT COST NEW	OPINION OF SITE VALUE = $
Source of cost data	Dwelling Sq. Ft. @ $ =$
Quality rating from cost service Effective date of cost data	Sq. Ft. @ $ =$
Comments on Cost Approach (gross building area calculations, depreciation, etc.)	
	Garage/Carport Sq. Ft. @ $ =$
	Total Estimate of Cost-New = $
	Less Physical / Functional / External
	Depreciation =$( )
	Depreciated Cost of Improvements =$
	"As-is" Value of Site Improvements =$
Estimated Remaining Economic Life (HUD and VA only) Years	Indicated Value By Cost Approach =$

PROJECT INFORMATION FOR PUDs (if applicable)

Is the developer/builder in control of the Homeowners' Association (HOA)? ☐ Yes ☐ No Unit type(s) ☐ Detached ☐ Attached

Provide the following information for PUDs ONLY if the developer/builder is in control of the HOA and the subject property is an attached dwelling unit.

Legal name of project

Total number of phases Total number of units Total number of units sold

Total number of units rented Total number of units for sale Data source(s)

Was the project created by the conversion of an existing building(s) into a PUD? ☐ Yes ☐ No If Yes, date of conversion

Does the project contain any multi-dwelling units? ☐ Yes ☐ No Data source(s)

Are the units, common elements, and recreation facilities complete? ☐ Yes ☐ No If No, describe the status of completion.

Are the common elements leased to or by the Homeowners' Association? ☐ Yes ☐ No If Yes, describe the rental terms and options.

Describe common elements and recreational facilities.

Small Residential Income Property Appraisal Report

File #

This report form is designed to report an appraisal of a two- to four-unit property, including a two- to four-unit property in a planned unit development (PUD). A two- to four-unit property located in either a condominium or cooperative project requires the appraiser to inspect the project and complete the project information section of the Individual Condominium Unit Appraisal Report or the Individual Cooperative Interest Appraisal Report and attach it as an addendum to this report.

This appraisal report is subject to the following scope of work, intended use, intended user, definition of market value, statement of assumptions and limiting conditions, and certifications. Modifications, additions, or deletions to the intended use, intended user, definition of market value, or assumptions and limiting conditions are not permitted. The appraiser may expand the scope of work to include any additional research or analysis necessary based on the complexity of this appraisal assignment. Modifications or deletions to the certifications are also not permitted. However, additional certifications that do not constitute material alterations to this appraisal report, such as those required by law or those related to the appraiser's continuing education or membership in an appraisal organization, are permitted.

SCOPE OF WORK: The scope of work for this appraisal is defined by the complexity of this appraisal assignment and the reporting requirements of this appraisal report form, including the following definition of market value, statement of assumptions and limiting conditions, and certifications. The appraiser must, at a minimum: (1) perform a complete visual inspection of the interior and exterior areas of the subject property, (2) inspect the neighborhood, (3) inspect each of the comparable sales from at least the street, (4) research, verify, and analyze data from reliable public and/or private sources, and (5) report his or her analysis, opinions, and conclusions in this appraisal report.

INTENDED USE: The intended use of this appraisal report is for the lender/client to evaluate the property that is the subject of this appraisal for a mortgage finance transaction.

INTENDED USER: The intended user of this appraisal report is the lender/client.

DEFINITION OF MARKET VALUE: The most probable price which a property should bring in a competitive and open market under all conditions requisite to a fair sale, the buyer and seller, each acting prudently, knowledgeably and assuming the price is not affected by undue stimulus. Implicit in this definition is the consummation of a sale as of a specified date and the passing of title from seller to buyer under conditions whereby: (1) buyer and seller are typically motivated; (2) both parties are well informed or well advised, and each acting in what he or she considers his or her own best interest; (3) a reasonable time is allowed for exposure in the open market; (4) payment is made in terms of cash in U. S. dollars or in terms of financial arrangements comparable thereto; and (5) the price represents the normal consideration for the property sold unaffected by special or creative financing or sales concessions* granted by anyone associated with the sale.

*Adjustments to the comparables must be made for special or creative financing or sales concessions. No adjustments are necessary for those costs which are normally paid by sellers as a result of tradition or law in a market area; these costs are readily identifiable since the seller pays these costs in virtually all sales transactions. Special or creative financing adjustments can be made to the comparable property by comparisons to financing terms offered by a third party institutional lender that is not already involved in the property or transaction. Any adjustment should not be calculated on a mechanical dollar for dollar cost of the financing or concession but the dollar amount of any adjustment should approximate the market's reaction to the financing or concessions based on the appraiser's judgment.

STATEMENT OF ASSUMPTIONS AND LIMITING CONDITIONS: The appraiser's certification in this report is subject to the following assumptions and limiting conditions:

1. The appraiser will not be responsible for matters of a legal nature that affect either the property being appraised or the title to it, except for information that he or she became aware of during the research involved in performing this appraisal. The appraiser assumes that the title is good and marketable and will not render any opinions about the title.

2. The appraiser has provided a sketch in this appraisal report to show the approximate dimensions of the improvements, including each of the units. The sketch is included only to assist the reader in visualizing the property and understanding the appraiser's determination of its size.

3. The appraiser has examined the available flood maps that are provided by the Federal Emergency Management Agency (or other data sources) and has noted in this appraisal report whether any portion of the subject site is located in an identified Special Flood Hazard Area. Because the appraiser is not a surveyor, he or she makes no guarantees, express or implied, regarding this determination.

4. The appraiser will not give testimony or appear in court because he or she made an appraisal of the property in question, unless specific arrangements to do so have been made beforehand, or as otherwise required by law.

5. The appraiser has noted in this appraisal report any adverse conditions (such as needed repairs, deterioration, the presence of hazardous wastes, toxic substances, etc.) observed during the inspection of the subject property or that he or she became aware of during the research involved in performing this appraisal. Unless otherwise stated in this appraisal report, the appraiser has no knowledge of any hidden or unapparent physical deficiencies or adverse conditions of the property (such as, but not limited to, needed repairs, deterioration, the presence of hazardous wastes, toxic substances, adverse environmental conditions, etc.) that would make the property less valuable, and has assumed that there are no such conditions and makes no guarantees or warranties, express or implied. The appraiser will not be responsible for any such conditions that do exist or for any engineering or testing that might be required to discover whether such conditions exist. Because the appraiser is not an expert in the field of environmental hazards, this appraisal report must not be considered as an environmental assessment of the property.

6. The appraiser has based his or her appraisal report and valuation conclusion for an appraisal that is subject to satisfactory completion, repairs, or alterations on the assumption that the completion, repairs, or alterations of the subject property will be performed in a professional manner.

Small Residential Income Property Appraisal Report File

APPRAISER'S CERTIFICATION: The Appraiser certifies and agrees that:

1. I have, at a minimum, developed and reported this appraisal in accordance with the scope of work requirements stated in this appraisal report.

2. I performed a complete visual inspection of the interior and exterior areas of the subject property, including all units. I reported the condition of the improvements in factual, specific terms. I identified and reported the physical deficiencies that could affect the livability, soundness, or structural integrity of the property.

3. I performed this appraisal in accordance with the requirements of the Uniform Standards of Professional Appraisal Practice that were adopted and promulgated by the Appraisal Standards Board of The Appraisal Foundation and that were in place at the time this appraisal report was prepared.

4. I developed my opinion of the market value of the real property that is the subject of this report based on the sales comparison and income approaches to value. I have adequate market data to develop reliable sales comparison and income approaches to value for this appraisal assignment. I further certify that I considered the cost approach to value but did not develop it, unless otherwise indicated in this report.

5. I researched, verified, analyzed, and reported on any current agreement for sale for the subject property, any offering for sale of the subject property in the twelve months prior to the effective date of this appraisal, and the prior sales of the subject property for a minimum of three years prior to the effective date of this appraisal, unless otherwise indicated in this report.

6. I researched, verified, analyzed, and reported on the prior sales of the comparable sales for a minimum of one year prior to the date of sale of the comparable sale, unless otherwise indicated in this report.

7. I selected and used comparable sales that are locationally, physically, and functionally the most similar to the subject property.

8. I have not used comparable sales that were the result of combining a land sale with the contract purchase price of a home that has been built or will be built on the land.

9. I have reported adjustments to the comparable sales that reflect the market's reaction to the differences between the subject property and the comparable sales.

10. I verified, from a disinterested source, all information in this report that was provided by parties who have a financial interest in the sale or financing of the subject property.

11. I have knowledge and experience in appraising this type of property in this market area.

12. I am aware of, and have access to, the necessary and appropriate public and private data sources, such as multiple listing services, tax assessment records, public land records and other such data sources for the area in which the property is located.

13. I obtained the information, estimates, and opinions furnished by other parties and expressed in this appraisal report from reliable sources that I believe to be true and correct.

14. I have taken into consideration the factors that have an impact on value with respect to the subject neighborhood, subject property, and the proximity of the subject property to adverse influences in the development of my opinion of market value. I have noted in this appraisal report any adverse conditions (such as, but not limited to, needed repairs, deterioration, the presence of hazardous wastes, toxic substances, adverse environmental conditions, etc.) observed during the inspection of the subject property or that I became aware of during the research involved in performing this appraisal. I have considered these adverse conditions in my analysis of the property value, and have reported on the effect of the conditions on the value and marketability of the subject property.

15. I have not knowingly withheld any significant information from this appraisal report and, to the best of my knowledge, all statements and information in this appraisal report are true and correct.

16. I stated in this appraisal report my own personal, unbiased, and professional analysis, opinions, and conclusions, which are subject only to the assumptions and limiting conditions in this appraisal report.

17. I have no present or prospective interest in the property that is the subject of this report, and I have no present or prospective personal interest or bias with respect to the participants in the transaction. I did not base, either partially or completely, my analysis and/or opinion of market value in this appraisal report on the race, color, religion, sex, age, marital status, handicap, familial status, or national origin of either the prospective owners or occupants of the subject property or of the present owners or occupants of the properties in the vicinity of the subject property or on any other basis prohibited by law.

18. My employment and/or compensation for performing this appraisal or any future or anticipated appraisals was not conditioned on any agreement or understanding, written or otherwise, that I would report (or present analysis supporting) a predetermined specific value, a predetermined minimum value, a range or direction in value, a value that favors the cause of any party, or the attainment of a specific result or occurrence of a specific subsequent event (such as approval of a pending mortgage loan application).

19. I personally prepared all conclusions and opinions about the real estate that were set forth in this appraisal report. If I relied on significant real property appraisal assistance from any individual or individuals in the performance of this appraisal or the preparation of this appraisal report, I have named such individual(s) and disclosed the specific tasks performed in this appraisal report. I certify that any individual so named is qualified to perform the tasks. I have not authorized anyone to make a change to any item in this appraisal report; therefore, any change made to this appraisal is unauthorized and I will take no responsibility for it.

20. I identified the lender/client in this appraisal report who is the individual, organization, or agent for the organization that ordered and will receive this appraisal report.

Small Residential Income Property Appraisal Report

File #

21. The lender/client may disclose or distribute this appraisal report to: the borrower; another lender at the request of the borrower; the mortgagee or its successors and assigns; mortgage insurers; government sponsored enterprises; other secondary market participants; data collection or reporting services; professional appraisal organizations; any department, agency, or instrumentality of the United States; and any state, the District of Columbia, or other jurisdictions; without having to obtain the appraiser's or supervisory appraiser's (if applicable) consent. Such consent must be obtained before this appraisal report may be disclosed or distributed to any other party (including, but not limited to, the public through advertising, public relations, news, sales, or other media).

22. I am aware that any disclosure or distribution of this appraisal report by me or the lender/client may be subject to certain laws and regulations. Further, I am also subject to the provisions of the Uniform Standards of Professional Appraisal Practice that pertain to disclosure or distribution by me.

23. The borrower, another lender at the request of the borrower, the mortgagee or its successors and assigns, mortgage insurers, government sponsored enterprises, and other secondary market participants may rely on this appraisal report as part of any mortgage finance transaction that involves any one or more of these parties.

24. If this appraisal report was transmitted as an "electronic record" containing my "electronic signature," as those terms are defined in applicable federal and/or state laws (excluding audio and video recordings), or a facsimile transmission of this appraisal report containing a copy or representation of my signature, the appraisal report shall be as effective, enforceable and valid as if a paper version of this appraisal report were delivered containing my original hand written signature.

25. Any intentional or negligent misrepresentation(s) contained in this appraisal report may result in civil liability and/or criminal penalties including, but not limited to, fine or imprisonment or both under the provisions of Title 18, United States Code, Section 1001, et seq., or similar state laws.

SUPERVISORY APPRAISER'S CERTIFICATION: The Supervisory Appraiser certifies and agrees that:

1. I directly supervised the appraiser for this appraisal assignment, have read the appraisal report, and agree with the appraiser's analysis, opinions, statements, conclusions, and the appraiser's certification.

2. I accept full responsibility for the contents of this appraisal report including, but not limited to, the appraiser's analysis, opinions, statements, conclusions, and the appraiser's certification.

3. The appraiser identified in this appraisal report is either a sub-contractor or an employee of the supervisory appraiser (or the appraisal firm), is qualified to perform this appraisal, and is acceptable to perform this appraisal under the applicable state law.

4. This appraisal report complies with the Uniform Standards of Professional Appraisal Practice that were adopted and promulgated by the Appraisal Standards Board of The Appraisal Foundation and that were in place at the time this appraisal report was prepared.

5. If this appraisal report was transmitted as an "electronic record" containing my "electronic signature," as those terms are defined in applicable federal and/or state laws (excluding audio and video recordings), or a facsimile transmission of this appraisal report containing a copy or representation of my signature, the appraisal report shall be as effective, enforceable and valid as if a paper version of this appraisal report were delivered containing my original hand written signature.

APPRAISER

Signature ____________________
Name ____________________
Company Name ____________________
Company Address ____________________
____
Telephone Number ____________________
Email Address ____________________
Date of Signature and Report ____________________
Effective Date of Appraisal ____________________
State Certification # ____________________
or State License # ____________________
or Other (describe) ____________ State # ____________
State ____________________
Expiration Date of Certification or License ____________________

ADDRESS OF PROPERTY APPRAISED

____
____

APPRAISED VALUE OF SUBJECT PROPERTY $ ____________

LENDER/CLIENT

Name ____________________
Company Name ____________________
Company Address ____________________
____
Email Address ____________________

SUPERVISORY APPRAISER (ONLY IF REQUIRED)

Signature ____________________
Name ____________________
Company Name ____________________
Company Address ____________________
____
Telephone Number ____________________
Email Address ____________________
Date of Signature ____________________
State Certification # ____________________
or State License # ____________________
State ____________________
Expiration Date of Certification or License ____________________

SUBJECT PROPERTY

☐ Did not inspect subject property
☐ Did inspect exterior of subject property from street
Date of Inspection ____________________
☐ Did inspect interior and exterior of subject property
Date of Inspection ____________________

COMPARABLE SALES

☐ Did not inspect exterior of comparable sales from street
☐ Did inspect exterior of comparable sales from street
Date of Inspection ____________________

Exterior-Only Inspection Residential Appraisal Report

File #

The purpose of this summary appraisal report is to provide the lender/client with an accurate, and adequately supported, opinion of the market value of the subject property.

SUBJECT

Property Address | City | State | Zip Code
Borrower | Owner of Public Record | County
Legal Description
Assessor's Parcel # | Tax Year | R.E. Taxes $
Neighborhood Name | Map Reference | Census Tract
Occupant ☐ Owner ☐ Tenant ☐ Vacant | Special Assessments $ | ☐ PUD | HOA $ | ☐ per year ☐ per month
Property Rights Appraised ☐ Fee Simple ☐ Leasehold ☐ Other (describe)
Assignment Type ☐ Purchase Transaction ☐ Refinance Transaction ☐ Other (describe)
Lender/Client | Address
Is the subject property currently offered for sale or has it been offered for sale in the twelve months prior to the effective date of this appraisal? ☐ Yes ☐ No
Report data source(s) used, offering price(s), and date(s).

CONTRACT

I ☐ did ☐ did not analyze the contract for sale for the subject purchase transaction. Explain the results of the analysis of the contract for sale or why the analysis was not performed.

Contract Price $ | Date of Contract | Is the property seller the owner of public record? ☐Yes ☐No Data Source(s)
Is there any financial assistance (loan charges, sale concessions, gift or downpayment assistance, etc.) to be paid by any party on behalf of the borrower? ☐ Yes ☐ No
If Yes, report the total dollar amount and describe the items to be paid.

NEIGHBORHOOD

Note: Race and the racial composition of the neighborhood are not appraisal factors.

Neighborhood Characteristics	One-Unit Housing Trends	One-Unit Housing	Present Land Use %
Location ☐ Urban ☐ Suburban ☐ Rural	Property Values ☐ Increasing ☐ Stable ☐ Declining	PRICE AGE	One-Unit %
Built-Up ☐ Over 75% ☐ 25–75% ☐ Under 25%	Demand/Supply ☐ Shortage ☐ In Balance ☐ Over Supply	$ (000) (yrs)	2-4 Unit %
Growth ☐ Rapid ☐ Stable ☐ Slow	Marketing Time ☐ Under 3 mths ☐ 3–6 mths ☐ Over 6 mths	Low	Multi-Family %
Neighborhood Boundaries		High	Commercial %
		Pred.	Other %

Neighborhood Description

Market Conditions (including support for the above conclusions)

SITE

Dimensions | Area | Shape | View
Specific Zoning Classification | Zoning Description
Zoning Compliance ☐ Legal ☐ Legal Nonconforming (Grandfathered Use) ☐ No Zoning ☐ Illegal (describe)
Is the highest and best use of the subject property as improved (or as proposed per plans and specifications) the present use? ☐ Yes ☐ No If No, describe

Utilities	Public	Other (describe)		Public	Other (describe)	Off-site Improvements—Type	Public	Private
Electricity	☐	☐	Water	☐	☐	Street	☐	☐
Gas	☐	☐	Sanitary Sewer	☐	☐	Alley	☐	☐

FEMA Special Flood Hazard Area ☐ Yes ☐ No | FEMA Flood Zone | FEMA Map # | FEMA Map Date
Are the utilities and off-site improvements typical for the market area? ☐ Yes ☐ No If No, describe
Are there any adverse site conditions or external factors (easements, encroachments, environmental conditions, land uses, etc.)? ☐ Yes ☐ No If Yes, describe

IMPROVEMENTS

Source(s) Used for Physical Characteristics of Property ☐ Appraisal Files ☐ MLS ☐ Assessment and Tax Records ☐ Prior Inspection ☐ Property Owner
☐ Other (describe) | Data Source(s) for Gross Living Area

General Description	General Description	Heating / Cooling	Amenities	Car Storage
Units ☐One ☐One with Accessory Unit	☐Concrete Slab ☐ Crawl Space	☐ FWA ☐ HWBB	☐ Fireplace(s) #	☐ None
# of Stories	☐Full Basement ☐ Finished	☐ Radiant	☐ Woodstove(s) #	☐ Driveway # of Cars
Type ☐Det. ☐Att. ☐S-Det./End Unit	☐Partial Basement ☐Finished	☐ Other	☐ Patio/Deck	Driveway Surface
☐Existing ☐ Proposed ☐ Under Const.	Exterior Walls	Fuel	☐ Porch	☐ Garage # of Cars
Design (Style)	Roof Surface	☐ Central Air Conditioning	☐ Pool	☐ Carport # of Cars
Year Built	Gutters & Downspouts	☐ Individual	☐ Fence	☐ Attached ☐ Detached
Effective Age (Yrs)	Window Type	☐ Other	☐ Other	☐Built-in

Appliances ☐Refrigerator ☐Range/Oven ☐Dishwasher ☐Disposal ☐Microwave ☐Washer/Dryer ☐Other (describe)
Finished area **above** grade contains: | Rooms | Bedrooms | Bath(s) | Square Feet of Gross Living Area Above Grade
Additional features (special energy efficient items, etc.)

Describe the condition of the property and data source(s) (including apparent needed repairs, deterioration, renovations, remodeling, etc.).

Are there any apparent physical deficiencies or adverse conditions that affect the livability, soundness, or structural integrity of the property? ☐ Yes ☐ No
If Yes, describe

Does the property generally conform to the neighborhood (functional utility, style, condition, use, construction, etc.)? ☐ Yes ☐ No If No, describe

Exterior-Only Inspection Residential Appraisal Report

File #

SALES COMPARISON APPROACH

There are comparable properties currently offered for sale in the subject neighborhood ranging in price from $ to $.

There are comparable sales in the subject neighborhood within the past twelve months ranging in sale price from $ to $.

FEATURE	SUBJECT	COMPARABLE SALE # 1		COMPARABLE SALE # 2		COMPARABLE SALE # 3	
Address							
Proximity to Subject							
Sale Price	$		$		$		$
Sale Price/Gross Liv. Area	$ sq. ft.	$ sq. ft.		$ sq. ft.		$ sq. ft.	
Data Source(s)							
Verification Source(s)							
VALUE ADJUSTMENTS	DESCRIPTION	DESCRIPTION	+(-) $ Adjustment	DESCRIPTION	+(-) $ Adjustment	DESCRIPTION	+(-) $ Adjustment
Sale or Financing Concessions							
Date of Sale/Time							
Location							
Leasehold/Fee Simple							
Site							
View							
Design (Style)							
Quality of Construction							
Actual Age							
Condition							
Above Grade Room Count	Total Bdrms. Baths	Total Bdrms. Baths		Total Bdrms. Baths		Total Bdrms. Baths	
Gross Living Area	sq. ft.	sq. ft.		sq. ft.		sq. ft.	
Basement & Finished Rooms Below Grade							
Functional Utility							
Heating/Cooling							
Energy Efficient Items							
Garage/Carport							
Porch/Patio/Deck							
Net Adjustment (Total)		☐ + ☐ -	$	☐ + ☐ -	$	☐ + ☐ -	$
Adjusted Sale Price of Comparables		Net Adj. % Gross Adj. %	$	Net Adj. % Gross Adj. %	$	Net Adj. % Gross Adj. %	$

I ☐ did ☐ did not research the sale or transfer history of the subject property and comparable sales. If not, explain

My research ☐ did ☐ did not reveal any prior sales or transfers of the subject property for the three years prior to the effective date of this appraisal.

Data source(s)

My research ☐ did ☐ did not reveal any prior sales or transfers of the comparable sales for the year prior to the date of sale of the comparable sale.

Data source(s)

Report the results of the research and analysis of the prior sale or transfer history of the subject property and comparable sales (report additional prior sales on page 3).

ITEM	SUBJECT	COMPARABLE SALE # 1	COMPARABLE SALE # 2	COMPARABLE SALE # 3
Date of Prior Sale/Transfer				
Price of Prior Sale/Transfer				
Data Source(s)				
Effective Date of Data Source(s)				

Analysis of prior sale or transfer history of the subject property and comparable sales

Summary of Sales Comparison Approach

Indicated Value by Sales Comparison Approach $

RECONCILIATION

Indicated Value by: Sales Comparison Approach $ Cost Approach (if developed) $ Income Approach (if developed) $

This appraisal is made ☐ "as is", ☐ subject to completion per plans and specifications on the basis of a hypothetical condition that the improvements have been completed, ☐ subject to the following repairs or alterations on the basis of a hypothetical condition that the repairs or alterations have been completed, or ☐ subject to the following required inspection based on the extraordinary assumption that the condition or deficiency does not require alteration or repair:

Based on a visual inspection of the exterior areas of the subject property from at least the street, defined scope of work, statement of assumptions and limiting conditions, and appraiser's certification, my (our) opinion of the market value, as defined, of the real property that is the subject of this report is $, as of , which is the date of the inspection and the effective date of this appraisal.

Exterior-Only Inspection Residential Appraisal Report

File #

ADDITIONAL COMMENTS

COST APPROACH TO VALUE (not required by Fannie Mae)

Provide adequate information for the lender/client to replicate the below cost figures and calculations.

Support for the opinion of site value (summary of comparable land sales or other methods for estimating site value)

ESTIMATED ☐ REPRODUCTION OR ☐ REPLACEMENT COST NEW	OPINION OF SITE VALUE			= $
Source of cost data	Dwelling	Sq. Ft. @ $		=$
Quality rating from cost service Effective date of cost data		Sq. Ft. @ $		=$
Comments on Cost Approach (gross living area calculations, depreciation, etc.)				
	Garage/Carport	Sq. Ft. @ $		=$
	Total Estimate of Cost-New			= $
	Less Physical	Functional	External	
	Depreciation			=$( )
	Depreciated Cost of Improvements			=$
	"As-is" Value of Site Improvements			=$
Estimated Remaining Economic Life (HUD and VA only) Years	Indicated Value By Cost Approach			=$

INCOME APPROACH TO VALUE (not required by Fannie Mae)

Estimated Monthly Market Rent $ X Gross Rent Multiplier = $ Indicated Value by Income Approach

Summary of Income Approach (including support for market rent and GRM)

PROJECT INFORMATION FOR PUDs (if applicable)

Is the developer/builder in control of the Homeowners' Association (HOA)? ☐ Yes ☐ No Unit type(s) ☐ Detached ☐ Attached

Provide the following information for PUDs ONLY if the developer/builder is in control of the HOA and the subject property is an attached dwelling unit.

Legal name of project

Total number of phases | Total number of units | Total number of units sold

Total number of units rented | Total number of units for sale | Data source(s)

Was the project created by the conversion of an existing building(s) into a PUD? ☐ Yes ☐ No If Yes, date of conversion

Does the project contain any multi-dwelling units? ☐ Yes ☐ No Data source(s)

Are the units, common elements, and recreation facilities complete? ☐ Yes ☐ No If No, describe the status of completion.

Are the common elements leased to or by the Homeowners' Association? ☐ Yes ☐ No If Yes, describe the rental terms and options.

Describe common elements and recreational facilities

Exterior-Only Inspection Residential Appraisal Report

File #

This report form is designed to report an appraisal of a one-unit property or a one-unit property with an accessory unit; including a unit in a planned unit development (PUD). This report form is not designed to report an appraisal of a manufactured home or a unit in a condominium or cooperative project.

This appraisal report is subject to the following scope of work, intended use, intended user, definition of market value, statement of assumptions and limiting conditions, and certifications. Modifications, additions, or deletions to the intended use, intended user, definition of market value, or assumptions and limiting conditions are not permitted. The appraiser may expand the scope of work to include any additional research or analysis necessary based on the complexity of this appraisal assignment. Modifications or deletions to the certifications are also not permitted. However, additional certifications that do not constitute material alterations to this appraisal report, such as those required by law or those related to the appraiser's continuing education or membership in an appraisal organization, are permitted.

SCOPE OF WORK: The scope of work for this appraisal is defined by the complexity of this appraisal assignment and the reporting requirements of this appraisal report form, including the following definition of market value, statement of assumptions and limiting conditions, and certifications. The appraiser must, at a minimum: (1) perform a visual inspection of the exterior areas of the subject property from at least the street, (2) inspect the neighborhood, (3) inspect each of the comparable sales from at least the street, (4) research, verify, and analyze data from reliable public and/or private sources, and (5) report his or her analysis, opinions, and conclusions in this appraisal report.

The appraiser must be able to obtain adequate information about the physical characteristics (including, but not limited to, condition, room count, gross living area, etc.) of the subject property from the exterior-only inspection and reliable public and/or private sources to perform this appraisal. The appraiser should use the same type of data sources that he or she uses for comparable sales such as, but not limited to, multiple listing services, tax and assessment records, prior inspections, appraisal files, information provided by the property owner, etc.

INTENDED USE: The intended use of this appraisal report is for the lender/client to evaluate the property that is the subject of this appraisal for a mortgage finance transaction.

INTENDED USER: The intended user of this appraisal report is the lender/client.

DEFINITION MARKET VALUE: The most probable price which a property should bring in a competitive and open market under all conditions requisite to a fair sale, the buyer and seller, each acting prudently, knowledgeably and assuming the price is not affected by undue stimulus. Implicit in this definition is the consummation of a sale as of a specified date and the passing of title from seller to buyer under conditions whereby: (1) buyer and seller are typically motivated; (2) both parties are well informed or well advised, and each acting in what he or she considers his or her own best interest; (3) a reasonable time is allowed for exposure in the open market; (4) payment is made in terms of cash in U. S. dollars or in terms of financial arrangements comparable thereto; and (5) the price represents the normal consideration for the property sold unaffected by special or creative financing or sales concessions* granted by anyone associated with the sale.

*Adjustments to the comparables must be made for special or creative financing or sales concessions. No adjustments are necessary for those costs which are normally paid by sellers as a result of tradition or law in a market area; these costs are readily identifiable since the seller pays these costs in virtually all sales transactions. Special or creative financing adjustments can be made to the comparable property by comparisons to financing terms offered by a third party institutional lender that is not already involved in the property or transaction. Any adjustment should not be calculated on a mechanical dollar for dollar cost of the financing or concession but the dollar amount of any adjustment should approximate the market's reaction to the financing or concessions based on the appraiser's judgment.

STATEMENT OF ASSUMPTIONS AND LIMITING CONDITIONS: The appraiser's certification in this report is subject to the following assumptions and limiting conditions:

1. The appraiser will not be responsible for matters of a legal nature that affect either the property being appraised or the title to it, except for information that he or she became aware of during the research involved in performing this appraisal. The appraiser assumes that the title is good and marketable and will not render any opinions about the title.

2. The appraiser has examined the available flood maps that are provided by the Federal Emergency Management Agency (or other data sources) and has noted in this appraisal report whether any portion of the subject site is located in an identified Special Flood Hazard Area. Because the appraiser is not a surveyor, he or she makes no guarantees, express or implied, regarding this determination.

3. The appraiser will not give testimony or appear in court because he or she made an appraisal of the property in question, unless specific arrangements to do so have been made beforehand, or as otherwise required by law.

4. The appraiser has noted in this appraisal report any adverse conditions (such as needed repairs, deterioration, the presence of hazardous wastes, toxic substances, etc.) observed during the inspection of the subject property or that he or she became aware of during the research involved in performing this appraisal. Unless otherwise stated in this appraisal report, the appraiser has no knowledge of any hidden or unapparent physical deficiencies or adverse conditions of the property (such as, but not limited to, needed repairs, deterioration, the presence of hazardous wastes, toxic substances, adverse environmental conditions, etc.) that would make the property less valuable, and has assumed that there are no such conditions and makes no guarantees or warranties, express or implied. The appraiser will not be responsible for any such conditions that do exist or for any engineering or testing that might be required to discover whether such conditions exist. Because the appraiser is not an expert in the field of environmental hazards, this appraisal report must not be considered as an environmental assessment of the property.

5. The appraiser has based his or her appraisal report and valuation conclusion for an appraisal that is subject to satisfactory completion, repairs, or alterations on the assumption that the completion, repairs, or alterations of the subject property will be performed in a professional manner.

Exterior-Only Inspection Residential Appraisal Report

File #

APPRAISER'S CERTIFICATION: The Appraiser certifies and agrees that:

1. I have, at a minimum, developed and reported this appraisal in accordance with the scope of work requirements stated in this appraisal report.

2. I performed a visual inspection of the exterior areas of the subject property from at least the street. I reported the condition of the improvements in factual, specific terms. I identified and reported the physical deficiencies that could affect the livability, soundness, or structural integrity of the property.

3. I performed this appraisal in accordance with the requirements of the Uniform Standards of Professional Appraisal Practice that were adopted and promulgated by the Appraisal Standards Board of The Appraisal Foundation and that were in place at the time this appraisal report was prepared.

4. I developed my opinion of the market value of the real property that is the subject of this report based on the sales comparison approach to value. I have adequate comparable market data to develop a reliable sales comparison approach for this appraisal assignment. I further certify that I considered the cost and income approaches to value but did not develop them, unless otherwise indicated in this report.

5. I researched, verified, analyzed, and reported on any current agreement for sale for the subject property, any offering for sale of the subject property in the twelve months prior to the effective date of this appraisal, and the prior sales of the subject property for a minimum of three years prior to the effective date of this appraisal, unless otherwise indicated in this report.

6. I researched, verified, analyzed, and reported on the prior sales of the comparable sales for a minimum of one year prior to the date of sale of the comparable sale, unless otherwise indicated in this report.

7. I selected and used comparable sales that are locationally, physically, and functionally the most similar to the subject property.

8. I have not used comparable sales that were the result of combining a land sale with the contract purchase price of a home that has been built or will be built on the land.

9. I have reported adjustments to the comparable sales that reflect the market's reaction to the differences between the subject property and the comparable sales.

10. I verified, from a disinterested source, all information in this report that was provided by parties who have a financial interest in the sale or financing of the subject property.

11. I have knowledge and experience in appraising this type of property in this market area.

12. I am aware of, and have access to, the necessary and appropriate public and private data sources, such as multiple listing services, tax assessment records, public land records and other such data sources for the area in which the property is located.

13. I obtained the information, estimates, and opinions furnished by other parties and expressed in this appraisal report from reliable sources that I believe to be true and correct.

14. I have taken into consideration the factors that have an impact on value with respect to the subject neighborhood, subject property, and the proximity of the subject property to adverse influences in the development of my opinion of market value. I have noted in this appraisal report any adverse conditions (such as, but not limited to, needed repairs, deterioration, the presence of hazardous wastes, toxic substances, adverse environmental conditions, etc.) observed during the inspection of the subject property or that I became aware of during the research involved in performing this appraisal. I have considered these adverse conditions in my analysis of the property value, and have reported on the effect of the conditions on the value and marketability of the subject property.

15. I have not knowingly withheld any significant information from this appraisal report and, to the best of my knowledge, all statements and information in this appraisal report are true and correct.

16. I stated in this appraisal report my own personal, unbiased, and professional analysis, opinions, and conclusions, which are subject only to the assumptions and limiting conditions in this appraisal report.

17. I have no present or prospective interest in the property that is the subject of this report, and I have no present or prospective personal interest or bias with respect to the participants in the transaction. I did not base, either partially or completely, my analysis and/or opinion of market value in this appraisal report on the race, color, religion, sex, age, marital status, handicap, familial status, or national origin of either the prospective owners or occupants of the subject property or of the present owners or occupants of the properties in the vicinity of the subject property or on any other basis prohibited by law.

18. My employment and/or compensation for performing this appraisal or any future or anticipated appraisals was not conditioned on any agreement or understanding, written or otherwise, that I would report (or present analysis supporting) a predetermined specific value, a predetermined minimum value, a range or direction in value, a value that favors the cause of any party, or the attainment of a specific result or occurrence of a specific subsequent event (such as approval of a pending mortgage loan application).

19. I personally prepared all conclusions and opinions about the real estate that were set forth in this appraisal report. If I relied on significant real property appraisal assistance from any individual or individuals in the performance of this appraisal or the preparation of this appraisal report, I have named such individual(s) and disclosed the specific tasks performed in this appraisal report. I certify that any individual so named is qualified to perform the tasks. I have not authorized anyone to make a change to any item in this appraisal report; therefore, any change made to this appraisal is unauthorized and I will take no responsibility for it.

Exterior-Only Inspection Residential Appraisal Report

File #

20. I identified the lender/client in this appraisal report who is the individual, organization, or agent for the organization that ordered and will receive this appraisal report.

21. The lender/client may disclose or distribute this appraisal report to: the borrower; another lender at the request of the borrower; the mortgagee or its successors and assigns; mortgage insurers; government sponsored enterprises; other secondary market participants; data collection or reporting services; professional appraisal organizations; any department, agency, or instrumentality of the United States; and any state, the District of Columbia, or other jurisdictions; without having to obtain the appraiser's or supervisory appraiser's (if applicable) consent. Such consent must be obtained before this appraisal report may be disclosed or distributed to any other party (including, but not limited to, the public through advertising, public relations, news, sales, or other media).

22. I am aware that any disclosure or distribution of this appraisal report by me or the lender/client may be subject to certain laws and regulations. Further, I am also subject to the provisions of the Uniform Standards of Professional Appraisal Practice that pertain to disclosure or distribution by me.

23. The borrower, another lender at the request of the borrower, the mortgagee or its successors and assigns, mortgage insurers, government sponsored enterprises, and other secondary market participants may rely on this appraisal report as part of any mortgage finance transaction that involves any one or more of these parties.

24. If this appraisal report was transmitted as an "electronic record" containing my "electronic signature," as those terms are defined in applicable federal and/or state laws (excluding audio and video recordings), or a facsimile transmission of this appraisal report containing a copy or representation of my signature, the appraisal report shall be as effective, enforceable and valid as if a paper version of this appraisal report were delivered containing my original hand written signature.

25. Any intentional or negligent misrepresentation(s) contained in this appraisal report may result in civil liability and/or criminal penalties including, but not limited to, fine or imprisonment or both under the provisions of Title 18, United States Code, Section 1001, et seq., or similar state laws.

SUPERVISORY APPRAISER'S CERTIFICATION: The Supervisory Appraiser certifies and agrees that:

1. I directly supervised the appraiser for this appraisal assignment, have read the appraisal report, and agree with the appraiser's analysis, opinions, statements, conclusions, and the appraiser's certification.

2. I accept full responsibility for the contents of this appraisal report including, but not limited to, the appraiser's analysis, opinions, statements, conclusions, and the appraiser's certification.

3. The appraiser identified in this appraisal report is either a sub-contractor or an employee of the supervisory appraiser (or the appraisal firm), is qualified to perform this appraisal, and is acceptable to perform this appraisal under the applicable state law.

4. This appraisal report complies with the Uniform Standards of Professional Appraisal Practice that were adopted and promulgated by the Appraisal Standards Board of The Appraisal Foundation and that were in place at the time this appraisal report was prepared.

5. If this appraisal report was transmitted as an "electronic record" containing my "electronic signature," as those terms are defined in applicable federal and/or state laws (excluding audio and video recordings), or a facsimile transmission of this appraisal report containing a copy or representation of my signature, the appraisal report shall be as effective, enforceable and valid as if a paper version of this appraisal report were delivered containing my original hand written signature.

APPRAISER

Signature ______________________
Name ______________________
Company Name ______________________
Company Address ______________________
____
Telephone Number ______________________
Email Address ______________________
Date of Signature and Report ______________________
Effective Date of Appraisal ______________________
State Certification # ______________________
or State License # ______________________
or Other (describe) ____________ State # ________
State ______________________
Expiration Date of Certification or License ______________________

ADDRESS OF PROPERTY APPRAISED

____
____

APPRAISED VALUE OF SUBJECT PROPERTY $ ______________________

LENDER/CLIENT

Name ______________________
Company Name ______________________
Company Address ______________________
____
Email Address ______________________

SUPERVISORY APPRAISER (ONLY IF REQUIRED)

Signature ______________________
Name ______________________
Company Name ______________________
Company Address ______________________
____
Telephone Number ______________________
Email Address ______________________
Date of Signature ______________________
State Certification # ______________________
or State License # ______________________
State ______________________
Expiration Date of Certification or License ______________________

SUBJECT PROPERTY

☐ Did not inspect exterior of subject property
☐ Did inspect exterior of subject property from street
Date of Inspection ______________________

COMPARABLE SALES

☐ Did not inspect exterior of comparable sales from street
☐ Did inspect exterior of comparable sales from street
Date of Inspection ______________________

Operating Income Statement

One- to Four-Family Investment Property and Two- to Four-Family Owner-Occupied Property

Property Address

Street City State Zip Code

General Instructions: This form is to be prepared jointly by the loan applicant, the appraiser, and the lender's underwriter. The applicant must complete the following schedule indicating each unit's rental status, lease expiration date, current rent, market rent, and the responsibility for utility expenses. Rental figures must be based on the rent for an "unfurnished" unit.

	Currently Rented	Expiration Date	Current Rent Per Month	Market Rent Per Month
Unit No. 1	Yes ___ No ___	______	$______	$______
Unit No. 2	Yes ___ No ___	______	$______	$______
Unit No. 3	Yes ___ No ___	______	$______	$______
Unit No. 4	Yes ___ No ___	______	$______	$______
Total			$______	$______

Utility Expense	Paid By Owner	Paid By Tenant
Electricity	☐	☐
Gas	☐	☐
Fuel Oil	☐	☐
Fuel (Other)	☐	☐
Water/Sewer	☐	☐
Trash Removal	☐	☐

The applicant should complete all of the income and expense projections and for existing properties provide actual year-end operating statements for the past two years *(for new properties the applicant's projected income and expenses must be provided).* This Operating Income Statement and any previous operating statements the applicant provides must then be sent to the appraiser for review, comment, and/or adjustments next to the applicant's figures *(e.g., Applicant/Appraiser 288/300).* If the appraiser is retained to complete the form instead of the applicant, the lender must provide to the appraiser the aforementioned operating statements, mortgage insurance premium, HOA dues, leasehold payments, subordinate financing, and/or any other relevant information as to the income and expenses of the subject property received from the applicant to substantiate the projections. The underwriter should carefully review the applicant's/appraiser's projections and the appraiser's comments concerning those projections. The underwriter should make any final adjustments that are necessary to more accurately reflect any income or expense items that appear unreasonable for the market. *(Real estate taxes and insurance on these types of properties are included in PITI and not calculated as an annual expense item.)* Income should be based on current rents, but should not exceed market rents. When there are no current rents because the property is proposed, new, or currently vacant, market rents should be used.

Annual Income and Expense Projection for Next 12 months

Income *(Do not include income for owner-occupied units)*	By Applicant/Appraiser	Adjustments by Lender's Underwriter
Gross Annual Rental *(from unit(s) to be rented)*	$ ______	$ ______
Other Income *(include sources)*	+ ______	+ ______
Total	$ ______	$ ______
Less Vacancy/Rent Loss	− ______ (%)	− ______ (%)
Effective Gross Income	$ ______	$ ______

Expenses *(Do not include expenses for owner-occupied units)*		
Electricity	______	______
Gas	______	______
Fuel Oil	______	______
Fuel (Type - ______)	______	______
Water/Sewer	______	______
Trash Removal	______	______
Pest Control	______	______
Other Taxes or Licenses	______	______
Casual Labor This includes the costs for public area cleaning, snow removal, etc., even though the applicant may not elect to contract for such services.	______	______
Interior Paint/Decorating This includes the costs of contract labor and materials that are required to maintain the interiors of the living units.	______	______
General Repairs/Maintenance This includes the costs of contract labor and materials that are required to maintain the public corridors, stairways, roofs, mechanical systems, grounds, etc.	______	______
Management Expenses These are the customary expenses that a professional management company would charge to manage the property.	______	______
Supplies This includes the costs of items like light bulbs, janitorial supplies, etc.	______	______
Total Replacement Reserves - See Schedule on Pg. 2	______	______
Miscellaneous	______	______
......	______	______
......	______	______
......	______	______
......	______	______
......	______	______
......	______	______
......	______	______
......	______	______
Total Operating Expenses	$ ______	$ ______

Freddie Mac Form 998 Aug 88 | **This Form Must Be Reproduced By Seller** Page 1 of 2 | Fannie Mae Form 216 Aug 88

Replacement Reserve Schedule

Adequate replacement reserves must be calculated regardless of whether actual reserves are provided for on the owner's operating statements or are customary in the local market. This represents the total average yearly reserves. Generally, all equipment and components that have a remaining life of more than one year—such as refrigerators, stoves, clothes washers/dryers, trash compactors, furnaces, roofs, and carpeting, etc.—should be expensed on a replacement cost basis.

Equipment	Replacement Cost		Remaining Life			By Applicant/ Appraiser	Lender Adjustments
Stoves/Ranges	@ $ ______	ea. ÷	____ Yrs. x	______	Units =	$ ______	$ ______
Refrigerators	@ $ ______	ea. ÷	____ Yrs. x	______	Units =	$ ______	$ ______
Dishwashers	@ $ ______	ea. ÷	____ Yrs. x	______	Units =	$ ______	$ ______
A/C Units	@ $ ______	ea. ÷	____ Yrs. x	______	Units =	$ ______	$ ______
C. Washer/Dryers	@ $ ______	ea. ÷	____ Yrs. x	______	Units =	$ ______	$ ______
HW Heaters	@ $ ______	ea. ÷	____ Yrs. x	______	Units =	$ ______	$ ______
Furnace(s)	@ $ ______	ea. ÷	____ Yrs. x	______	Units =	$ ______	$ ______
(Other)	@ $ ______	ea. ÷	____ Yrs. x	______	Units =	$ ______	$ ______
Roof	@ $ ______	÷	____ Yrs. x	One Bldg. =		$ ______	$ ______

Carpeting (Wall to Wall)

		Remaining Life		
(Units)	____ Total Sq. Yds. @ $____ Per Sq. Yd. ÷	____Yrs. =	$ ______	$ ______
(Public Åreas)	____ Total Sq. Yds. @ $____ Per Sq. Yd. ÷	____Yrs. =	$ ______	$ ______

Total Replacement Reserves. (Enter on Pg. 1) $ ______ $ ______

Operating Income Reconciliation

$ ______ – $ ______ = $ ______ ÷12 = $ ______
Effective Gross Income — Total Operating Expenses — Operating Income — Monthly Operating Income

$ ______ – $ ______ = $ ______
Monthly Operating Income — Monthly Housing Expense — Net Cash Flow

(Note: Monthly Housing Expense includes principal and interest on the mortgage, hazard insurance premiums, real estate taxes, mortgage insurance premiums, HOA dues, leasehold payments, and subordinate financing payments.)

Underwriter's instructions for 2-4 Family Owner-Occupied Properties

- If Monthly Operating Income is a positive number, enter as "Net Rental Income" in the "Gross Monthly Income" section of Freddie Mac Form 65/Fannie Mae Form 1003. If Monthly Operating Income is a negative number, it must be included as a liability for qualification purposes.

- The borrower's monthly housing expense-to-income ratio must be calculated by comparing the total Monthly Housing Expense for the **subject property** to the borrower's stable monthly income.

Underwriter's instructions for 1-4 Family Investment Properties

- If Net Cash Flow is a positive number, enter as "Net Rental Income" in the "Gross Monthly Income" section of Freddie Mac Form 65/Fannie Mae Form 1003. If Net Cash Flow is a negative number, it must be included as a liability for qualification purposes.

- The borrower's monthly housing expense-to-income ratio must be calculated by comparing the total monthly housing expense for the borrower's **primary residence** to the borrower's stable monthly income.

Appraiser's Comments *(Including sources for data and rationale for the projections)*

Appraiser Name ______ Appraiser Signature ______ Date ______

Underwriter's Comments and Rationale for Adjustments

Underwriter Name ______ Underwriter Signature ______ Date ______

DIRECT CAPITALIZATION (IRV)

DIRECT CAPITALIZATION (IVR)

DIRECT CAPITALIZATION (VIR)

MULTIPLIERS (GRM)

MULTIPLIERS (GIM)

MULTIPLIERS (VIM)

(Net Operating) Income ÷ Value = (Capitalization) Rate

Common application:

- Used to extract a direct capitalization rate from comparable data when the value (usually sale price) and the comparable's NOI are known

(Net Operating) Income ÷ (Capitalization) Rate = Value

Common application:

- Used to find the value of a subject property when NOI and the direct capitalization rate are known

(Gross) Rent x GRM = Value

Common application:

- Used most often for residential properties where rent from living unit(s) is the primary or consistent source of income
- Monthly gross rent is used (unless otherwise noted)
- Gross rent does not include any losses or expense items!

Value x (Capitalization) Rate = (Net Operating) Income

Common application:

- Used to identify the NOI of comparable data when the value (usually sale price) and the direct capitalization rate are known

Value ÷ (Gross) Income or rent = Multiplier

Common application:

- Used to derive either a GRM or a GIM from comparable data
  - Gross rent (usually monthly) is used to derive a GRM
  - Gross rent plus other income (usually annual) is used to derive a GIM

(Gross) Income x GIM = Value

Common application:

- Used most often for properties that have a consistent source of income in addition to the rent from unit(s)
- Income includes rent and other income
- Can be derived and applied as an EGIM or a PGIM
- Annual gross income is used (unless otherwise noted)
- Gross income does not include any losses or expense items!

NET OPERATING INCOME (NOI)

RESERVES FOR REPLACEMENT

VACANCY LOSS

BAND OF INVESTMENT

MORTGAGE CONSTANT

OPERATING EXPENSES

Estimated cost of replacement ÷ Number of years until replacement is anticipated = Annual Reserve

(Divide the annual amount by 12 to determine a monthly replacement reserve)

Common application:

- Calculation of operating expenses

PGI (Potential gross income)

- Vacancy and Collection Losses

=EGI (Effective gross income)

-Operating Expenses

=NOI (Net operating income)

Common application:

- Component of direct capitalization: NOI ÷ Capitalization Rate = Value

---

Mortgage Component + Equity Component = Overall Capitalization Rate (R_O)

Annual debt service ÷ Mortgage amount = Mortgage constant (R_M)

Mortgage constant x LTV (percent financed) = Mortgage Component

Equity Dividend (R_E) x Percent of Investment = Equity Component

Common application:

- Used to develop an overall capitalization rate (R_O)

Total number of days of vacancy for all units ÷ Total calendar days (Number of units x 365) = Rate of vacancy (%)

Common application:

- Calculation of effective gross income

Fixed Expenses + Variable Expenses + Reserves for Replacement = Operating Expenses

Common application:

- Component of a calculation to determine net operating income (NOI)
- Debt service (mortgage payment), depreciation, etc., are not operating expenses

Annual debt service (principal and interest payment) ÷ Mortgage amount = Mortgage constant

Common application:

- Used in the band of investment technique to represent the ratio of annual debt service to the dollar amount financed

Glossary of Key Terms

A

Amortization Elimination of a debt with a series of equal payments (principle and interest) at regular time intervals.

Anticipation An economic theory that says value is created by the expectation of future benefits, such as profit, pleasure, tax shelter, production, income, etc. Anticipation is the foundation for the income approach.

Appraiser's Peers Other appraisers with expertise and competency in a similar type of assignment.

Appurtenant Rights Rights that go with ownership of real property. They are usually transferred with the property, but may be sold separately. This is a legal term referring to both physical and non-physical appurtenances.

Assumptions That which is taken to be true.

B

Balance A condition that exists in the real estate market when there are slightly more homes available than buyers.

Band of Investment A technique for determining an overall capitalization rate by weighting and combining the various components of an investment.

Bracketing A process in which an appraiser identifies a probable value range, most often by identifying values of properties that are inferior and those that are superior. The appraiser then determines where an opinion of value for the subject should fall within that range.

Buyer's Market A situation in the real estate market in which buyers have a large selection of properties from which to choose.

C

Change A principle affecting value in real estate that says all factors that influence real estate—physical, economic, governmental, and social—are constantly changing, and, thus, property value itself is subject to constant change.

Characteristics of Value Also known as D-U-S-T. The characteristics of value are Demand, Utility, Scarcity, and Transferability.

Client The party (or parties) who engage an appraiser (by employment or contract) in a specific assignment.

Comparable Property Possesses many of the same appeal factors, but the buyer for one property may not necessarily be interested in the comparable property.

Competition Two or more parties, properties, etc., trying to obtain the same thing.

Competitive Property Those that compete head to head. A potential buyer for one property would also be interested in the competitive property.

Compound Interest Interest paid on previously earned interest based on the original principal amount. The more frequent the compounding period and the higher the effective interest rate, the greater the impact on the calculation.

Conditions of Sale Atypical motivations of the parties of a transaction (usually make the sale non-arm's length).

Conformity The theory that says a particular property achieves its maximum value when it is surrounded by properties that are similar in style, function, and utility. Also called **Homogeneity**.

Contract Rent What tenants are actually paying in rent, as stated in the terms of the lease.

Contributory Value The theory that a particular item or feature of a property is worth only what it actually contributes in value to that parcel of real estate.

Credible Worthy of belief.

D

Date of Report An indication of the perspective from which the appraiser is examining the market.

Debt Service The amount of funds required to make periodic payments of principal and interest to the lender.

Decline The third stage a neighborhood goes through in its life cycle, when property values begin to fall as demand falls.

Deed An instrument that conveys the grantor's interest in real property.

Deficit Rent The resulting difference when the market rent exceeds the contract rent.

Direct Capitalization An income method that converts a property's single-year net operating income (NOI) into a value indication by applying an overall capitalization rate: NOI ÷ Overall Capitalization Rate = Value.

Discount Points An amount paid to a lender (1% of loan amount) when a loan is made to make up the difference between the current market interest rate and the rate a lender gives a borrower on a note. Discount points increase a lender's yield on a note, allowing the lender to give a borrower a lower interest rate.

Discounting The process, by some investors, that uses the principles of TVM to convert future income or cash flows into present value, at a specified interest rate.

District The narrowest of definitions of a market area. A district is an area consisting of one particular land use, such as multi-family residential, commercial, industrial, etc.

Dominant Tenement A property that benefits from an easement.

E

Easement A right to use some part of another person's real property for a particular purpose. An easement is irrevocable and creates an interest in the property.

Easement Appurtenant An easement that burdens one parcel of land for the benefit of another.

Easement in Gross An easement that benefits a person instead of a particular property; there is a dominant tenant, but no dominant tenement.

Effective Date Establishes the context for the value opinion.

Effective Gross Income (EGI) Potential gross income, less vacancy and collection losses.

EGIM A factor derived and applied using EGI—the amount after estimated vacancy has been deducted from PGI.

Elements of Comparison Characteristics of a property or a transaction that can be used to explain differences in the price paid in a transaction.

Equity Capitalization Rate The capitalization rate applied to the expectation of return on equity (symbolized by R_E).

Excess Rent The resulting difference when the contract rent exceeds the market rent.

Excess Site A site that is not needed to support the existing improvements or highest and best use. Could have sell-off potential or be needed for future expansion of the existing or anticipated improvements.

Extraordinary Assumption An assignment-specific assumption as of the effective date regarding uncertain information used in an analysis which, if found to be false, could alter the appraiser's opinions or conclusions.

F

Fee Simple The greatest estate (ownership) one can have in real property; it is freely transferable and inheritable, and of indefinite duration, with no conditions on the title. Often called **fee simple absolute** or **fee title**.

Fixed Expenses Ongoing operating expenses that do not vary based on occupancy levels of the property (e.g., taxes and insurance).

Functional Utility When a building has the adequate design and features to be used as intended.

Future Value Amount of money that an investment (either a single payment or an annuity) at a fixed interest rate, for a specified period of time, will grow to in the future.

G

General Data Information that covers the forces that affect property values, but are not directly related to a particular property. General data covers **p**hysical, **e**conomic, **g**overnmental, and **s**ocial factors (**P E G S**) and can be local or national.

Gentrification The process of rapid revitalization of properties in a neighborhood, which causes current residents to be displaced.

Gross Adjustments The overall total of all adjustments applied regardless of whether the adjustment is applied as a positive or a negative. (For example, a +$1,000 and a -$1,000 adjustment would result in $2,000 gross adjustments.)

Gross Income Multiplier (GIM) A factor that takes into account income derived from all sources of a property (e.g., vending, storage units).

Gross Lease A property lease for which the landlord pays all expenses related to the operation of the property.

Gross Rent Multiplier (GRM) A factor derived from comparable rental data, which is then used to develop an opinion of value of the subject property.

Growth The first stage a neighborhood goes through in its life cycle, when property values rise as development activity begins and continues.

H

Highest and Best Use The most profitable, legally permitted, economically feasible, and physically possible use of a property.

Hypothetical Condition A condition, related to a specific assignment, which is contrary to what is known by the appraiser to exist on the effective date of the assignment results, but is used for the purpose of analysis.

I

Intended Use The use(s) of an appraiser's reported appraisal or appraisal review assignment results, as identified by the appraiser based on communication with the client at the time of the assignment.

Intended User The client and any other party as identified, by name or type, as users of the appraisal or appraisal review report by the appraiser, based on communication with the client at the time of the assignment.

IVR A formula or technique that derives an overall capitalization rate: Income (NOI) ÷ Value (Sale Price) = Rate.

J

Jurisdictional Exception An assignment condition established by applicable law or regulation, which precludes an appraiser from complying with a part of USPAP.

L

Lease Conveyance of a leasehold estate from the fee owner to a tenant; a contract for which one party pays the other rent in exchange for possession of real estate.

Leased Fee Estate The landlord's ownership interest in property.

Leased Fee Interest Defined by the amount of contract rent over and above market rent.

Leasehold Estate An estate that gives the holder (tenant) a temporary right to possession, without title. Also called **Less-than-Freehold Estate**.

Leasehold Interest Defined by the amount of rent that is less than market rent (amount of difference between contract and market rent).

Lessee A person who leases property; a tenant.

Lessor A person who leases property to another; a landlord.

Life Estate A freehold estate that lasts only as long as a specified person lives.

Life Tenant Someone who owns a life estate; the person entitled to possession of the property during the measuring life.

Limiting Conditions Statement by the appraiser explaining the framework used to reach the appraisal value.

Linkages The proximity of property to common destinations and conveniences, and the time required to reach those places.

M

Market Area The broadest of all terms identifying the boundaries of a particular area. Market area takes into account the land uses and characteristics of typical market participants within the defined area.

Market Rent What the property could rent for in the open market if currently vacant and available.

Mortgage Capitalization Rate A return on the money lent in an investment (symbolized by R_M).

Mortgage Constant The ratio between annual debt service and loan principal.

Multiplier A factor that is derived from market data and applied to the subject's market rent or income to produce a value indication in an income approach.

N

Negative Leasehold When contract rent is more than market rent (an advantage to the lessor).

Neighborhood Any constant, contiguous area that may be identified by similar characteristics of physical boundaries.

Net Adjustments The sum of the adjustments taking into account whether the adjustment was a positive or a negative. (For example, a +$1,000 and a -$1,000 adjustment would result in $0 net adjustments.)

Net Lease A property lease for which the tenant pays all utilities and certain expenses, in addition to rent payments.

Net Operating Income Income after expenses.

O

Operating Expenses Day-to-day costs of running a building, like repairs and maintenance, but not including debt service or depreciation.

Overage Rent A percentage of business sales a tenant's business has generated paid in addition to rent payments.

Overall Capitalization Rate Used to interpret a property's single year net operating income to the property's value using direct capitalization (symbolized by R_O).

Overall Yield Rate Considers a series of annual figures over the entire investment period as well as reversion.

P

Paired Data Analysis The process of determining the value of specific property characteristics or features by comparing pairs of similar properties. Also called **Matched Pair Analysis**.

Partial Interest Any interest in real estate that one may have, other than the full bundle of rights.

PGIM A factor derived from, and applied to, the total gross income generated by the property without vacancy being considered.

Positive Leasehold When contract rent is less than market rent (an advantage to the lessee).

Potential Gross Income (PGI) The income that could be produced by a property in an ideal situation, with no vacancy or collection losses.

Present Value An amount today that is equivalent to a future payment, or series of payments (annuity), based on a specified interest rate, for a specific period of time.

Primary Data Data that is obtained directly by the appraiser.

Principle of Consistent Use Holds that land cannot be valued for one use, while the improvements are valued at another use.

Progression A principle that says the value of a home is positively affected by the other homes in an area. Usually said about the "worst" home in the "best" area.

Q

Qualitative Analysis A method used after any quantitative adjustments have been applied that employs the appraiser's judgment in forming opinions relying on such methods as relative comparison analysis (bracketing), ranking analysis, and/or personal interviews. The method requires good judgment and reasoning skills of the appraiser.

Quantitative Adjustments A method that requires the recognition of the differences between the comparable data and the subject property and assigning either a market derived dollar or percentage amount as an adjustment.

R

Reconciliation Analyzing the values derived from the different appraisal approaches to arrive at a final opinion of value.

Regression A principle that says the value of a home is negatively affected by the other homes in an area. Usually said about the "best" home in the "worst" area.

Regression Analysis A statistical measure that attempts to ascertain the source of change in variables.

Remainderman The party in a life estate who is entitled to the remainder of the property interest after the life estate is terminated.

Rent Roll Briefly details the unit information, such as lease terms, contract rent, as well as the effective date of the leases that are in place for the property.

Rent Survey A compilation of the rents being generated (and often rent history) in a particular market for a particular property type.

Reserves for Replacement An amount of money set aside for future replacement of major items, such as the roof or heating system. Also called **Reserves**.

Reverse Polish Notation (RPN) A formal logic system used in the HP-12C calculator that allows mathematical equations to be expressed by pressing the arithmetic operations key (+, -, x, ÷) after the numbers or variables have been keyed.

Reversionary Benefit Typically a sum, often stated in a dollar amount, that a property owner will receive when or if he sells the property at the end of the investment term.

Revitalization The final stage a neighborhood goes through in its life cycle, when property values rise again as demand increases, resulting in increased renovation and rehabilitation. *See:* **Gentrification.**

S

Scatter Diagram Graphs used to study the relationship between two variables.

Scope of Work The type and extent of research and analyses in an appraisal or appraisal review assignment.

Secondary Data Data that is compiled by other parties and used by the appraiser.

Seller's Market A situation in the real estate market where sellers can choose from a large number of buyers looking for property in an area.

Servient Tenement A property that is burdened by an easement.

Sinking Fund Factor Amount set aside on a periodic basis so that, when compounded at a given interest rate for a defined term, it will accumulate to a specified future sum.

Specific Data Information that is relevant to the subject property. There are two types of specific data.

Stability The second stage a neighborhood goes through in its life cycle, when the area is built up to the point where there is little, if any, vacant property. Also called **equilibrium.**

Substitution Theory that an informed buyer will not pay more for a home than a comparable substitute.

Surplus Site A site that is not needed for the highest and best use of the subject and does not have potential for sell-off or an autonomous highest and best use.

T

Timeshares Grant the right to use (or possess) a property for a specified period of time (the right may or may not be accompanied with an ownership interest in the property).

Time Value of Money (TVM) The concept that a dollar today is usually worth more than receiving a dollar at some point in the future.

U

Unit of Comparison A component with which a property can be divided for the purpose of comparison such as square foot, living unit, etc.

V

Variable Expenses Operating expenses necessary to the property, but usually dependent on the property's occupancy level.

VIM A formula used to derive the appropriate multiplier from the transaction data: V (sale price) ÷ I (gross monthly rent) = M (multiplier).

W

Workfile The documentation necessary to support the appraiser's analyses, opinions, and conclusions.

Index

M

N

O

P

Q

R